# Rebranding Islam

APARC
STANFORD
IIS

THE WALTER H. SHORENSTEIN
ASIA-PACIFIC RESEARCH CENTER

Studies of the Walter H. Shorenstein Asia-Pacific Research Center

Andrew G. Walder, General Editor

The Walter H. Shorenstein Asia-Pacific Research Center in the Freeman Spogli Institute for International Studies at Stanford University sponsors interdisciplinary research on the politics, economies, and societies of contemporary Asia. This monograph series features academic and policy-oriented research by Stanford faculty and other scholars associated with the Center.

# Rebranding Islam

PIETY, PROSPERITY, AND A SELF-HELP GURU

*James Bourk Hoesterey*

Stanford University Press

Stanford, California

Stanford University Press
Stanford, California

Portions of Chapters 1 and 6 are reprinted from an essay titled "Marketing Morality: The Rise, Fall and Rebranding of AA Gym," which appeared in *Expressing Islam: Religious Life and Politics in Indonesia*, edited by Greg Fealy and Sally White, 2008, © 2008 Institute of Southeast Asian Studies, Singapore, https://bookshop.iseas.edu.sg. Reprinted by permission.

Portions of Chapters 1 and 6 previously appeared in an essay titled "Aa Gym: The Rise, Fall, and Re-branding of a Celebrity Preacher," published in *Inside Indonesia*, no. 90 (2007). Reprinted by permission.

Portions of Chapter 4 previously appeared in an essay titled "Prophetic Cosmopolitanism: Islam, Pop Psychology, and Civic Virtue in Indonesia," published in *City & Society*, no. 24 (2012). Reprinted by permission.

All photos by the author unless otherwise noted.

Printed in the United States of America on acid-free, archival-quality paper

Library of Congress Cataloging-in-Publication Data

Hoesterey, James Bourk, 1975–author.
 Rebranding Islam : piety, prosperity, and a self-help guru / James Bourk Hoesterey.
  pages cm—(Studies of the Walter H. Shorenstein Asia-Pacific Research Center)
 Includes bibliographical references and index.
 ISBN 978-0-8047-9511-1 (cloth : alk. paper)—
 ISBN 978-0-8047-9637-8 (pbk. : alk. paper)
 1. Gymnastiar, Abdullah, 1962-. 2. Muslim religious leaders—Indonesia—
Biography. 3. Celebrities—Indonesia—Biography. 4. Self-help techniques—
Religious aspects. 5. Muslims—Religious life—Indonesia. 6. Indonesia—Religious
life and customs. 7. Islam—Psychology. I. Title. II. Series: Studies of the Walter H.
Shorenstein Asia-Pacific Research Center.
 BP80.G93H64 2015
 297.4092—dc23
 [B]
                              2015007275
 ISBN 978-0-8047-9638-5 (electronic)

Typeset by Bruce Lundquist in 11/14 Adobe Garamond

*For my parents*

# Contents

# Preface

I first came to this project through my own befuddlement with the phrase *Manajemen Qolbu* (Heart Management). I was preparing a guest lecture about Islam in Indonesia for Charles Hirschkind's course Anthropology of Religion at the University of Wisconsin. A year after 9/11 and just weeks after the deadly bomb blasts in Bali in 2002, I wanted to provide a portrait of Islam beyond bombs and veils. That very week the *New York Times* published "A TV Preacher to Satisfy the Taste for Islam Lite," an article in which Jane Perlez describes a young, hip preacher—Aa Gym—and his Islamic self-help program of Manajemen Qolbu. I was curious about this peculiar linguistic hybrid that conjured both English and Arabic roots. Despite a year of intensive Indonesian language training and several stints living in Indonesia, at that time I had never even heard of the word *qolbu*. A bit embarrassed, I consulted the most respected Indonesian dictionary. *Qolbu* was not to be found. I then proceeded to a dictionary devoted to Indonesian Islam (Federspiel 1995). Still no *qolbu*. Next, I e-mailed an esteemed anthropologist of emotion with decades of experience in Indonesia. Never heard of it. With a couple of notable exceptions (Stange 1984), scholars writing about emotion in Indonesia had not really noticed *qolbu*.[1] This was due, in part, to a generation of emotion studies in Indonesia that approached the study of emotion largely in localized terms of ethnicity and ethno-psychology, neglecting how Islam might offer cultural constructs and moral models of affect. Beginning perhaps with Margaret Mead and Gregory Bateson in Bali during the 1930s, and carried on by Clifford Geertz during the 1960s and a generation of scholars in the 1980s, anthropologists of Indonesia have been interested in the cultural, not religious, construction of emotion. Geertz wrote about both religion and emotion, but seldom in terms of religious models of emotion. And for Geertz, Islam itself was a "thin veneer" overlying Hindu-Buddhist mystical practices and courtly restraint (1960b; Woodward 1989).

But the story is more complex. Even if scholars of Indonesia had been attuned to religious idioms of affect, they still would not have written about *qolbu*. The word has only recently entered the everyday national lexicon in Indonesia. Aa Gym brought the word *qolbu*—largely confined to the walls of Islamic schools—into the national public sphere and the religious marketplace of Islamic self-help. This relatively recent transformation in the national discourse about emotion marks an interesting shift in terms from the *hati* (the seat of the emotions, the liver) and the Javanese "logic of the *rasa*" (Stange 1984) toward a decidedly Islamic understanding of the heart.

However, by 2005 the word *qolbu* was ubiquitous in the national and religious imaginary. In spoken speech, Indonesians still use the word *hati*, but *qolbu* had acquired a cultural, religious, and market cachet in the public sphere and national imaginary. For example, popular television preacher Jefri al-Buchori occasionally hosted the morning television show *The Qolbu Touch* (*Sentuhan Qolbu*); then-head of Indonesia's People's Consultative Assembly (MPR), Hidayat Nur Wahid, wrote the book *The Qolbu Touch in the Qur'an*; and, of course, Aa Gym even trademarked Manajemen Qolbu as MQ. His devotees listened to his radio show *MQ Pagi*, watched televised sermons produced by MQTV, and joined his piety and prosperity training seminars, MQ Training. Beyond the world of popular preachers, Islamist politicians, and Islamic training seminars, in the early 1990s academic psychologists in Indonesia formed the Association for Islamic Psychology, launched the academic publication *Journal of Islamic Psychology* (*Jurnal Psikologi Islami*) in 2004, and led divisive campaigns in universities to separate those academics who subscribed to Western secular models of the mind from those who promoted Islamic understandings of the mind, self, and soul. The popularity of Aa Gym and Manajemen Qolbu is thus part of a widespread convergence of Islam and psychology across diverse organizational and institutional settings. My task was to try to make some sense of these encounters—who, where, how, why, and to what social, economic, and political effect?

Like ethnographies, field sites are made, not found (Heider 1988). In terms of methodological strategies, I followed George Marcus's advice (1998, 90–91) for conducting multisited ethnography: "follow the people" (in this case, Aa Gym) and "follow the thing" (Manajemen Qolbu). Over the course of two years of fieldwork (September 2005–July 2007) and several subsequent visits (August 2008, June 2009, July 2010, July 2012, and August 2014), I shadowed Aa Gym, collecting unique observations and insights about his role as public figure, the specific kind of religious authority he wielded, and how he navigated networks of religious, business, and political elite and then mobilized them for his personal, corporate, and political causes. Second, I also followed "the thing," tracing the social life of Manajemen Qolbu (MQ) to understand its multiple discursive genealogies that connect with Islamic and Western psychological sciences and circulate within the market niche of Islamic self-help psychology.

It would be difficult to overstate Aa Gym's celebrity status at the time I began fieldwork in 2005. In a country where even the most famous movie stars can walk freely in Jakarta's supermalls without being mobbed, Aa Gym had no hope of making it through a crowd without his bodyguards. Even then, it typically involved countless handshakes, group photos, and selfies. He even claims to have set a national record for being the most photographed Indonesian ever. With thousands of visitors getting their pictures taken with Aa Gym every weekend, I am not inclined to dispute that claim. I am grateful to Aa Gym for welcoming me into his Islamic school and permitting me to chronicle his life, from the proud moments of national celebrity to the dark and difficult days of public humiliation. I gathered ethnographic information and leveraged that data for my own professional, and ultimately financial, ends.

Yet ethnography is more than simple extraction. It is also embedded in exchange. When I present this research for academic audiences, I am often asked, What (if anything) did Aa Gym get out of having me around? Why even allow me to travel with him and chronicle his life (especially his fall from grace)? For the most part, Aa Gym described my presence as an opportunity to show an American "the beauty of Islam." I arrived in 2005 amid an ongoing "war on terror," and he joked that he wished I were a CIA agent so I could tell President Bush that Islam is not a violent faith. Beyond the geopolitics of America's war on terror, when he was young, Aa Gym had a very positive experience with American missionaries, and I suspect that also played a role in his warm welcome.

I traveled with Aa Gym throughout Indonesia as he preached to tens of thousands of admiring followers, observed the production of television

programs, and accompanied Aa Gym as he met with politicians, bureau-
crats, and businesspeople. I usually traveled with his advance team, two
or three assistants who arrived a few days prior to liaise with the inviting
committees, double-check travel routes, and verify the stage and sound
setup. I observed long conversations, and occasional arguments, about who
would get to sit next to Aa Gym, dine at his table, or sit at adjacent tables.
During informal interviews with local committee members, I got a sense
of how local cultural brokers pulled together private and government funds
to sponsor Aa Gym's visits, which could cost thousands of dollars for lo-
gistics, police, crowd control, advertising, and the preacher's honorarium. I
often rode with Aa Gym during these visits, especially when his motorcade
would circle the town square after his sermon, and Aa Gym would rise out
of the sunroof and wave to his adoring fans, who shouted warm greetings
as he passed by. News spread quickly when he visited local restaurants, and
soon dozens of onlookers, mostly his female admirers, gathered outside in
the hopes of catching a glimpse of Aa Gym.

Gender played an important role in Aa Gym's widespread popularity. As
I will discuss, Aa Gym presented himself as the ideal of modern Muslim
masculinity—the gentle, romantic, self-made family man—and his audiences were overwhelmingly women. Whereas much of the literature has
divided the intellectual labor into studies of Muslim femininity *or* masculinity, I bring these categories together in a single analytical frame in order
to better understand how feminine fantasy is informed by understandings
about ideal Muslim masculinity (at least in this particular hetero-normative
articulation). Of course, ideas about gendered propriety influenced the social spaces in which I could speak with women as well as the sorts of questions I could ask. My gendered positionality as a male certainly influenced
my fieldwork, data, and analysis. My status as a man, however, did not
prevent me from eliciting meaningful accounts about women's emotional
and economic connection with Aa Gym. Indeed, I spent much of my weekends speaking with women's pilgrimage groups as they waited in line to get
their picture taken with Aa Gym. I also attended public events tailored for
women, such as the launching of Betty Y. Sundari's book, *A Muslim Woman
Becomes CEO: Come On, Become a Momtrepreneur*. I also served as a guest
speaker for an MQTV training seminar, "The Spiritual Power of Women."
Although I cannot claim any privileged insider perspective, the seminar offered yet another opportunity to understand the cultural ideals of gender,

emotion, and family espoused by popular icons of feminine piety, such as celebrity actress Astri Ivo. And when Aa Gym fell from public grace, women had no problem expressing their anger and sense of betrayal.

At both the pinnacle of popularity and during his downfall, Aa Gym graciously provided access to different contexts, moments, discussions, and decisions. When I first asked Aa Gym for copyright permission for MQ Photo's portrait of Aa Gym standing boldly in front of a fighter jet, and disclosed that the image would be used for an article about his downfall, he simply replied, "Please feel free to use any documentation you have, as long as you first consult your conscience." This was a testament to his cooperation with my project, and I have taken his request to heart. Along the way, Aa Gym offered commentary on his understanding of his role as a public figure as well as his diverse relationships with Muslim clerics, national politicians, and wealthy investors.

Just weeks into my research, Aa Gym invited me to join an eight-car caravan for family vacation at the end of Ramadan 2005. Professing one's friendship and sympathetic connection with interlocutors has long been a trope in anthropological research and writing. I do not wish to extol or exaggerate my close connection with Aa Gym. Nonetheless my access to Aa Gym, and my relationships with his family and inner circle, did afford a unique glimpse into the phenomenon of Muslim televangelism, Islamic psychology, and popular culture. Aa Gym often invited me to join him onstage, especially during his stock sermon on "the beauty of differences." He introduced me as his American anthropologist friend, Aa Jim (our running joke was that he was Aa Gym, pronounced with a hard "G," and I was his sidekick Aa Jim). "Hey Mr. *Aa Jim*. Did you place an order with Allah, asking to be born with white skin?" And in what eventually turned into a scripted performance, I would reply, "No, Aa [elder brother]." Then he would continue, "And did you put in a request to be born in America, that land of Mr. George W. Bush?" After a little more banter, Aa Gym quoted from the Qur'an to remind the audience that Allah, if so inclined, could have made all ethnic groups and nationalities the same. But Allah chose not to and decreed that religions and nations are to compete with each other in good deeds. I had become part of the road show—a small price to pay for the opportunity to travel with Aa Gym around the country. Much like his devotees, and perhaps like many other ethnographic encounters, my relationship with Aa Gym was marked by economic and emotional exchange.

To "follow the thing," I traced how Manajemen Qolbu Training integrated Western psychology and then stripped it of its secular garb, adorning it instead with teachings from the Qur'an and stories of the Prophet Muhammad. At Daarut Tauhiid—Aa Gym's Islamic school, television studios, and training complex—I worked closely with several trainers whose job was to design, market, and conduct MQ Training. I participated in meetings and observed firsthand how these trainers drew from a broad range of Islamic and Western sources. I looked on as they refined MQ Training and pitched training seminars to human resources managers of privately owned companies and state-owned enterprises. MQ Training at Daarut Tauhiid generated the bulk of the non-MQTV-related revenues—to the tune of five hundred dollars per person for week-long training groups of approximately fifty employees.[2] Daarut Tauhiid had the capacity and resources to host about eight groups a week. I joined dozens of corporate MQ Training cohorts and "spiritual tourist" groups during their visits to Daarut Tauhiid. Weekends could begin as early as 3:00 a.m. with prayers and *dzikir* (mindfulness of God) recitation inside the mosque in the mornings, continuing with seminar classes and group meals during the day, culminating each evening in coffee and conversation in the open-air lobby of the MQ Guest House. As I got further into my research, I also surveyed other popular Islamic training programs to get a better sense of the range of both Islamic training and Muslim *trainers* in Indonesia.[3]

I developed my ideas on marketing and Aa Gym's personal brand during ongoing conversations with leading figures in the marketing and business seminar circuit. One of these, Hermawan Kartajaya, was Indonesia's self-proclaimed "marketing guru." President of one of Indonesia's most successful marketing firms, Kartajaya popularized his theory of a historical marketing trajectory that began with appeals to the rational, then to the emotional, and now to the spiritual values of customers—or "spiritual marketing." Even though he was not Muslim, Kartajaya was a keen observer of religious marketing and coauthored the best-selling book *Syariah Marketing*. He also coauthored books with Aa Gym and frequently appeared on the seminar circuit with other popular Muslim trainers and business leaders. After initially meeting Kartajaya at a seminar on "Spiritual Capital," we met several times to discuss Aa Gym as a spiritual marketer and the booming culture of corporate seminars in Indonesia. Eventually Kartajaya asked me to become a trainer for his marketing firm. I was hired to develop and deliver marketing seminars on "Ethnographic Marketing." These were the sorts of serendipity that shaped my fieldwork.

Without wishing to romanticize "street corner" ethnography (Whyte 1943), I was fortunate to be able to conduct the vast majority of my fieldwork within one hundred meters of a single street corner at Aa Gym's Islamic school. To give a sense of the spatial layout of Aa Gym's Islamic school, a sprawling complex tucked away in a crowded suburb on the slopes of northern Bandung, this ethnographic crossroads was directly across from the mosque, which was in front of Aa Gym's mini-mart, next to the training classrooms, diagonally across from the MQ Fashion store, which was next to Aa Gym's Islamic bank office, which was near the souvenir shop, up the alley from Aa Gym's home, which was across the courtyard from MQTV, just down another side street from the MQ Publishing company, across from the sound production company, and near the MQ Guest House, diagonal from the souvenir shop, which, to come full circle, gets us back to the mosque.

Aa Gym seldom missed a piece of the economic action. An admirer of vertical integration business models, he owned the guest houses where the corporate trainees stayed, the cleaning business that washed the sheets, the restaurants that catered the food, the mini-mart that sold snacks and toiletries, the nearby pharmacy, and even funded profit-sharing initiatives for dozens of small-scale food, clothing, and souvenir vendors inside the complex. He frequently sold Daarut Tauhiid display space for various promotional and marketing ventures of both private corporations (such as Honda) and state-owned enterprises (such as PERTAMINA Oil).

Part of Aa Gym's business success was due to an adept ability to cultivate personal relationships with Indonesia's financial and political brokers. A parade of politicians, Muslim leaders, foreign dignitaries, and academics came to visit Aa Gym on a regular basis. Each weekend, thousands of "spiritual tourists" and corporate trainees toured the complex, prayed in the mosque, and purchased Aa Gym souvenirs to take home to family and friends. I enjoyed countless conversations, coffees, and lunches with a diverse range of Indonesians (Muslims and non-Muslims alike) who made the pilgrimage to Daarut Tauhiid, and I even met with some of them in their homes when I traveled with Aa Gym.

Aa Gym left Bandung every Monday afternoon and typically returned by Thursday evening to deliver his national radio sermon. Each Monday morning, I would join the approximately seven hundred other employees for a weekly sermon and motivation session before Aa Gym left town. As an honorary member of Daarut Tauhiid, I was expected to arrive promptly for these weekly sessions and to conform to the male dress code of dark pants and long-sleeved formal white shirt. Occasionally some of my friends and interlocutors would ask jokingly when I was going to fully comply with the dress code: "Hey, *Aa Jim*, why do you always seem to remember everything except for the white *peci* hat?" Donning this hat would mean that I had converted to Islam. Their playful kidding aside, Aa Gym made it clear that compulsion was not allowed in Islam. Whether I became Muslim, he assured me, was an issue between God and me.

It would be impossible to provide an in-depth analysis of the twenty-plus corporate divisions within Daarut Tauhiid and MQ Corporation. I conducted a preliminary visit to every subsidiary but later focused my efforts on those most relevant to my ethnographic questions and theoretical interests. I did not have a rigid schedule that dictated certain months for researching each division at Daarut Tauhiid. Instead I structured my calendar in a way that would allow me to research what departments defined as their most important activities and propagation (*dakwah*; Arabic, *da'wah*). I worked with MQTV during the times when they were most intensively designing, programming, and producing Aa Gym's television shows (usually the couple of months before Ramadan). I sat in production meetings while marketing directors discussed how to best promote Aa Gym. I listened as producers decided which psychologist to invite for an episode of Aa Gym's prime-time program *Voice of the Heart* (*Suara Hati*). I also interviewed several popular preachers, public icons, and industry executives involved with Islamic media and self-help psychology.

I met with writers and editors at Aa Gym's publishing company (MQS), worked alongside employees as they prepared their booth for the Islamic Book Fair in Jakarta, and followed the successes and failures of various MQS self-improvement books. I learned even more about the Islamic publishing industry during several long conversations and interviews with Haidar Bagir, the president-director of Mizan Press. These experiences do not figure heavily in this book, yet they were important to my broader understandings of the Islamic self-help industry.

I also devoted a lot of time working with the executive board and staff of Aa Gym's moral movement, Gema Nusa. I participated in the "Training of Trainers" retreat, where representatives from over thirty provincial offices convened in Jakarta to learn Gema Nusa's civic volunteer and organizational management curriculum. During my trips with Aa Gym, I attended the formal declarations of the provincial offices in North Sumatra, West Sumatra, and South Kalimantan. I gained insights into some of the local politics of becoming a Gema Nusa leader, and I got a sense of how Gema Nusa also spread through some of the organizational structures and economic players involved in Aa Gym's multilevel marketing and consumer goods company, MQ Barokah (MQ Blessings).

These ethnographic encounters reflect my main methodological strategies and the ethnographic contexts in which they unfolded. I collected hundreds of qualitative surveys and conducted a range of formal interviews. I gained important perspectives through conversations with Indonesian scholars and greatly appreciate their invitations to present my research at several universities and academic forums in Indonesia. The insights of these colleagues and interlocutors were especially valuable during the immediate aftermath of Aa Gym's downfall, when I had to rethink my prior assumptions, working theories, and future research agenda. This book examines the phenomenon of Muslim televangelism from different ethnographic contexts and theoretical perspectives. It is about the rise and fall of a celebrity preacher, yet it is about much more than the biography of a single preacher. It is about how a popular-culture niche of Sufis and self-help gurus has managed to recalibrate religious authority, Muslim subjectivity, and religious politics in post-authoritarian Indonesia. Popular culture is a fickle thing, though. Styles go in and out of vogue, and pop icons rise and fall. This book is a reluctant truce in my thinking and writing.

# Acknowledgments

Hutang emas dapat dibayar
Hutang budi dibawa mati
Debts of gold can be repaid
Debts of kindness we take to the grave

—*Indonesian couplet*

I have had the great fortune to accumulate many debts of kindness along the meandering path that led to the research and writing of this book. As this book project nears its end, I get the privilege and pleasure to reflect on the people and places that have shaped both research and researcher. I am indebted to so many for their time, generous engagement, intellectual insights, incisive critiques, and kind encouragement along the way. Formal acknowledgments cannot adequately express my gratitude to the several institutions, departments, and colleagues that have helped to shape this book.

I first became interested in the academic study of emotion as a high school intern at Southern Methodist University, where Buck Hampson introduced me to observational research in the field of clinical psychology. Two decades later, Buck continues to be a wonderful mentor and friend. When I was an undergraduate psychology major at Marquette University, Marvin Berkowitz, James Grych, and Tony Kuchan continued to guide my interest in emotion. When my interests gradually shifted toward the cultural dimensions of emotion, my anthropology professor Alice Kehoe encouraged me to consider graduate training in anthropology.

When I began my MA in anthropology under the guidance of Karl Heider at the University of South Carolina, I could barely place Indonesia on a map and had never heard of Clifford Geertz. In his seminars, Karl introduced me to the anthropological study of Indonesia, emotion, ethnographic film, and cinema studies. Through his everyday example, he taught me the importance of humility and collegiality. Laura Ahearn, Ann Kingsolver, and Tom Leatherman introduced me to anthropological theory and continue to offer encouragement when our paths cross. During a year of intensive Indonesian language study at Cornell University, Betty Chandra, Krishna Darma, and John Wolff were brilliant (and patient) teachers, and the Center for Southeast Asian Studies provided a warm welcome. Richard Baxstrom added welcome levity to our language study, and over the years I have learned much from his innovative approach to cinema in Southeast Asia.

This project took shape within, and between, two vibrant intellectual communities at University of Wisconsin–Madison: the Department of Anthropology and the Center for Southeast Asian Studies (CSEAS). It would be difficult to overstate the time, generosity, and unfailing support of Ken George. In what came to be known as "idea badminton," Ken guided me as I tried, in fits of starts and stops, to articulate what this project might become, always encouraging me to follow my curiosity. In the years since, Ken has continued to offer warm counsel and sharp insights. Kirin Narayan contributed her wonderful energy, wit, and wisdom, and her seminar on ethnographic writing compelled me to consider issues of voice, narrative, and characterization. Historian of science and medicine Warwick Anderson encouraged me to investigate the historical legacies, transnational flows, and social life of Islamic psychology. Katherine Bowie, Charles Hirschkind, Maria Lepowsky, Paul Nadasdy, Larry Nesper, Frank Solomon, and the late Neil Whitehead generously offered their time and expertise along the way. The CSEAS was a wonderful community of interdisciplinary inquiry, and I am especially grateful to Mike Cullinane, Anne Hansen, Ellen Rafferty, Andy Sutton, and Mary Jo Wilson. Conversations with fellow graduate students Sarah Besky, Yosef Djakababa, Eric Haanstad, Jennifer Munger, Alex Nading, Natalie Porter, Fadjar Thufail, and Kent Wisniewski pushed me to articulate the relevance of my work beyond Indonesia, and I remain grateful for their continued advice and friendship.

Several scholars beyond UW-Madison also helped to shape this project during the initial stages of research and writing. Robert Hefner commented on an early grant proposal, visited Daarut Tauhiid during my fieldwork, and has continued to provide abiding mentorship and encouragement. Anna Gade generously offered her encyclopedic knowledge about Islam and emotion when she was a scholar-in-residence in Madison during the summer of 2004, and she continues to offer wisdom and guidance in the study of Islam. And Peter Mandaville, ever since his visit to Daarut Tauhiid in 2007, has been an invaluable interlocutor about Islam, media, and politics. Other scholars who shared their own insights during visits to Daarut Tauhiid include Art Buehler, miriam cooke, M. B. Hooker, Julia Day Howell, Bruce Lawrence, Tim Lindsey, Hans Pols, Julia Suryakusuma, and Nelly van Doorn-Harder. Byron Good and Mary-Jo DelVecchio Good were wonderful interlocutors when I presented my research at the Islamic University of Indonesia (UII). They, along with Michael Fischer and Mary Steedly, offered helpful insight, questions, and encouragement when I presented my research at Harvard University's School of Social Medicine.

I am also grateful to other interlocutors along the way who posed provocative questions during presentations at Boston University (CURA, The Institute on Culture, Religion, and World Affairs); Indonesian Institute for Sciences (LIPI); New College of Florida (Department of Anthropology); Islamic University of Bandung (Department of Psychology); National Islamic University-Syarif Hidayatullah (UIN, Center for the Study of Islam and Society); Stanford University (Asia Pacific Research Center); University of Michigan (Stephen M. Ross School of Business); World Affairs Council (San Francisco); and the Centers for Southeast Asian Studies (CSEAS) at Cornell University, Northern Illinois University, University of Michigan, University of Wisconsin–Madison, UCLA, and University of California, Berkeley.

This book evolved over the course of fellowships, and I appreciate these institutions and colleagues for their warm collegiality and generous support of my research. During my time at the Shorenstein Asia Pacific Research Center at Stanford University (2009–2010), my thinking benefited from Don Emmerson's indefatigable curiosity and unfailing collegiality. I am also grateful to other scholars-in-residence during that time, Marshall Clark, Juliet Piet, Thitinan Pongsudhirak, Sudarno Sumarto, and Christian von Luebke. In the Islamic World Studies Program at Lake Forest College (2010–2011), Cathy Benton, Hasan Kösebalaban, and Ahmad Sadri, each in their own ways, offered important guidance as I continued to revise the book and figure out how to write and teach about Islam.

During my time at University of Michigan (2011–2012), I am especially indebted to Allen Hicken for his efforts to host my ACLS New Faculty Fellow grant at the CSEAS and the Center for International and Comparative Studies. I also offer my gratitude to several other scholars and students affiliated with CSEAS: Ismail "Aji" Alatas, Saul Allen, Dan Birchok, John Ciorciari, Nancy Florida, Linda Lim, Rudolf Mrazek, Charley Sullivan, and Kate Wright. In the Department of Anthropology, I enjoyed conversations with Webb Keane, whose engagement with my 2011 talk at CSEAS pushed me to better articulate my arguments about interpellation, sincerity, and scandal. It was also a pleasure to talk with Stuart Kirsch, who graciously commented on a draft book chapter about reality-TV production in Papua. At Michigan State University, Mohammed Ayoob, Siddharth Chandra, Beth Drexler, and Mara Leichtman were wonderful interlocutors who warmly welcomed me to lectures and workshops in Islamic studies, Asian studies, and anthropology.

In my current home at Emory University, I am privileged to have wonderful colleagues in the Departments of Religion, Anthropology, Film and Media Studies, Islamic Civilizations (ICIVS), and the Graduate Division of Religion (GDR). In the West and South Asian Religions course of study in the GDR, I have learned from the scholarship and collegiality of John Dunne, Joyce Flueckiger, Marko Geslani, Arun Jones, and Sara McClintock. Joyce Flueckiger, Vernon Robbins, and Don Seeman have been wonderful mentors; Gary Laderman has been a steady source of guidance, humor, and good music; and Bobbi Patterson has blessed my family with her friendship and grace.

The Departments of Anthropology and Film and Media Studies have each welcomed me into their communities, and I am especially grateful for the collegiality of Matthew Bernstein, Jenny Chio, Carla Freeman, Bruce Knauft, Peter Little, David Nugent, Chikako Ozawa-del Silva, and Michael Peletz. And Vince Cornell warmly welcomed me as a faculty member in the Islamic Civilizations PhD program (ICIVS). This book builds on Vince's arguments about exemplary authority, and our conversations about Aa Gym and Al-Ghazālī pushed me to expand the arguments advanced in Chapter 5 about an Islamic ethics of vision. It has also been a pleasure to work alongside additional ICIVS colleagues as we launched our PhD program, especially Sam Cheribi, Rkia Cornell, Scott Kugle, Roxani Margariti, Abdullahi an-Naim, Gordon Newby, and Devin Stewart. I have also benefited from the insights and intellect of several current and former Emory students working in Indonesia, including Claire-Marie Hefner, Mohammed Nasir, and Siti Sarah Muwahidah.

Many other colleagues and mentors over the last decade have helped broaden my understanding of Indonesia and sharpen my analysis of Islam. Without the space for detail here, I list many in the hopes that each of them will know the specific workshop, panel, collaboration, or late-night conference conversation in which their insights and observations helped to shape this book: Ed Aspinall, Tauhid Nur Azhar, Azyumardi Azra, Joshua Barker, Greg Barton, Richard Baxstrom, Suzanne Brenner, Michael Buehler, Robin Bush, Siddharth Chandra, Aryo Danusiri, Dadi Darmadi, Yosef Djakababa, Christopher Duncan, Greg Fealy, Richard Fox, Nelden Djakababa Gericke, George Gmelch, Sharon Gmelch, Jeff Hadler, Nelly van Doorn-Harder, Adam Harr, Karl Heider, Charles Hirschkind, Doug Hollan, Julia Day Howell, Carla Jones, Eunsook Jung, Arsalan Khan, Doreen Lee, Mara Leichtman, Rob Lemelson, Johan Lindquist, Brent Luvaas, Peter Mandaville, Rich Martin, Rusdi Maslim, Jeremy Menchik, Yasmin Moll, Rudolf Mrazek, Wazhmah Osman, Jolanda M. Pandin, Jim Peacock, Tom Pepinsky, Hans Pols, Rachel Rinaldo, Kathy Robinson, Daromir Rudnyckyj, Laurie Sears, Nancy Smith-Hefner, David Strohl, M. A. Subandi, Sukidi, Eric Tagliocozzo, Fadjar Thufail, Philips Vermonte, C. W. Watson, Andrew Weintraub, Marina Welker, Sally White, and Kent Wisniewski.

I am forever indebted to Bob Hefner, Carla Jones, and Michael Peletz for graciously reading the entire manuscript and for their deep knowledge, sharp insights, and incisive critiques. Their respective scholarship has greatly influenced my own thinking about anthropology, Islam, and Southeast Asia, and I could not have asked for more generous readings and critical reflections. Eric Haanstad, Ron Lukens-Bull, Kristin Phillips, and David Strohl also provided careful readings, encouraging comments, and critical reflections on the introduction and specific chapters during the final editing. Each has made this a better book, though undoubtedly it falls short. At Stanford University Press, Anne Fuzellier, Jenny Gavacs, and James Holt gracefully guided this book throughout the process, and I am grateful to Cynthia Lindlof for her masterful copyediting.

I am grateful to several organizations whose support helped fund different stages of the research and writing for this book, including a Fulbright Hays Award; an Andrew W. Mellon Foundation fellowship in Islamic World Studies at Lake Forest College; American Council of Learned Societies New Faculty Fellows award; University of Wisconsin (Center for Southeast Asian Studies; Department of Anthropology; Global Studies Program); and Stanford University (Shorenstein Asia Pacific Research Center). I would also like to thank Emory College of Arts & Sciences and the James T. Laney Graduate School for subvention support for the index and map.

None of this research would have been possible without my extended family (*keluarga besar*) at Daarut Tauhiid (DT) who welcomed me into their offices, homes, and lives. Telling me that he wanted to provide me the opportunity to see the "real" Islam, Aa Gym warmly welcomed me into the DT community and allowed me to chronicle his personal triumphs and his public defeats. I have tried to do so with both a critical eye and respectful tone. Aa Gym's family always made me feel welcome. I am especially grateful Ibu Yetty Rohayati, Apa Engkus Kuswara, Aa Deda, Pak Wahyu, Pak Dudung, Teh Betty, Teh Nggen, Teh Ninih, Teh Rini, and Teh Mira. Others at DT were especially helpful during my research, including Pak Budi Faisal, Pak Palgunadi, Pak Eko, Pak Achmad, and Ibu Khairati. DT employees at the secretary and security offices in Bandung and Jakarta, especially Bang Herdan, Bang Jaka, Mas Hendra, and Teh Popon, shared Aa Gym's itineraries to help me plan my research schedule and graciously coordinated my travel with him. Several trainers from MQ Training and LP2ES invited me into their creative processes of developing curriculum, especially Pak Sena, Pak Yana, Ustad Komar, Mas Amri, Kang Fahri, and Kang Bagja. Gema Nusa representatives provided extraordinary access to, and insights about, their mission to cultivate civic virtue. I especially appreciate Pak Mukhlis, Pak Umar Hadi, Pak Anas, Mas Rosidin, Kang Opick, Mas Obest, and Kang Fuad. Employees at MQ Publishing, including Pak Bambang, Kang Denny, and Mas Abdul, shared their insights and experience in the burgeoning industry of Islamic publishing. Last, friends at MQ Travel added warm friendship and great humor during our English-language classes.

Several prominent Indonesian trainers generously shared their time and perspectives, including Ary Ginanjar Agustian, Jamil Azzaini, Marwah Daud Ibrahim, Tung Desem Waringin, and Andrie Wongso. I gained a much broader perspective about aspirational piety and Islamic psychology over the course of several conversations with Haidar Bagir and his colleagues at Mizan Press and Mizan Productions, especially Putut Widjanarko, M. Deden Ridwan, and Cecep Romli. At MarkPlus & Co., Hermawan Kartajaya, Michael Kartajaya, Jacky Mussry, and Taufik shared their encyclopedic knowledge of marketing in Indonesia and have continued to offer their perspectives on Aa Gym as a religious marketer. Dr. Muhamad Hisyam, my research sponsor at the Indonesian Institute of Sciences, shared his insights about religious authority in the public sphere. I could not have managed all of my data without the brilliant help of Arif Doeya, who worked as my research assistant in rural West Sumatra in 1998 when he was just sixteen years old. When our paths crossed again in 2006, Arif was an undergraduate student at the prestigious Bandung Institute of Technology (ITB) and graciously agreed to help me, yet again, to transcribe what seemed like endless sermons and television shows.

I had the privilege of having two foster families during my time in Indonesia. Relatives of my friend Fadjar Thufail, Bu It and Om As, welcomed me into their home in Jakarta as if I were their own son. When I returned to Jakarta for subsequent visits, I frequently stayed with my friend Yosef Djakababa and his sister Nelden, who became like my brother and sister. After spending weeks shadowing Aa Gym, I always looked forward to taking a short break, hopping the train to Jakarta, and enjoying a couple of days of relaxing dinners and inspiring conversations with Yosef, Nelden, and friends. I am also grateful to AMINEF staff, especially Nellie Paliama, for their generous kindness and warm hospitality..

This book would never be possible without the enduring love and support of my own family. Mark Twain once remarked that, when he was a boy of fourteen, his father was so ignorant that he could hardly stand it. But by the time Twain turned twenty-one, he was amazed at how much his old man had learned in just seven years. And so it has been with my own gradual understanding of and appreciation for my parents, Dick and Marybeth Hoesterey. Each in their own way, my parents have always provided unconditional love, support, and wisdom. They never asked me how I would ever get a job in anthropology or whether I might prefer graduate school in law, medicine, or business. Instead, they visited Indonesia, learned more about Islam, and generously found ways to help keep me afloat at pivotal points during graduate school. My siblings, Brian, Julie, Mark, and Sarah, have each influenced me in their own ways, all of them serving as a constant reminder of the more important and enduring things in life. They have always been there for me—and that is the debt of kindness one takes to the grave. If none of this would have been possible without my parents, none of it would have much meaning or joy without the friendship, faith, humor, advice, and love of my wife, Kristin Phillips. I am blessed to share this journey with you and our beloved boys, Burke and Marcus.

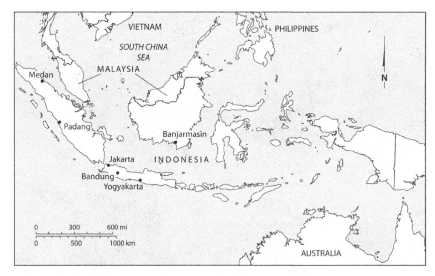

MAP I.I. The author traveled with Aa Gym in each city noted on the map. Daarut Tauhiid is located in Bandung.

FIGURE I.I. Aa Gym swarmed by the audience after a sermon in Padang, West Sumatra.

# Authority, Subjectivity, and the Cultural Politics of Public Piety

This book is about the rise and fall of celebrity preacher Kyai Haji Abdullah Gymnastiar. Known affectionately across the Indonesian archipelago as "Aa Gym" (elder brother Gym), he rose to fame with his message of MQ, or Manajemen Qolbu (Heart Management). MQ blends Sufi ideas about the ethical heart with self-help slogans of Western popular psychology. Despite Aa Gym's lack of formal religious education, he carefully crafted his public image as a pious family man and doting husband, which made him especially popular among Indonesian women. His reputation as a savvy entrepreneur also resonated with the aspirations of middle-class Muslims who seek both piety and prosperity. Aa Gym trademarked Manajemen Qolbu as MQ, and his companies sold products ranging from MQ Training and MQ inspirational text messages to MQ Cola and MQ Shampoo. Millions of viewers tuned in for his Sunday television show, over one hundred radio stations broadcast his morning program, and thousands of spiritual tourists and corporate trainees flocked to his Islamic school each week. Ranked among the "50 Most Important Muslims" worldwide, Aa Gym was keen to parlay his public pulpit into political capital (Esposito and Kalin 2009). Then, at the peak of his popularity in 2006, Aa Gym fell from grace when a secret went public. His female followers, feeling heartsick and betrayed, publicly shred photographs of their once-beloved guru; television executives canceled his lucrative contracts; powerful politicians kept their distance; and his Islamic school and MQ Training complex became a ghost town.

The rise and fall of Aa Gym raises important questions about religious authority, Muslim subjectivity, and the cultural politics of public piety:

How could a young man without formal religious education become Indonesia's most celebrated preacher? How might Aa Gym's story suggest a new kind of religious authority quite different from a more conventional cleric's erudition in Islamic jurisprudence? How can an understanding of the rise of Muslim self-help gurus—and their Islamic popular psychology—shed light on the anxieties and aspirations of middle-class Muslims in Indonesia? How might Aa Gym's political engagements on the public stage compel scholars to reimagine the relationship between popular culture and political Islam? And what does his abrupt fall from grace reveal about the cultural and market politics of religious authority and public piety?

In this book I chronicle the phenomenon of Aa Gym as a way to examine new trends in religious authority, to explore the religious and economic desires of an aspiring middle class, and to inquire about the political predicaments bridging self and state. I follow Aa Gym as he circulates, connects, and occasionally collides with the religious, financial, and political elite. It is a world of Sufis and self-help gurus, piety and anxiety, products and brands, patrons and politicians. Thus, tracing the life and career of a celebrity preacher affords a unique vantage point from which to comment on wider conversations concerning authority, subjectivity, and public piety in post-authoritarian Indonesia. In what follows I frame my research on Aa Gym and Manajemen Qolbu within a broader inquiry in the social life of psychology. Next, I describe my approach to the study of global Muslim networks and the deployment of genealogy as method, noting how it differs from recent scholarship linking Southeast Asia with the Middle East. The remainder of the introduction outlines the three main sections of the book: (1) religious authority; (2) Muslim subjectivity; and (3) the politics of public piety.

## An Anthropology of Islamic Psychology

During my first month of fieldwork, Aa Gym invited me inside his home office while he prepared his Thursday-evening radio sermon, broadcast across the archipelago on Indonesia's national radio station. He sat with his legs propped up, his reflexologist working out the kinks. Aa Gym alternated between two books. The first, *Parting the Curtain to God*, was a formal exegesis of the Qur'an by the prominent Indonesian scholar Quraish Shihab. I was surprised to see this juxtaposed with the second book: an Indonesian translation of *Chicken Soup for the Philosopher's Soul*. Perplexed,

I glanced at his bookcases nearby. Stacked comfortably beside his collection of Abū Ḥāmid al-Ghazālī's treatises on the heart were translated books by American pop psychologists and management gurus: Daniel Goleman's *Emotional Intelligence*; Steven Covey's *Seven Habits of Highly Effective People*; Dale Carnegie's *Guide to Enjoying Your Life and Work*; *The Millionaire Mind*; *Anybody Can Do Anything*, and so on. When I asked (somewhat dubiously) Aa Gym about his interests in Western popular psychology and management, he replied gently with a hadith (saying from the Prophet): "The Prophet Muhammad, peace be upon him, tells us that 'we must go as far as China to seek knowledge.' . . . We can take wisdom [*hikmah*; Arabic, *ḥikma*] from this book. . . . All knowledge ultimately comes from God."

Aa Gym promoted Manajemen Qolbu as a moral psychology of the heart, as practical Islamic wisdom that would help Indonesians in their pursuit for both piety and prosperity. Manajemen Qolbu blends Sufi ideas of the heart with Western pop psychology and corporate models of human resources training. *Qolbu* is the Islam-inflected Indonesian rendering for the Arabic word *qalb*, roughly translated as the "heart." Aa Gym designed, packaged, and sold MQ Training for "spiritual tourists"[1] and corporate trainees who, by the thousands, made the weekend pilgrimage to his school, studio, and training complex, Daarut Tauhiid. MQ Training begins with a Power-Point slide of the tranquil waters of a mountain lake and quotes a saying of the Prophet Muhammad: "Verily, inside the body there is a piece of flesh. If that flesh is pure, the whole body is pure. If it is soiled, then so too is the entire body. Know that this is the *qalb*."[2] In Sufi psychology the heart is a moral organ, and the cultivation of a pure heart (*qolbun salim*; Arabic, *qalb sālim*) is integral to the ethical pursuit to purify the self (*tazkiyah al-nafs*; Arabic, *tazkiyat al-nafs*), ideally culminating in a tranquil inner self devoted to God (*nafs al-mutma'inna*; Arabic, *al-nafs al-muṭma'inna*).[3] The cultivation of a soft and pure heart is necessary for the word of God to enter one's consciousness and transform one's moral subjectivity.[4]

My ethnographic focus on Islamic psychology does not fall neatly into the category of psychological anthropology. There is nothing inherently "Islamic" about *Psikologi Islami*. The Indonesian use of the phrase denotes its adjectival sense (similar to anthropology's own turn toward speaking about the cultural), in which a generation of Muslim pop preachers and self-help gurus in Indonesia have interpreted global psychological sciences (including works by Muslims) and then reinscribed them with religious meaning, legitimacy, and authority. In this book I bring what we might call the anthropology *of* psychology[5] to bear on discussions in Islamic studies and anthropology concerning religious authority, subjectivity, and politics.[6] An anthropology *of* psychology steers clear of the assumptions that plagued psychological anthropology from its early days in culture and personality theory, in which the psychological was understood as an interior state of subjectivity, and the ethnographer's task was to map out a discrete ethno-psychology unique to a particular ethnic group.

Rather than individual emotion and interiorized subjectivity, I am more concerned with the social life of psychology, how popular psychologies travel across borders, circulate within market niches, and are reinscribed in specific religious and political contexts. Invoking Edward Said's concept of traveling theory, Peter Mandaville has observed, "And so theory travels. That which 'is' in one place elsewhere becomes undone, translated, reinscribed; this is the nature of translocality: a cultural politics of *becoming*" (2001, 84; emphasis in original). For the middle class of contemporary Indonesia, Islamic popular psychology resonates with a form of aspirational piety that emphasizes the process of becoming one's true self—pious Muslim, loving partner, savvy entrepreneur, and virtuous citizen.

I am especially interested in *Psikologi Islami* as it informs the political projects of, and social imaginaries about, the nation-state.[7] In this respect, this book builds on legacies of the historical study of psychology,[8] as well as studies of postcolonial science and medicine,[9] in which psychology is understood in terms of power and politics, not simply culture and personality. Ashis Nandy eloquently describes this distinction:

> I have *not* tried to interpret here Indian personality or culture. . . . Instead, I have presumed certain continuities between personality and culture and seen in them political and ethical possibilities. These possibilities are sometimes accepted and sometimes not. In other words, I have tried to retain the critical edge of depth psychology but shifted the locus of criticism from the purely psychological to the psycho-political. There is in these pages an attempt to demystify conventional psychological techniques of demystification. (1983, xviii–xix; emphasis in original)

Inspired by Nandy (and others),[10] I approach *Psikologi Islami* as multiple, transnational bodies of expert knowledge that Indonesian Muslims summon, mobilize, and contest as they navigate the religious and political entanglements between self, market, and state. Islamic psychology and its self-help gurus contribute to the broader repertoire of ethical cultivation practiced by Indonesian Muslims. *Psikologi Islami* is thus one among many ways of being both modern and Muslim.

I also engage and build on the impressive body of scholarship on the cultural and market politics of Islam in Indonesia.[11] Aa Gym rose to fame within the particular religious, economic, and political context of post-authoritarian Indonesia. Whereas public and political expressions of Islamic piety were intensely regulated during much of Suharto's rule (1965–1998), the transition to democratic governance accelerated the proliferation and privatization of media that made possible new media forms and religious figures. On the other hand, the liminal years of democratic transition also brought revelations of mass state violence and related anxieties about authenticity and political uncertainty. The flip side of these anxieties was hope for new beginnings, less corruption, and a gentler state apparatus. Islamic psychology emerged from this blend of anxiety and hope during uncertain times. Alongside the structural reforms mandated by an International Monetary Fund (IMF) bailout in 1998 was resurgence in public dialogue about Islamic entrepreneurship and business ethics. As both entrepreneur and citizen-believer, Aa Gym offered a model of religious and civic authenticity during a post-authoritarian climate of uncertainty and hope. In this respect, Aa Gym represents a new sort of public figure in the religious and political landscape of contemporary Indonesia. Yet at the same time he is only the latest in a centuries-long story of popular preachers who parallel more formal, elite establishments of religious learning (Berkey 2001). At issue is how we conceive of historical precedents, where we look for transnational linkages, and how we understand global Muslim networks.

## Popular Islam, Orthodoxy, and Genealogy as Method

Historians and anthropologists have offered important insights into the literary, religious, and political connections linking Southeast Asia with North Africa and the Middle East.[12] This excellent body of work makes the case for the "long view" of history, or what the French Annales school of historical writing has dubbed the *longue durée*. As such, the emphasis on history, mobility, and the transmission of Sufi practices provides a welcome corrective to previous scholarship about Indonesia that viewed Islam as a "thin veneer" of essentially Hindu-Buddhist practice (e.g., Geertz 1960b).[13] Michael Laffan (2003) has argued in his critique of Benedict Anderson's (1990) theory of nationalism that global Muslim networks and the rise of print capitalism among Indonesian nationalists in Cairo and Mecca also played an important role in forging Indonesian nationalism. Hence, this body of work on global Muslim networks focuses on the long view of history and insists that an understanding of Islam in Indonesia must account for global networks of religious knowledge and practice.

By focusing on the long view, however, we miss the novel role of new figures of religious authority, different demarcations of religious knowledge, and innovative engagements with media technologies. This focus on the Middle East sheds little light on how popular Islam and *Psikologi Islami* in contemporary Indonesia actually connect with the pop psychology and self-help gurus of the West—not just exegetical texts and religious scholars residing in the Middle East. A generation of young Muslim entrepreneurs across the globe—from Jakarta, Indonesia, to Cairo and Ankara—now summon Western pop psychologists and New Age gurus in order to produce religious knowledge, claim religious legitimacy, and engage in the politics of the nation-state. This is not to dismiss the long view of history or to deny the importance of centers of religious learning in the Middle East. It is to say, however, that genealogies of knowledge and practice that connect Bandung, Indonesia, with 1970s New Age from Santa Cruz deserve as much attention as their links with nineteenth-century Cairo.

But which genealogies should we follow? How does the privileging of particular genealogies reflect a certain politics of authority and authenticity? Allow me to briefly sketch out an understanding of genealogy as methodology in the wider context of Talal Asad's important work to shift scholarly understanding away from a Geertzian emphasis on meaning, belief, and cultural systems. Drawing on his notion of Islam as "discursive tradition," Asad advances a post-structuralist approach to how religious tradition and orthopraxy are constituted and contested within relationships of power and knowledge (1986, 14; 1993; 2003). Methodologically, Asad advocates for the study of genealogies of discursive traditions within a "historical grammar of concepts" (2003, 189). When Asad first defined this approach to the study of religion, he deployed a broad understanding of the porosity and geographical reach of genealogies, "whose elements are never fully integrated, *and never bounded by the geographical limits of the Middle East*" (1986, 11; emphasis in original). However, in Asad's more recent contributions to the study of religion (1993, 2003), there appears to be an unfortunate constriction concerning what counts as discursive tradition. Where, geographically, should we follow genealogies of religion? Must we trace a genealogy of discursive traditions within the historical grammar of concepts from the Middle East and Enlightenment Europe? What counts as discursive tradition and correct practice?

Asad directs much of his attention to historical transformations of Islamic jurisprudence (*fiqh*) (2003, 205–256). Legal reasoning is undoubtedly an important domain, and historical and ethnographic studies of Islamic courts have generated compelling ethnographic insights into the relationship between Islam and the modern state (Naim 2008; Peletz 2002, 2013). However, the genealogies of knowledge and forms of religious reasoning related to popular Islam fall well under the radar of Asad's interest in Islamic jurisprudence. We must venture well beyond the medieval Middle East and Enlightenment Europe. Popular Islam is part of a different Islamic genre of moral aphorisms that guide everyday moral comportment (*adab*). We can trace the genealogy of popular Islam back to medieval philosophy and advice-centered (*nasihat*; Arabic, *naṣīḥa*) traditions of moral-political criticism in the Middle East (Asad 1993, 200–238), but not exclusively so. We can follow the genealogy of Western popular psychology back to Enlightenment philosophy and the Kantian championing of individuality and rationality, yet this would fail to account for how the discursive traditions of Western psychology were forged in conversation with an imagined "East." Islamic psychology, and popular Islam more broadly, is thus a sort of unconventional orthodoxy (and orthopraxy, as we will see) that constitutes a discursive tradition with plural origins in both form and content.

These psychological discourses and material manifestations integrate multiple historical genealogies and understandings of religious doctrine and practice. Consider a few brief examples of how Islamic psychology draws from multiple sources and claims to legitimacy and relevance. Contemporary Saudi cleric Dr. Aidh bin Abdullah al-Qarni's 2007 book *Laa Tazhan* (Don't be sad) was arguably *the* most popular Islamic self-improvement book during my fieldwork. As for other links to the Middle East and North Africa, Indonesia's Mizan Press translated a book by the Egyptian human resources consultant Dr. Ibrahim Elfiky, marketed as the "World's Maestro Motivator" and promoter of the therapeutic and professional values of "Neuro-linguistic Programming" (NLP).[14] Finally, Ary Ginanjar's popular ESQ Training (Emotional Spiritual Quotient) creatively blended Islamic ethics with American pop psychologist Daniel Goleman's concept of emotional intelligence (Rudnyckyj 2010). It is difficult to explain these examples of global, psychologized, and hypermodern forms of Islamic knowledge and practice simply in terms of the *longue durée* of networks between Indonesia, North Africa, and the Middle East. Such an analysis might shed important light on how Ibn ʿAṭāʾ Allāh al-Iskandarī's *Al-Ḥikam* (1984) made its way to an Islamic school in West Java, but it does not explain how a young man of modest means and no formal religious education managed to transform its practical theology into a massive empire of Islamic self-development during a particular moment of political democratization in late capitalist modernity.

There is also the problem of origins, authenticity, and the assumptions behind concepts like hybridity and syncretism. Manajemen Qolbu is a blend—as all cultural projects undoubtedly are—yet this does not imply any prior, timeless, coherent cultural forms. Many scholars rightly note that, at one level, every cultural form is hybrid and shaped by history. But we should also ask, How do Indonesians grant legitimacy to expertise that is perceived to be from global psychological sciences? Interestingly, the understanding of neuro-linguistic programming by the Egyptian human resources expert Elfiky is actually based on a self-improvement technique popularized by American firewalking expert Tolly Burkan and his self-help protégé Anthony Robbins. As Loring Danforth (1989) observed, the firewalking movement itself was premised on a romanticization of "Eastern" religious practice.[15]

In 2006 MQ trainers paid hundreds of dollars to attend Anthony Robbins's firewalking training seminar in Jakarta, and they subsequently developed a firewalking training seminar at Daarut Tauhiid. Islamic psychology in contemporary Indonesia thus draws from several genealogies of religious and scientific knowledge. Here, it is difficult to articulate clear-cut "genealogies of religion" that can be neatly traced back to either Western Enlightenment or medieval Islamic philosophy and jurisprudence (Asad 1993, 2003). The case of *Psikologi Islami* requires us to examine multiple genealogies and related models of self and subjectivity that, at times, resonate across seemingly incommensurate historical, ethical, and philosophical divides. And with respect to Aa Gym's newfound psycho-religious authority, he parlayed his public pulpit into a political project to reform self and state. In the remainder of the Introduction, I explore what the rise and fall of Aa Gym and Manajemen Qolbu might tell us about the cultural production of (1) religious authority, (2) Muslim subjectivity, and (3) the politics of public piety.

*Marketing Islam: Public Figures, Personal Brands,
and the Emotional Economy of Religious Authority*

The phenomenon of Aa Gym offers an interesting lens through which to examine the corporatization of religious authority within a marketplace of Islamic modernity. As a celebrity sensation, Aa Gym is emblematic of a recent wave of preachers in Muslim societies worldwide who have adeptly managed media technologies and made innovative claims to religious authority.[16] Anthropologists, historians, and political scientists have explored these new forms of religious authority as part of a post-Habermasian attempt to understand Islamic publics and their counter-publics. In their classic work *Muslim Politics*, Dale Eickelman and James Piscatori (1996) argued that the global Islamic revival of the late twentieth century produced a "fragmentation" of religious authority in the Muslim world. Similarly, Eickelman and Anderson's ([1999] 2003) influential volume on new media in Islamic public spheres explores how new voices of authority mobilize media technologies to contend with (and provide alternatives to) the more conventional forms of authority enjoyed by more orthodox clerics (*ulama*; Arabic, *'ulamā'*).[17] Over the course of several decades, Muslim societies have experienced the impact of new media, the formation of new publics (and counter-publics), and the rise of new public figures.[18] Experienced worldwide, but in different local and transnational contexts, the proliferation of media technologies inspired a new generation of Muslim figures of modernity (professors, painters, and "media mufti") who claim to speak for Islam.[19]

The figure of the televangelist can be understood within this broader shift in the study of new media, religious authority, and Islamic publics. In Indonesia and elsewhere, the privatization and proliferation of television and social media, as well as an emerging middle class, created the structural possibilities and social spaces for a new kind of public figure: the Muslim television preacher, or what I refer to as tele-*dai*. I prefer this term for a couple of reasons. First, popular preachers in Indonesia prefer the Arabic word *dā'ī* (literally, one who calls people to the faith). Second, the term "televangelist" conjures images, memories, and moral judgments of American televangelists in the 1980s (Harding 2000) that do not easily map onto the phenomenon of Muslim television preachers in contemporary Indonesia. However, this is not to say that Muslim televangelism is not without scandal.

The Muslim television preacher emerged as an important figure of Muslim modernity, and Aa Gym was its prototype. In an innovative experiment, Joshua Barker and Johan Lindquist (2009) asked colleagues, myself included, to contribute short essays about salient "figures of modernity" through which to understand the social, cultural, and political shifts in contemporary Indonesia. Drawing on Raymond Williams's (1976) concept of "keywords," Barker and Lindquist envisioned figures of modernity, in part, as a methodological experiment to consider the ideological constitution (and contestation) of Indonesian modernity (2009, 35–36). Among many others, these figures of modernity included "telecommunications expert," "spiritual trainer," "career woman," and the "tele-*dai*." As a figure of modernity, the Muslim television preacher symbolizes an idealized blend of Islam, media, and technology that resonates with an aspirational form of piety. Aa Gym was arguably the most prominent of several television preachers and a related cohort of Islamic "trainers" (they used the English word) who successfully promoted their formulas for piety and prosperity. As preacher, entrepreneur, and pop psychologist, Aa Gym was an icon of public piety through which millions of Indonesians could project, discuss, lament, and rejoice in their own anxieties and aspirations.

Aa Gym certainly had predecessors in Indonesia. C. W. Watson (2005b) notes the popularity of preacher and film star KH Zaenuddin MZ. Known as the "Preacher with a Million Followers," Zaenuddin MZ also starred as the moral protagonist in several Islam-themed films during the 1980s and 1990s, such as Chaerul Umam's *Nada dan Dakwah* (Tone and Islamic outreach). Whereas Zaenuddin MZ is a predecessor with respect to the history of television and film, I would argue that the importance and success of Aa Gym and Manajemen Qolbu owes more to the campus outreach movements of the late 1970s and early 1980s. Imaduddin Abdulrahim's "Mental Training" seminars at the Salman mosque at Bandung Institute of Technology (ITB) were especially important in providing a template for Islamic training. Robert Hefner describes the Salman mosque movement as "the new Muslim activism par excellence" (2000, 123). The Salman mosque training itself was part of a broader engagement with psychology and the medium of Islamic training. In his pioneering work on Indonesia's modernist movement Muhammadiyah during the 1970s, James Peacock provides the first ethnographic description of "Islamic training" in Indonesia (1978b, 95). Peacock noted the explicit usage of the English phrase "social psychology" as part of a broader field of Islamic knowledge. Thus, in terms of Aa Gym's predecessors providing a context for the kind of public figure he would become, we should be mindful of both celebrity preachers such as Zaenuddin MZ and the "Islamic training seminar" as a new discursive tradition.

With respect to comparable popular preachers in other Muslim societies, Aa Gym bears striking resemblance to television preachers Amr Khaled of Egypt (Wise 2003; Moll 2012), Yaşar Nuri Öztürk in Turkey (Öncü 2006), and Cherif Haidara of Mali (Schulz 2006; Soares 2005) and the best-selling author al-Qarni of Saudi Arabia. If one were to search for an American comparison, Aa Gym could aptly be described as a combination of prosperity gospel televangelist Joel Osteen and TV psychologist Dr. Phil (Einstein 2008), with Oprah Winfrey's power of the personal brand (Lofton 2011). Without the erudite education of orthodox clerics, Muslim celebrity preachers have nonetheless managed to attract huge followings and to garner novel forms of religious authority.

There has been a tendency, however, to think about the authority of popular preachers as merely epiphenomena of new media technologies and structural forces. While such considerations help explain the broad political and economic forces that created the possibilities for the rise, proliferation, and privatization of new media and celebrity preachers, they do not shed light on why *particular* preachers have become so popular. Nor does an emphasis on media alone tell us much about how such figures have parlayed their celebrity pulpit into political capital. What exactly was it about Aa Gym and Manajemen Qolbu that resonated with the desires and anxieties of a particular religious and consumerist public in Indonesia? What does this say about his specific form of religious authority? Why did he suffer a fall from public grace for something that might have gone unmentioned had Aa Gym been an orthodox *ulama*?

As a public figure, Aa Gym is more celebrity guru than Sufi saint. To understand Aa Gym's particular form of religious authority, we must consider his conscious marketing strategy to build the personal brand of the modern Muslim man: shrewd entrepreneur, ideal family man, and manager of his own heart. With respect to Aa Gym's particular niche of religious authority, he draws from the techno-scientific allure of global psychological sciences yet also offers Manajemen Qolbu as an Islamic corrective to the (purportedly) secular foundations of Western psychology. In doing so, Aa Gym positions himself as a popular preacher whose work is to provide Muslims with the practical "how-to" knowledge of applying Islamic teachings to everyday life. In Indonesian bookstores, many of his books appear in the "Applied Psychology" (*Psikologi Terapan*) rather than the "Islam" section. As Aa Gym readily admits, without formal religious training he does not fit neatly into the category of a religious scholar. Further, he is careful not to encroach on the exegetical and jurisprudential authority of religious scholars (*ulama*). Instead, he garners a particular form of religious authority, in part, through his ability to transform diverse forms of psychological knowledge (*ilmu psikologi*) into everyday religious wisdom (*hikmah*). His honorific title "older brother" (Aa) connotes one to whom one turns for personal advice, not a religious scholar one might consult for sound theological judgments.

Aa Gym preaches Manajemen Qolbu through his own life story. He promotes himself as the embodiment of piety and prosperity. Aa Gym's religious authority found its market niche within the burgeoning Islamic self-help industry. The Islamic revival of the 1970s and 1980s, coupled with drastic increases in literacy rates among Indonesians, led to a vast expansion of the Islamic publishing industry. C. W. Watson (2005a, 209) observed that self-help books for family and career represent the most significant surge in the Islamic publishing industry of post-authoritarian Indonesia.[20] As a public figure of Muslim modernity, Aa Gym straddled the social, religious, and economic spaces between pop preacher and pop psychologist, televangelist and trainer. His self-help program of Manajemen Qolbu was not just about managing hearts but also about achieving success. After decades of corruption and nepotism, Indonesians once again placed their hopes in the possibilities of entrepreneurship and social mobility, of piety and prosperity. Aa Gym's self-help formulas for success gave a religious foundation and economic direction to these hopes, desires, and anxieties. He offered his own life story—from rags to riches, from naughty youngster to pious family man and successful entrepreneur—as proof that anything was possible. "God has already decreed our fortunes," he told his followers. "Our job is to maximize our initiative in order to meet up with material fortune."

The affective tone of aspirational piety is about tomorrow's possibilities, not today's reality. Aa Gym—owner of twenty companies, who serenades his wife on national TV—embodies and conjures a larger-than-life, futuristic, cutting-edge sort of supermodernity, what I have described as *Islam mutakhir*, or "Islam on the cutting-edge" (Hoesterey 2012, 57). Self-help psychology meets the Qur'an. The Prophet Muhammad meets multilevel marketing. This photo of the pop preacher–cum–fighter pilot provides a striking visual image of this kind of Muslim modernity—a far cry from the elderly

FIGURE I.2. Aa Gym in flight suit prior to riding in F5-E Tiger fighter jet. Courtesy of
Daarut Tauhiid.

bearded cleric. MQ trainees and spiritual tourists can purchase the photo as a keepsake of their visit to his Islamic school, for a price of course.

The MQ emphasis on psychological knowledge as religious wisdom differs from the bodies of knowledge and judicial injunctions summoned by conventional clerics whose influence is more firmly rooted in issues of jurisprudence. Unlike such clerics, Aa Gym is not remotely interested in issuing a *fatwā*, and he consciously deferred to the authority of established *ulama* on issues of jurisprudence. Instead, Aa Gym appeals to Islamic sensibilities regarding everyday ethical comportment and the moral psychology of the heart. Jurisprudence and comportment are not necessarily mutually exclusive, but it is helpful to acknowledge these two semiautonomous spheres of influence on both religious authority and Muslim subjectivity. In his invitation for scholars to pursue the "anthropology of *adab*," Ebrahim Moosa describes *adab* in terms of a "disposition toward knowledge . . . the attitude and disposition that enables one to experience the effects of knowledge and be transformed by its animation in the self" (2005, 210). I examine Aa Gym's Manajemen Qolbu Training as a technology of self that privileges psychological expertise and operates within the market niche of self-development.

This knowledge of the *practical application* of Islamic ethics appeals to Muslims searching for ways to bring Islamic teachings into their everyday lives. Aa Gym tells his followers that Manajemen Qolbu provides just such a practical method of self-improvement. He promotes this approach with the acronym BASIS. Teachings must be *Benar* (true); *Aplikatif* (applicable); *Sederhana* (simple); *Inovatif* (innovative); and *Solutif* (solution-oriented). Frederic Volpi and Bryan Turner admonish scholars of Islam to more fully appreciate this distinction between different kinds of religious knowledge and authority. Theoretical knowledge about the text itself, they argue, is distinct from practical knowledge about how to best integrate religious knowledge into everyday life (2007, 12). Whereas religious scholars argue about exegetical interpretation, Aa Gym offered a "how-to" program for happiness in this life and the hereafter. And he offered his personal story as proof that a pious Muslim can have both personal fortune and family harmony.

Aa Gym built his own brand of Muslim masculinity, and his religious authority hinged on his image as moral exemplar. In sermons and training seminars, Aa Gym narrated his life story as evidence of the efficacy of Manajemen Qolbu. As Vincent Cornell (1998) has argued with respect to Sufi sainthood, an understanding of "exemplary authority" allows us to go

FIGURE I.3. Aa Gym, Teh Ninih, and their seven children at Idul Fitri celebration at the end of Ramadan, October 24, 2006. Photo by author.

beyond Weberian explanations of charisma and contextualize it within the dynamics of the preacher-disciple relationship. At public events Aa Gym typically introduced himself with a seven-minute video autobiography, what he refers to as his *Qolbugrafi* (Aa Gym: Just as he is). With a catchy sound track, the video biography is a montage of Aa Gym at work and play— in the boardroom, skydiving with Indonesian special forces, scuba diving, playing paintball during an outbound corporate training seminar, spending time with family, and hanging out with rickshaw drivers on the roadside. Then words flash on the screen: "There is no success without bravery." Aa Gym carefully crafted and consciously nurtured this personal brand. Even Indonesia's leading marketing guru, Hermawan Kartajaya, affectionately referred to him as a "spiritual marketer." In a poster that hangs on the wall of Aa Gym's bookstore, he provides advice on how to market oneself.

Aa Gym skillfully crafted his personal brand within the religious marketplace of Islamic televangelism and self-help psychology. I want to be clear that I do not distinguish a supposedly "authentic" Islam from its commoditized versions, as if Muslim practice of the "Chicken Soup for the Soul"

FIGURE 1.4. The poster reads: "Success Marketing Yourself. 3 A: I am peaceful with you; I make you happy; I am useful to you."

variety is inherently superficial, its leaders conniving and its followers wandering aimlessly in the fog of false consciousness. Much like fundamentalist Christians, televangelists and self-help gurus are often viewed as the "repugnant cultural other" (Harding 1991). During my first week of fieldwork, a senior Indonesian scholar and liberal activist scoffed when he learned that I was researching Islamic self-help: "It's about the economy, stupid!" he retorted in English. While I appreciated the witty turn of phrase (harkening back to James Carville during Clinton's successful 1992 presidential campaign), there is a tendency within the academy to dismiss such figures as charlatans driven by material desire alone. It is indeed about the economy, but it is also about a real, lived Islam. By taking branding seriously as part of Aa Gym's religious outreach (*dakwah*), we can better understand how Aa Gym publicly positioned himself as a particular kind of public figure. His form of religious authority depended on the affective and economic exchange relationship between a marketer-preacher and his consuming devotees. In other words, religious authority must be understood as a form of exchange, mediated by the brand. William Mazzarella has argued, "The practice of branding is built on a metaphor of gift exchange" (2003, 53). The value of a brand is subject to an affective allegiance, an intersubjective trust between preacher and disciple regarding the veracity of the brand narrative.

However, consumers are fickle and brands come and go. Aa Gym's fall from grace provides the sharp relief of how religious brands can unravel. As Constantine V. Nakassis notes, "To study the brand requires that we situate our analysis in moments when the brand is invoked but also called into question, bracketed, refashioned, or negated. In such moments, new performative values, forms of politics, and social formations emerge through, but in constant tension with, the brand" (2013, 110). We can understand Aa Gym's religious authority in the marketing parlance of brand equity. The value of his personal brand, and legitimacy of his religious authority, thus hinges on the intersubjective economic and affective relationship between preacher and disciple, producer and consumer.

My interest in the role of marketing bridges conversations about new media and religious authority in Islam with anthropological inquiries into "market Islam" and branding as social and practice.[21] Expanding on Patrick Haenni's (2005) concept of "l'Islam de marché," Daromir Rudnyckyj (2009a) advances the useful concept of "market Islam" as a lens through which to understand religious practice in the broader socioeconomic context of privatization and neoliberal economic policy in Indonesia. Rudnyckyj (2010) provides valuable insights into the religio-economic ways in which privatizing companies invest in Islamic training as one way to discipline its workers. I would like to broaden the scope of market Islam, however, in order to investigate the ideas and practices that go into marketing products and public icons deemed as Islamic. I am more concerned with the *marketing of* Islam than the broader structures of economic globalization in which Islamic self-cultivation occurs.

Religious marketing can also shed light on the production and consumption of religious knowledge and authority. Dorothea Schulz, in her study of Malian popular preacher Cherif Haidara, implores scholars to consider "the ways in which material objects, consumption practices, and certain forms of media engagements are constitutive of religious experience, authority, and legitimacy" (2006, 223; see also Özyürek 2004). Viewed from this perspective, virtue and religious authority can be asserted, contested, and negotiated *through* the consumption of popular culture products deemed Islamic (Jones 2010c, 618). Likewise in Indonesia, the consumption of preacher-as-brand was precisely the means by which many of Aa Gym's female followers cultivated personal virtue and tended to the economy of affect in the family. Their consumption practices catapulted Aa Gym into stardom on the national stage and, in the process, lent a marketized legitimacy to his religious authority.

Aa Gym's admirers believed in, and fantasized about, the personal brand of Aa Gym. This brand was not simply a visible logo or trademark but also a story—a brand narrative—of Aa Gym as doting husband and successful entrepreneur. Mara Einstein, media studies scholar and former marketing executive, examines branding practices and exchange relationships in her research about American televangelists and self-help gurus such as Rick Warren, Joel Osteen, Dr. Phil, and Oprah. Einstein argues that, "with a combination of on-air charisma and off-air commerce," these public figures have become personal "faith brands" (2008, 14; see also Lofton 2011). Previous studies of the commodification of religious symbols have often focused on how tangible commodities shed light on changing religious ideas and state politics (Starrett 1995; Özyürek 2006). Attention to these intangible "faith brands" offers a fresh perspective to better understand how Aa Gym claimed legitimacy, the ways he marketed MQ as an Islamic commodity, and the subsequent consumption patterns that both affirmed and challenged his authority.

The newfound religious authority of Muslim self-help gurus depended on their ability to transform psychological knowledge into religious wisdom and, equally important, to market themselves as the embodiment of their formulas for success. The power of the personal brand, however, depends on the affective and economic exchanges between preacher-producers and consuming devotees. When a personal secret went public, his devotees no longer trusted the brand and Aa Gym lost his exemplary authority. This is not to reduce religious authority to rational logics of a mystified market; rather it illuminates how the exemplary authority of Aa Gym rested on the public belief (and, eventually, the refusal to believe) in the brand narrative of Aa Gym as loving husband, wealthy entrepreneur, and master of his *qolbu*.

Within this religious marketplace of Muslim modernity, Aa Gym's female devotees enjoyed a new form of consumer power, whereby their refusal to believe the story challenged his particular kind of religious authority and severed the affective-economic exchange relationship on which such authority (and public visibility) rested. By turning to marketing as religious practice, I am able to explain Aa Gym's particular form of religious authority in a way that does not simply place it within the rise of new media or a vague Weberian notion of personal charisma. My explanation of Aa Gym's religious authority in terms of his personal brand explains both his rapid rise to fame and his dramatic fall from public grace.

## Managing Muslim Hearts: Ethics, Affect, and Subjectivity before and beyond Neoliberalism

Aa Gym preaches Manajemen Qolbu as a practical guide to ethical self-discipline, one that encourages reflection on one's emotions and the cultivation of bodily habits purported to lead to piety, prosperity, and the common good. In his study on ethical self-formation in an Islamic counter-public in Egypt, Charles Hirschkind (2006) argued that the neo-Enlightenment privileging of rational public debate neglects the importance of ethical self-fashioning and the cultivation of pure hearts that allow one to be receptive to God's message. Hirschkind draws attention to the mediated cultivation of Islamic sensibilities and virtue through listening to, and talking about, cassette sermons. Drawing on Michel Foucault (1988), Hirschkind examines cassette sermon audition as a "technology of self," arguing that part of the moral work of listening to sermons is developing the inner disposition, the open heart, of an ethical listener.

In this book I engage and build on a burgeoning body of literature about ethical self-cultivation. I examine how Manajemen Qolbu—as a technology of Islamic personhood—summons psychological knowledge to shape economic and civic subjectivity. Taking cues from the work of Foucault and others on the moral-political work of "psy-discourses" and technologies of self (Foucault 1988; Rose 1996, 1999), I analyze Islamic idioms of affect and ethics as they are summoned, articulated, and mobilized within the economic and ethical debates of the nation-state. I discuss how MQ Training encourages trainees to fashion two complementary dimensions of subjectivity—the enterprising self and the virtuous citizen. With respect to the former, I examine MQ Entrepreneur Training to better understand how Islamic training offers moral models and embodied exemplars of the "ethical entrepreneur." MQ Civic Training, on the other hand, turns its attention toward the ethical and affective habits of the virtuous citizen. Technologies of psychology and self, then, are also technologies of nation and state.[22]

The aura of scientific and psychological expertise has led to new classes of experts (in Indonesia and elsewhere) whose proclaimed knowledge naturalizes colonial and postcolonial projects of capitalist modernity (Jones 2010a; Li 2007; Mitchell 2002; Prakash 1999; Strassler 2009b). As Carla Jones argues, "Expertise is never generic but, rather, addresses particular subjects in highly specific ways" (2010a, 270). In the case of Aa Gym, his authority and authenticity rested on proclaimed expertise in the psychology of the heart. Islamic psychology promised to allay the anxieties and bolster the aspirations of the Muslim middle class. Nikolas Rose (1989, 1999) and scholars in the field of "Critical Psychology" (e.g., Parker 2006) advance a Foucauldian approach to psychological expertise. Rose argues that "psy-discourses" provided the very expertise, categories, and modes of self-discipline that were compatible with liberalism and democracy (1999, vii) and served to justify, even naturalize, neoliberal logics of the free market and a belief in an autonomous, self-enterprising subject (1999; Rose and Miller 2008).

My ethnographic engagement with MQ Entrepreneur Training bridges Rose's concern for the disciplinary power of psychology and self-cultivation with Ong's (2006) attention to neoliberal techniques of self-engineering and capital accumulation. To refer to this strictly in terms of neoliberalism, however, might be somewhat misleading. In anthropology, the term "neoliberalism" is so ubiquitous that it appears to have lost its conceptual moorings. What exactly do scholars mean when they deploy the term "neoliberalism"? What political projects and analytical vantage points does a focus on neoliberalism privilege? And what does an emphasis on neoliberalism assume and occlude? Islamic popular psychology in Indonesia, at least at first glance, appears to conform to a neoliberal ethos of the ethical subject who cultivates an individual entrepreneurial ethic, within a supposedly free and private market, rather than looks to the state for support. In one sense, the Indonesian case would seem to fit David Harvey's oft-cited definition of neoliberalism as "a theory of political economic practices that proposes that human well-being can best be advanced by liberating individual entrepreneurial freedoms and skills within an institutional framework characterized by strong private property rights, free market, and free trade" (2005, 2). The importance of economic globalization notwithstanding, Andrew Kipnis raises concern about the pervasive and imprecise use of the term "neoliberalism," arguing that overuse risks "a reification that occludes more than it reveals" (2007, 384). Kipnis argues that neoliberalism takes many forms and thus must be understood in particular political, economic, and religious contexts.[23] He also warns scholars from privileging the analytical model of neoliberalism over other forms of national, religious, and legalist governance (397n13).

Likewise, Aihwa Ong recognizes that "neoliberalism" is not a neat and tidy concept of ideas in the abstract that are somehow implemented everywhere to the same effect. Emphasizing the "exceptions" of neoliberalism as it is manifest in actual practices, Ong observes, "As an array of techniques centered on the optimization of life, neoliberalism migrates from site to site, interacting with various assemblages that cannot be analytically reduced to cases of a uniform global condition of 'Neoliberalism' writ large" (2006, 14). Similarly, in the case of Indonesia, political scientist Edward Aspinall remarks that, over the course of three decades, the neoliberalism in Indonesia "has become diluted, hybridized, and delinked from many of its foundational theories. . . . In this perspective, neoliberalism is as much a cultural phenomenon as it is a political or economic one" (2013, 28).[24] And so it is with Aa Gym's Islamic formulas for financial fortune. With its get-rich-quick formulas from Euro-American popular psychology and management theory, MQ Entrepreneur Training invokes *Islamic*—not just Euro-American neoliberal—models of the self-enterprising subject that emphasize that capital accumulation can help one fulfill religious financial obligations (*zakat*; Arabic, *zakāh*) and propose that piety can lead to riches on earth and in the afterlife. In the case of models for citizenship, Aa Gym's psy-discourses of civic duty summon the civic legacy of the Prophet Muhammad as much as they provide a liberal-secular template of democratic citizenship. Rather than privilege one over the other, I explore the resonances between neoliberal techniques of the self and Islamic modes of subjectivity.

Daromir Rudnyckyj paints a similar picture in his innovative research on ESQ Training in Indonesia. Led by popular trainer Ary Ginanjar, ESQ Training enjoyed widespread popularity among middle-level management during the 2000s. Rudnyckyj (2009b) advances the idea of "spiritual economies" as a corrective to Jean Comaroff and John Comaroff's (1999, 2001) notion of "occult economies," in which spirituality is understood as a retreat from oppressive structures of the "culture of neoliberalism." Based on his observations of ESQ Training at state-owned company Krakatau Steel, Rudnyckyj argues that Islamic corporate training "is as much the Islamization of neoliberalism as it is the neoliberalization of Islam" (2009a, 131). I am also cautious to not cede Muslim subjectivity to the intellectual imperialism of neoliberalism—as if it were a singular phenomenon that neatly replicates itself around the world. While acknowledging the importance of neoliberal ideals of self-enterprise, I would also argue that we run the risk of recolonizing anthropology by imposing the category of neoliberalism as a tidy, universal explanation. Neoliberalism alone cannot account for the global spread of psy-discourses and related techniques of self-enterprise and capital accumulation. Islamic concepts of ethics and economy are also at play.[25] At the same time, Michael Peletz (2013) also suggests that scholars should use the term "Islamization" with more precision, noting that processes of corporatization and bureaucratization, not Islamization, more aptly characterize the major developments in Malaysia's Islamic courts over the last two decades.

The trainers and trainees of MQ Entrepreneur Training articulate these psy-discourses of self and wealth and reinscribe them with Islamic idioms of the self, fortune, and ethics. If we look historically at the early twentieth century, it becomes clear that, decades prior to the privatization and liberalization of the Indonesian marketplace, modern Islamic organizations during late colonialism and the nationalist movement were also preoccupied with cultivating self-enterprising Muslims. Explanations that fall back on contemporary global structures of neoliberalism often fail to acknowledge the historical genealogies of local modes of self-governance and the enterprising self. With respect to the crafting of capitalist subjects and Muslim entrepreneurs in contemporary Indonesia, I am interested in how the self-help market has flourished as part of a broad, renewed emphasis on such Islamic business, or *Ekonomi Santri*, in post-authoritarian Indonesia. I describe how MQ Entrepreneur Training incorporates the capital accumulation program of American guru Robert Kiyosaki and reinscribes it with Islamic idioms of faith and fortune. In MQ Entrepreneur Training, religious practices such as the nonobligatory prayers performed to invite personal fortune (*solat duha*; Arabic, *ṣalāt al-ḍuḥā*) play an increasingly important role in the formation of ethical entrepreneurs. Televangelist Yusuf Mansur, one of Aa Gym's close friends, developed a training program (The Power of Charity) that summons Islamic teachings to proclaim that giving charity can lead to fortune. The more you give, the more you get.

With these ethnographic and theoretical considerations in mind, I ask, What are the limits to the globalization of neoliberal ideals of the entrepreneurial and civic subject? How do MQ trainers and trainees play with the resonances, as well as the points of departure, among multiple models of the capitalist entrepreneur subject offered by Western self-help psychology and *Psikologi Islami*? As I argue, this play between Islam and psychology reframes Islamic discursive traditions and recalibrates the prophetic tradition with new, psychologized imaginations of the Prophet Muhammad in which he is reckoned as "Super Leader & Super Manager."

MQ Training also reimagines the Prophet Muhammad in terms of civic virtue and the ideal citizen-subject. Aa Gym promoted a vision of civic virtue that embodied the Prophet Muhammad's example of "leading through service." During months of fieldwork with Aa Gym's civic organization Movement to Build the Conscience of the Nation (Gema Nusa), I worked alongside Gema Nusa workers in the main Bandung office, observed executive board meetings, and attended the launching of regional Gema Nusa offices in North Sumatra, South Kalimantan, and South Sulawesi.[26] In March 2006, leaders from each provincial office gathered in Jakarta for MQ Civic Training. These provincial leaders would return to their home offices and lead similar training seminars for their civic volunteers (*sukarelawan*).

MQ Civic Training invoked psycho-religious knowledge as a way to provide a model of the "good Muslim citizen." I consider how MQ Civic Training offers multiple psycho-religious understandings for civic participation, especially for those civic volunteers bestowed with leadership positions in Gema Nusa. Once again MQ trainers summon the techno-scientific allure of global psychology as well as the moral gravitas of Islamic history and tradition. I describe how trainers cast the psychological profile of the Prophet Muhammad as the moral exemplar of the citizen-believer. Or, as one trainer explained in the psychologized terms of the Myers-Briggs personality inventory, Muhammad was the exemplary "ESFJ" (Extraverted Sensing Feeling Judging; servant leader). By privileging the prophetic tradition in terms of both entrepreneurial ethos and civic virtue, these trainers do not simply summon psychological expertise. They offer what they deem to be a corrective to secular psychology and proclaim that Islam completes our understanding of psychological expertise. MQ Civic Training thus recalibrates the prophetic tradition within Islam and transforms the intersubjective relationship between prophet and practitioner. Similar to MQ Entrepreneur Training, the training for civic volunteers does not reproduce some overarching model of the liberal citizen of the world but instead frames diversity, tolerance, and citizenship within an Islamic ethics of civic virtue.

## Feeling like a State: Pornography, Pop Preachers, and the Ends of Political Islam

The inaugural Indonesian edition of *Playboy* magazine hit the streets of Jakarta in 2006. At the time, Indonesia's Parliament was in the midst of drafting controversial anti-pornography legislation. Whereas hard-liner organizations like the Islamic Defenders Front (FPI) ransacked *Playboy*'s Jakarta office, groups advocating the arts and women's rights bemoaned elements of the anti-pornography bill that they perceived as the increasing Islamization of Indonesia. Aa Gym preached that, with regard to the temptations of sexual vice, Indonesians should remember Allah's command to "lower the gaze." For Aa Gym, lowering the gaze was an ethical act that cultivated shame and steered the heart from vice to virtue. In this moral psychology, "shame is noble." Similar to the way in which Aa Gym popularized *qolbu* as an Islamic concept of the heart, Aa Gym's strategy vis-à-vis the state was to summon state officials—even Indonesia's president—to publicly perform their sense of shame. Aa Gym's "shaming of the state" is a political strategy aimed to assert the moral authority of Islam in relation to the state.

Aa Gym framed affective and ethical discipline in terms of the "personal and political virtues" of the citizen-believer (Hirschkind 2001a, 4). My attention to the politics of affect, ethics, and popular culture converges with ongoing conversations about the nature of political Islam—how to define it, where to look for it, and how to study it. Scholars have searched for terminology that best expresses the diverse political aspirations, predicaments, and contexts in which Muslims mobilize Islam's texts, traditions, and symbols. Unfortunately, though, much of this search has focused narrowly on explicit efforts to establish an Islamic state. This preoccupation with the inability of Islamists to achieve their dreams of the caliphate led noted French scholar Olivier Roy to famously declare the "failure of political Islam" (1994; see also Roy 2004; Kepel 2004). Unfortunately, defining political Islam in terms of electoral politics and formal institutions overlooks other ways of being political and of exerting influence on the state, other—of the many— "faces of political Islam" (Ayoob 2008).

Sociologist Asef Bayat proposed the idea of "post-Islamism" as a way to think about political Islam beyond the formation of a global caliphate (1996, 2007, 2013). Bayat developed the term as a way to understand the aspirations and strategies of disillusioned Islamists in postrevolutionary Iran. Bayat defines post-Islamism as simultaneously a sociological condition and a political project that turns away from Islam as political ideology directed at the formation of an Islamic state and toward an emphasis on Islam's compatibility with democratic governance. Whereas Islamists promoted religion and duty, post-Islamists were more concerned with religiosity and rights (2013, 8). Bayat has also cautioned that "the advent of post-Islamism does not necessarily mean the historical end of Islamism. What it means is the birth, out of the Islamist experience, of a qualitatively different discourse and practice" (2005, 5). Bayat's attention to post-Islamist politics in Iran and Egypt—among youth, women, and intellectuals—goes beyond electoral politics and the global caliphate in order to investigate alternative forms of political Islam.

Post-Islamism constitutes a different way of imagining what it means to be political and exactly how one should go about it. It is certainly not a retreat from politics. As Peter Mandaville has discerned:

> The post-Islamism we have in mind, then, is not one that describes the demise of efforts to establish an Islamic social order. It is most definitely not, as Roy and Kepel seem to see it, the acceptance by Islamists of Francis Fukuyama's thesis

regarding the "end of history." . . . The challenge of moving beyond Islamism . . . is about widening the boundaries of what counts as Muslim politics. (2007, 348–351)

To aspire toward the establishment of an Islamic social order constitutes a markedly different notion of the political than to aim to restore the Islamic caliphate. Further still, post-Islamism is not confined to the familiar institutional bases and social spaces of Islamism. Many middle-class Muslims now look to other arenas of public life—from fashion to finance, recitation to rock music—in which to be politically active.

This brings us into the realm of popular culture. Indonesia, a country where Muslim celebrities vie for public office and presidents consult with televangelists, provides an instructive case study to understand how political Islam is linked with popular culture. Putting it more forcefully, Ariel Heryanto proclaims that popular culture is "at the very heart of Indonesian national politics" (2008, 34). In contrast to political scientists who look to political economy and electoral politics to gauge the social and political force of Islam in Indonesia (e.g., Mujani and Liddle 2010), anthropologists have tended to locate and interpret political Islam in public culture, fashion, education, cinema and the arts, and televangelism.[27] This focus on public culture does not, however, negate the importance of the state. Rather than privilege popular Islam over the state, I am concerned with those precise moments when popular culture converges with the state—its institutions and actors, its language and affect.

Indonesia presents a challenging model for understanding religion and politics. Michael Buehler (2008) and Robin Bush (2008) astutely note the irony that it has actually been secular-nationalist parties—not Islamist parties—who have deployed idioms of Islamic ethics and proposed local Sharia-inspired ordinances, presumably in their quest to consolidate political power (see also Aspinall 2013; Fealy 2008). Yet even these keen insights concerning the ostensibly secular mobilization of Islamic symbolism run the risk of reducing religion to an instrumentalist function of politics. The underlying assumption seems to be that power brokers politicize religion for personal or political party gains. This may indeed be the case, but it cannot tell the entire story.

What if this line of reasoning were reversed? What if we imagine the possibility, as Benedict Anderson suggested decades ago, "of religious people using politics for religious ends" (1977, 22).[28] For Aa Gym, *dakwah* was not a means for politics; rather, politics was a means for *dakwah*. Aa Gym mobilized political networks within the state, business, and civil society in an effort to create what he describes as "a culture of shame." In Aa Gym's vision, the state plays a role in this political project, but official state power is not the end goal. He does not seek to replace the state but rather to endow the state with the aura of an ethical affect and to summon state actors to serve as vanguards for public ethics.

This is an important distinction for understanding how Aa Gym imagined his relationship with the state and for our understanding of political Islam more broadly. To work within the boundaries of the modern nation-state is not necessarily a retreat from Islamist politics, nor is it simply an attempt to establish Sharia law by stealthy means (see Aspinall 2013). Popular Islam can indeed be political, but it requires a more nuanced understanding of both politics and the state. As Aa Gym rose to national fame and was invited to preach at various state functions, he carefully cultivated religio-political connections with diverse state actors. When *Playboy* magazine came to Indonesia, Aa Gym leveraged his role as celebrity preacher to summon many of these actors—including then-President Yudhoyono—to publicly perform their personal piety. His cries for moral reform may not have been as loud as the Council of Indonesian Ulama (MUI) or as violent as the FPI. Nonetheless, Aa Gym adeptly leverages his celebrity status and public image to discipline the state with Islamic idioms of vice and virtue, ethics and affect.

Before proceeding to Aa Gym's political strategies, allow me to describe my understanding of the state and how we might approach it from an ethnographic perspective. In light of Phillip Abrams's seminal article "Notes on the Difficulty of Studying the State" (1988), social scientists are increasingly wary of reifying the state, presenting the state as undifferentiated monolith, thereby giving the state an agency of its own. Scholars have also challenged the very idea of state sovereignty, arguing that the state is neither completely hegemonic nor everywhere homogeneous. Subsequently they have turned their gaze to the everyday rituals of the state and the social spaces in which state power is constituted, deployed, and contested (van Klinken and Barker 2009). Aa Gym's strategy to shame the state suggests that we might productively bridge the study of the state with the anthropology of emotion.

During the 1980s anthropologists critiqued assumptions in psychology and psychological anthropology that conceived of emotion in terms of interior feelings and offered an alternative approach that understood emotion in the context of language and power. In their groundbreaking volume, Catherine A. Lutz and Lila Abu-Lughod (1990) cogently argue that emotion is public and political, not simply private and personal. Whereas some scholars in anthropology, cultural studies, and elsewhere prefer that we differentiate between the terms "emotion," "affect," and "sentiment," I use these terms interchangeably.[29] I am especially interested in how emotion (affect, or sentiment) can be officially mandated or subtly summoned by the state and its citizenry. In their 1988 study of postrevolutionary Iran, Mary-Jo DelVecchio Good and Byron Good argued that "anthropologists have tended to neglect the role of the state in authorizing or prescribing particular forms of emotional discourse, in mobilizing those sentiments through civic rituals, [and] in interpreting emotional actions in relation to state ideology and political purposes" (1988, 59). The authors describe how the Iranian state promoted nationalist ideals of mourning, grief, and sadness during the 1980s when it was at war with Iraq (57).

Likewise, Ann Stoler's (2009) work on affect and desire in the Dutch East Indies argues that colonial governance was preoccupied with affective discipline. Arguing against postcolonial theorists of science and technology who privilege colonial rationality (e.g., Prakash 1999), Stoler describes colonial statecraft as "affective mastery": "At issue was the emotional economy of empire, and how colonial states intervened in shaping which feelings mattered, who had a right to them, and how they were politically framed" (2009, 68–69). In both postrevolutionary Iran and the colonial Dutch East Indies, states mobilized discourses of affect as a way to discipline their subjects.

The Indonesian state during the New Order also attempted to cultivate a particular affective sensibility of civic devotion, especially among the wives of civil servants (Brenner 1998). In post-authoritarian Indonesia, however, citizen-subjects and Islamic organizations are now trying to discipline the state (Wilson 2008). Aa Gym employs Islamic idioms of moral affect to discipline the state. What does it mean, though, for a state to be disciplined by affect? What specific form does discipline take? Aa Gym rose to fame during a time of ongoing public revelations about massive state-sponsored violence under Suharto's New Order regime. Though newly democratic, the Indonesian state in the early 2000s did not enjoy much moral authority or religious legitimacy. Various state and civil society organizations began to jockey to speak for Islam and to instruct the state in such matters. This strategy builds on personal relationships with state actors, and the disciplining of the state takes the form of a summoning of state officials to publicly perform their sense of shame.

To better understand Aa Gym's framing of shame as a form of political affect capable of being performed by state actors, I find it useful to draw from Begoña Aretxaga's work on the state as affect, fantasy, and "fictional reality" (2000). In her posthumously published essay "Maddening States," Aretxaga argues that scholars must focus on "the actual social and subjective life of this formation we call the state" (2003, 401). Aa Gym wanted to enshroud the state with a sense of shame, thereby publicly and ritually endowing it with a certain subjectivity of its own. My attention to this shaming of the state raises broader questions about Islam, politics, and public piety in post-authoritarian Indonesia: How does the disciplinary power of ethical speech shape how state actors publicly perform the political work, affective tone, and moral obligations of the state? How does ethical speech shape the relationship and power relations between Islam and the state?

My concept of "shaming the state" is also inspired by Asef Bayat's concept of the "socialization of the state." Writing about Egypt's "passive revolution" in the 1990s, Bayat argues that the Islamist movement "*socialized the state* to the society's prevailing sensibilities, and by penetrating the state apparatus helped create a kind of 'secularreligious' state" (2007, 166; emphasis in original). In this case the state acquiesced to some Islamist demands, if only to then portray the state as the true vanguard of Islam. Bayat interprets socialization of the state as the inverse of Foucault's governmentality (204). I appreciate this Foucauldian reading, which, in the case of Aa Gym summoning state actors, also provides an analytical lens through which to view state actors disciplining themselves on the public stage. However, I would like to push the analysis in a somewhat different direction. I am interested in the specific *form* of ethical discipline, the rhetorical and religious ways in which Aa Gym tries to discipline the state.

Aa Gym's shaming of the state is decidedly not a public scolding but rather a public invitation—a summoning of the state—to embody an ethical affect of shame. Or, to invoke Althusser, we could say that Aa Gym "interpellated" state actors to assume an affective subject position. Althusser understood the formation of subjectivity in terms of the dialectical recognition between the state and its citizenry. According to Althusser, the "Ideological State Apparatus"—much like a traffic cop saying "Hey, You there!"—interpellates, or hails, its citizenry into particular subjects (1972, 174–175). The case of Aa Gym, however, suggests a different scenario in which Aa Gym hails the state, interpellating its actors to publicly perform their sense of shame. It is an invitation to publicly display one's civic virtue and sense of shame. Aa Gym's strategy is thus to endow the state with, and invite state actors to publicly perform, an ethical affect of shame. Thus, my work bridges an inverse reading of Althusser's idea of interpellation with Aretxaga's ideas about the "subjective life of the state" in order to better understand the political life of Islamic psychology.

## Architecture of the Book

In this introductory chapter I sketched the ethnographic context, theoretical terrain, and comparative reach of this research. The remainder of the book is structured around three themes: religious authority (Chapters 1 and 2); Muslim subjectivity (3 and 4); and the politics of public piety (5 and 6). In Chapter 1, I describe Aa Gym as a figure of Muslim modernity who— despite his lack of formal religious education—managed to carve a peculiar niche of religious authority and political voice. I interpret his rise to fame within the broader context of hope, uncertainty, and aspirational piety during the early years of post-authoritarian Indonesia.

In Chapter 2, I cast the nets beyond Aa Gym to describe how a new generation of Muslim trainers draws from multiple genealogies of knowledge to create, package, and sell what is now known as *Psikologi Islami*. The figure of the Muslim trainer certainly does not possess the sort of authority enjoyed by more orthodox Muslim scholars who peddle their own knowledge in terms of jurisprudence; instead, trainers cater to the practical application, the "how-to" of religious knowledge. And the genealogies of religion bounce back and forth between fourteenth-century Cairene mystics to 1970s Northern California New Age gurus, from twelfth-century philosophers in Persia to twenty-first-century pop psychologists in Indonesia.

I describe the process of how Aa Gym transformed the popular science findings of an atheist Japanese scientist's research on the "power of water" into a psycho-religious treatise on the beauty of Islamic concepts of affective discipline and moral comportment. I then broaden my analysis to include a range of popular Islamic training programs to outline the emergence of a new figure of psycho-religious authority—the Muslim trainer. By exploring the widespread popularity of such training programs among urban middle-class Muslims, private-sector companies, and government agencies, I demonstrate how these Muslim trainers have also become significant figures of Muslim modernity.[30] Muslim trainers, with their formulas for worldly riches and heavenly redemption, have also become important proponents of the shift toward an Islamic economy in Indonesia. This niche of Islamic knowledge and practice, especially its appeal to global psychologies, is popular precisely because of its appeal to the "cutting edge," or *mutakhir*, of science, psyche, and technology.

The second section of the book examines Manajemen Qolbu Training—as a technology of the self—through the lens of Muslim subjectivity. In Chapter 3, I turn to MQ Entrepreneur Training to examine the extent to which we can understand aspirational piety in post-authoritarian Indonesia in terms of the global spread of neoliberal ideals and forms of self-discipline. As noted previously, I argue that even though certain ideals and practices of a neoliberal enterprising self are at play, we must take seriously the historical legacies of an Islamic ethics of capital accumulation in colonial, postcolonial, and post-authoritarian Indonesia. Through a detailed description of the design and implementation for MQ Entrepreneur Training, I detail how Western self-help psychology is reinscribed with Islamic ideals of economic justice, wealth distribution, and capital accumulation. All of this suggests a more complicated subjectivity not reducible to nebulous neoliberal logics or mystified market forces.

In Chapter 4, I turn the discussion of Muslim subjectivity toward the figure of the civic volunteer. Once again, trainers operate as cultural brokers that invoke Western psychological knowledge in their quest to forge Islamic concepts of civic virtue. Islamic ideals of civic virtue and Muslim citizenship, however, cannot be reduced to an understanding of neoliberal "flexible citizenship" (Ong 1999), nor does Appiah's (1997, 618) notion of "rooted cosmopolitanism" or Bhabha's (1996) concept of "vernacular cosmopolitanism" quite capture the synergies and tensions between ethnic, religious, and national allegiances. Trainers evoke the Myers-Briggs personality test, but as part of a different story that frames the Prophet Muhammad as the ideal citizen. Islamic notions of civic virtue and Muslim cosmopolitanism are thus in conversation with, not distinct from, global discourses of self, psychology, and society. What I refer to as "prophetic cosmopolitanism" is only vernacular insofar as it engages the discursive traditions of Islam and the national ideals of citizenship. We might think of prophetic cosmopolitan-ism as a genre, not the vernacular, of Muslim cosmopolitanism.

The final section of the book turns to the politics of Islamic psychology and public piety. In Chapter 5, I describe how Aa Gym mobilizes a public ethics of vision and shame in order to discipline state officials. Specifically, I trace how Aa Gym and others sought to reframe public meanings of shame (*malu*) by promoting an Islamic understanding of shame as a noble emotion inti-mately connected with ethical and bodily discipline. In this respect, I bridge the study of political affect with theories of subjectivity and the state to de-scribe how, and to what political effect, Aa Gym summons the state to serve as the moral guardian of Islamic public ethics. My attention to the convergence of politics and popular culture sheds light on forms of political Islam beyond the ballot box.

In Chapter 6, I tell the story of Aa Gym's dramatic fall from public grace. Feeling heartbroken and betrayed, Aa Gym's female admirers boycotted his self-help seminars, television executives canceled his contracts, and his business empire began to crumble. This moment of national scandal and social rupture, when public moral debate crystallized around public piety and fallen preachers, brings the cultural politics of religious authority and public piety into sharp relief. Unlike more orthodox preachers, Gymnas-tiar garnered a different, more ephemeral form of religious authority that was subject to the exchange relations of a new, marketized preacher-disciple relationship. Religious authority in late capitalist modernity—as claimed by self-help gurus and challenged by consuming devotees—is made public and negotiated through exchange processes of commodification and con-sumption. The story comes full circle, with a distressed Aa Gym turning to techniques of self-help psychology to help him manage his own heart. In a short conclusion based on subsequent visits to Daarut Tauhiid as recently as August 2014, I provide some reflections about the rise, fall, and rebranding of Aa Gym and Manajemen Qolbu.

# *Religious Authority*

# CHAPTER I

# Rebranding Islam
## Autobiography, Authenticity, and Religious Authority

> Aa Gym does not only preach about peace, harmony, simple living, and
> honest, socially-responsible business practices. He also offers an example
> through his everyday actions. He has already practiced what he preaches.
>
> —*Hermawan Kartajaya, Indonesia's "marketing guru"*[1]

On the eve of the fiftieth anniversary celebration of the Asian-African
Conference in 2005, Aa Gym admonished Muslim leaders to become more
savvy about marketing the "beauty of Islam." He used this occasion to
explain his strategy for religious propagation (*dakwah*) in terms of "the
wisdom of durian fruit." Likening Muslim leaders to marketers and Islam
to a fruit, Aa Gym declared: "Even a ripe, delicious durian won't sell if a
person does not know how to market it wisely." For Aa Gym, the form of
*dakwah* was as important as its content. Islam was not just a religion to be
lived but also a product to be packaged and sold. When I began research
in 2005, Aa Gym had promoted, trademarked, and licensed Manajemen
Qolbu through nationally televised sermons, self-help books, and Islamic
training seminars. His multilevel marketing firm MQ Baroqah (MQ Blessings) sold a diverse range of consumer and household products ranging
from halal cosmetics and Qolbu Cola to MQ Noodles and "Pure MQ"
mineral water.[2] Indonesia's leading marketing guru hailed Aa Gym as a
"spiritual marketer."[3] Aa Gym turned himself into an icon of Islamic virtue, his turban into a trademark, and "Aa Gym" into a name brand. Aa
Gym was the guru of virtue, his mantra was MQ, and his mission was to
rebrand the public face of Islam.

Marketing is more than bold brands, creative logos, and catchy jingles. It
is about building relationships between producers, products, and consumers.
Aa Gym's personal brand is more than a logo, trademark, or image. It is at
once a story and a pastoral relationship. Aa Gym's national image and thera-

peutic style of preaching are rooted in discursive traditions of advice giving (*nasihat*; Arabic, *naṣīḥa*) as examined by Asad (1993, 200–238). However, Indonesians describe this affect-laden and interpersonal preacher-disciple relationship not only in terms of *nasihat* but also with the acronym *curhat* for *curahan hati*, literally "an outpouring of the heart." When Aa Gym was only beginning to make a name for himself in the early 1990s, his earliest students gathered several times a week for his "Sermon to Cool the Heart" (*Taushi-yah Penyejuk Hati*). Solahudin notes that—even before Aa Gym attained national stature—the most common answer for why people attended was that Aa Gym "cools their heart" and "touches their heart" (1996, 85). Thus, public sermons, corporate seminars, and television programs were placed within the social and affective registers of a "heart-to-heart" conversation.

A focus on religious brands offers an important glimpse into the relationships between marketing and modernity, preacher and brand, autobiography and authority. Aa Gym carefully cultivated his brand—a persona and narrative as self-help guru, shrewd entrepreneur, and doting husband that mediated economic and affective relationships with his followers. As Mara Einstein observed with respect to Oprah, Dr. Phil, and Joel Osteen in America, "branding . . . occurs through the creation of stories or myths surrounding a product" (2008, 12; see also Lofton 2011; Luvaas 2013; Mazzarella 2003). The power of Aa Gym's brand, and the religious authority it presumes, relies on his public image as a pious, successful, devoted, and dreamy man who can restrain negative emotions but also share his soft and romantic side. Even when thousands of women are squished into a hot and impersonal stadium crowd, many still describe the encounter in terms of a "heart to heart." Considering Aa Gym as both celebrity preacher and personal brand contributes to an understanding of the production of religious authority and the moral economy of the preacher-disciple relationship. Kenneth M. George, in his book about Indonesian painter A. D. Pirous, asks readers to think about Pirous's paintings (and the stories about them) as "points of human encounter": "As he makes his way in his lifeworld, his works and ideas belong not just to him, but to others as well. They are the places where he is in expressive dialogue with predecessors and peers, with his nation, with ideas about art, and with God" (2010, 5). Likewise, we would do well to understand religious brands in terms of narrative, encounter, and exchange.

In this chapter I map out different moments of exchange—both affective and economic—between preacher and devotee, producer and consumer, brand and fantasy. This is not to pit "superficial" marketing against "authentic" religion but rather to better understand the ways in which knowledge and authority are constituted and contested within the preacher-disciple relationship and the marketplace of modernity. Religious branding is part of a broader framework of Islamization, corporatization, and privatization of post-authoritarian Indonesia. Even decidedly non-Islamic corporations tried to capitalize on the believed intimacy between preacher and disciple. For example, as part of an effort to thank its female customers for making the Mio the most popular motorcycle among Indonesian women, Yamaha partnered with MQTV to launch an eight-city customer relations tour, aptly titled "Touching the Heart with Love." Aa Gym was the headliner. A Japanese transnational corporation hires a celebrity preacher to market its women's motorcycle brand in terms of the heart. Religious branding in a neoliberal age.

Patrick Haenni (2005) and Daromir Rudnyckyj (2009a, 2010) advance the idea of "market Islam" as a way to understand religious practice in late

FIGURE I.I. Mio motorcycle display and stage for Aa Gym's sermon for Yamaha's "Touching Hearts with Love" campaign.

capitalist modernity. In this reckoning, Islam is commensurable with market capitalism but not simply reducible to neoliberal logics (see also Hefner 2012; Nasr 2009; Osella and Osella 2009; Soares and Osella 2009). Without undercutting the importance of political and economic forces of privatization and liberalization in Indonesia, I am more interested in the marketing *of* Islam and its influence on *dakwah*, religious authority, and the preacher-disciple relationship. Aa Gym's religious authority in the public sphere was based on the story—the brand narrative—of Aa Gym as the master of his own heart and the embodiment of everyday ethics. In this chapter I reflect critically on how Aa Gym told his life history—in his autobiography, televised sermons, and everyday encounters—as a way to position himself as a public figure, to legitimate his claims to religious authority, and to cultivate the economic and affective allegiance of his followers.

Aa Gym's life story is not confined to a book or a video. It is a living history that he repeatedly narrates during his sermons and public appearances. For years, Aa Gym preached before stadium crowds by day and dined with politicians and Muslim leaders by night. On each occasion, he used examples from his own life to teach lessons about everyday ethics. Whether at dinner with the mayor of Padang, the governor of Central Kalimantan, or the ambassador of Afghanistan, Aa Gym made sure that an LCD projector was ready to screen an abridged, seven-minute version of his video autobiography. With microphone in hand, Aa Gym provided a live running commentary: "See, Pak. That was when I went scuba diving with the military special forces [Kopassus]. It really required concentration." When the video had finished, he would encourage applause and then begin a casual (but consistently routine) story about his life: humble roots; embracing Islam, family, and entrepreneurial ventures; and current success and happiness. After taking some questions, he would sing a couple of songs, often concluding with John Denver's "Country Road" (as a child, he often listened to his father's eight-track recordings of John Denver and other hits from the West). His advance team always made sure there was a karaoke keyboard ready and waiting, the song queued. I observed this sequence of events every time I accompanied Aa Gym on trips across Indonesia and each weekend at Daarut Tauhiid when he met with pilgrims and trainees. In this chapter I describe how Aa Gym built his personal brand and reflect on how it afforded a particular form of religious authority.

## From Neighborhood Preacher to National Celebrity: The Political and Economic Contexts of Stardom

Aa Gym's rise to fame as a television preacher must be understood within the context of the easing of media restrictions during the latter years of the New Order regime (1965–1998). In 1975 Suharto introduced what would become known as the SARA doctrine, which, in effect, prohibited overt media discussion of four issues that the state viewed as capable of eroding nationalist sentiment: *Suku* (ethnicity); *Agama* (religion); *Ras* (race); and *Antargolongan* (social class). During most of Suharto's rule, Indonesia had only one television channel, the state-run TVRI. Only in 1987 were private channels permitted to operate, although program content was still heavily censored and had to promote the five pillars of the nationalist state ideology of *Pancasila* (van der Pool 2005, 11).[4] During the late 1980s and early 1990s, however, Suharto embraced what he termed "cultural Islam" and endorsed the founding of an Islamic newspaper, Islamic bank, and the Association for Indonesian Muslim Intellectuals (ICMI; George 1998; Hefner 2000). Thus, even though there may have been a market for Islamic programming during the Islamic revival of the 1980s, politics of state censorship restricted any political overtones of religious programming (van der Pool 2005, 16). Even state-run religious TV programs were largely confined, barren production sets with aging clerics discussing Islamic jurisprudence—a far cry from the extremely choreographed Islamic TV that emerged after Suharto's downfall.

In 1990 Aa Gym officially founded Daarut Tauhiid in the very neighborhood in which he grew up. What started as two rented rooms in 1990 would become a multi-million-dollar enterprise with over twenty businesses under the parent company, MQ Corporation. His popularity grew steadily during those first few years, and demand for his humorous and practical sermons grew beyond Bandung. In 1992, *Time* magazine in Asia referred to him as Indonesia's "Holy Man," and in 1993 he was featured on the cover of the respected Indonesian national weekly magazine *Tempo*. During the mid-1990s, Aa Gym realized that his popularity had caught the nervous attention of Suharto, Indonesia's authoritarian ruler who remained concerned about political Islam. Aa Gym and Daarut Tauhiid leaders gleefully recollected a story about Suharto's New Order government sending intelligence agents to spy on Aa Gym's sermons and activities. As the story goes, these intelligence officials inevitably realized that Aa Gym had nothing to hide, confessed to him about their covert activities, and asked for forgiveness.

These claims aside, Aa Gym surely knew that Suharto had jailed Muslim figures (such as Imaduddin Abdulrahim) whenever their popularity was deemed a threat to the New Order. Another one of Aa Gym's predecessors of sorts was Zaenuddin MZ, known as the "preacher with a million followers." He was a star in some of the earliest *dakwah* films of the 1980s and 1990s, often playing the wise senior elder with the moral authority to intervene and resolve conflict. However, Zaenuddin MZ's following sharply declined once he began to more explicitly engage in party politics. It was this sociopolitical context in which Aa Gym learned the value of publicly declaring himself apolitical. Even though Suharto stepped down in 1998, Aa Gym refused to openly declare his allegiance to any political party. Interestingly, he and his advisers referred to their ostensibly apolitical stance in terms of the English marketing parlance of "positioning." Even in 2006, when he mapped out a clearly political strategy to rally popular support for controversial anti-pornography legislation, Aa Gym reminded his closest advisers, "Our positioning is neutral. Our role is to calm national tensions and encourage respectful dialogue. That's it." Aa Gym was always cognizant of the positioning of his personal brand on the public stage, and he devoted special attention to be sure that he did not divide his following along political lines.

With the widespread proliferation and privatization of media during post–New Order Indonesia, television producers and advertisers enthusiastically embraced Islam-inspired programming and even organized special committees to Islamize their image. In the process, Islam accrued a certain market value. This was especially the case during Ramadan, when television preachers began to appear on nearly every channel. Aa Gym's preaching style was well suited to this medium. In 2000, Aa Gym had his national television debut on SCTV with the program *Indahnya Kebersamaan* (The beauty of togetherness). Aa Gym's appeal to togetherness, with its explicit focus not just on the Muslim community but on Indonesia as a diverse nation emerging from the grip of authoritarian rule, can be understood within the social-political milieu of post–New Order Indonesia. Suharto fell in 1998, but by 2000 the jubilant calls for reform (*reformasi*) had often given way to the realities of new political factions competing for power and money. As an ardent nationalist, Aa Gym genuinely wanted Indonesia to prosper, and he was troubled by the interreligious clashes in Indonesia in areas with a higher percentage of Christians, such as Central Sulawesi and the Moluccas. Despite sharp criticism from some conservative *ulama*, Aa Gym preached in a Christian church when conflict in Central Sulawesi—not inherently religious, but cast in terms of religion—resulted in widespread violence. The photograph is even included in his autobiography. As a marketer, Aa Gym had a keen understanding of how to increase his stature and moral authority by placing himself at the center of national events—clashes in Sulawesi, the 2002 bomb blast in Bali, and the 2004 tsunami in Aceh. Aa Gym was developing his public persona as the nation's therapist-in-chief, carefully weaving the personal through the political, and vice versa.

Although Aa Gym's television debut was in 2000, he solidified his standing as a national figure during a nationally broadcast sermon live from Istiqlal mosque in December 2001 when he was invited to preach before an audience that included politicians, foreign dignitaries, and then-President Megawati Sukarnoputri. As usual, he offered religious wisdom in the form of everyday anecdotes, humorous asides, and the occasional quotation, in Arabic, of passages from the Qur'an. Actually Aa Gym hardly spoke any Arabic, but he was well aware of the power of language, especially the capacity for a well-placed quote in Arabic to assert one's religious authority. Soon after this sermon "Aa Gym" was a household name throughout Indonesia.

With his newfound popularity, Aa Gym also began to parlay his celebrity status into political capital. In early 2003 he mobilized thousands of supporters to protest the impending American war in Iraq. With the vast majority of Indonesians against American imperialism in Muslim countries, Aa Gym could afford to be political when it concerned international affairs. In a clever marketing move, he asked attendees to paint their clothes in red, and, on his cue, everyone fell to the ground in an effort to simulate the needless deaths that would inevitably occur. This "die-in" proved to be a great photo-op for the evening news. More important, it caught the attention of foreign diplomats who were anxious to cultivate allies in the so-called war on terror. Aa Gym's autobiography includes his letter to President George W. Bush. With a strategic rhetorical style to which I return in Chapter 5—he does not condemn America but instead invites America to act in accordance with purportedly noble values. It was an ethical summons. When Aa Gym refused to meet with Bush when he visited Bali for a few hours (a story Aa Gym loves to recount), General Colin Powell arranged to meet with Aa Gym, and Western diplomats began to visit Daarut Tauhiid as part of their official diplomatic circuit with Muslim leaders. Aa Gym had the shrewd ability to use his popularity to enter the political arena and, in turn, to seize such moments of political and moral debate to further advance his own standing and interests as both preacher and entrepreneur.

In the following years Aa Gym continued to test the political waters, but from a safe vantage point. In 2004 he produced a talk show to discuss the upcoming 2004 elections. The title *Ada Aa Gym* is an acronym for *Aman dan Akur a la Aa Gym* (Safe and orderly, like Aa Gym). The acronym can also imply "Here is Aa Gym." He kept party politics at a distance but tried to interject moral lessons along the way. His rhetorical style was gentle and friendly. He was careful not to condemn any specific individual; instead he summoned state actors to publicly perform their piety and virtue. Aa Gym continued to refine this strategy of moral invitation—of summoning the state—during controversies surrounding *Playboy* magazine and a banned film. Aa Gym was learning the value of speaking about the political in terms of the personal.

### Aa Gym's Autobiography: Of Self, Family, and Nation

Like any story (or ethnography), life histories are plagued by the ambitions, proclivities, and anxieties of the storyteller. Aa Gym's official autobiography, *Aa Gym: Just as He Is*—available as both a book and a video—must be understood within this context of Aa Gym's public maneuvering for relevance, authority, and legitimacy. Whereas the subtitle insinuates a folksy sort of candidness (especially the original Indonesian subtitle *Apa Adanya*), Aa Gym carefully crafted his biography—what he refers to as his *qolbugrafi*—to brand himself as a particular kind of religious figure who wielded a specific sort of religious wisdom. This positioning was directed not just at his admirers but especially at his critics. The challenge was to position his role as a public figure in a way that carved out his own niche of authority without encroaching on the terrain of more orthodox religious scholars. It was not an easy balancing act.

Not everyone in Indonesia was enchanted by Aa Gym's rapid rise to fame. One Salafist ridiculed Manajemen Qolbu as being caught in the "prison of Sufism" (Al-Mukaffi 2003). From other perspectives, liberal intellectuals and religious scholars sneered at his lack of religious education and his claim to have received religious knowledge directly from God (*ilmu laduni*; Arabic, *al-'ilm al-ladduni*). Ulil Abshar Abdullah, a prominent liberal Muslim scholar in Indonesia, once scoffed at Aa Gym as the "Britney Spears of

Islam." His detractors were seldom vocal, but, when asked, Muslim intellectuals would readily admit that they believe his teachings are shallow and superficial. Nonetheless many public figures and Muslim intellectuals also agreed to serve on the advisory board for his moral movement.

Aa Gym's autobiography serves in part as a rejoinder to these, and other, public challenges to his authority. As the director of Aa Gym's publishing company, Bambang Trim, acknowledges in the introduction: "It may very well be the case that this book becomes a response to other published books that raise topics about the position of Aa Gym in the arena of Islamic propagation. The idea: books must speak with [other] books, books must be answered by [other] books—this is part of the culture of Islamic intellectualism" (Gymnastiar 2003, x). Through a critical reading of autobiography, then, we can better understand how Aa Gym positions himself within the broader religious, political, and economic debates of the nation.

His life story, we are told, demonstrates that one can attain both worldly riches and heavenly redemption. The success story of "Aa Gym the entrepreneur" was not limited to his autobiography. It was also the focus of countless magazine covers and popular books on business. His face adorns the cover of the 2004 book *Success Stories: Muslim Businesspeople in Indonesia*, which includes a VCD titled *Who Wants to Be a Muslim Billionaire?* Aa Gym's success story also serves as a case study in the 2006 book *Imitating the Business Keys of 50 Successful Entrepreneurs* (*Nyontek Kiat Bisnis 50 Entrepreneurs Sukses*). Aa Gym's cutting-edge blend of Islam, technology, media, and management was also lauded in the 2005 Ramadan special issue of *Gatra* magazine that featured icons of Islamic business.

Aa Gym's video autobiography explains his rags-to-riches success story, from roadside meatball soup vendor to president of a multi-million-dollar business empire. Next, a self-help slogan flashes on the screen: "There is no success without courage." Anyone can succeed—as long as he or she is willing to use his MQ formula (and Daarut Tauhiid's official motto) of *Dzikir* (mindfulness of God; Arabic, *dhikr*), *Fikir* (cognitive effort; Arabic, *fikr*), and *Ikhtiar* (self-initiative; Arabic, *ikhtiyār*). *Dzikir*, a popular (albeit not exclusively) Sufi practice, refers to being mindful of God through recitation. *Fikir*, the cognitive capacity of humans, should be exercised through personal initiative, or *ikhtiar*. Whereas in Arabic *ikhtiyār* literally means "choice," the Indonesian word connotes self-initiative or effort. Aa Gym's teachings on entrepreneurship promote the maximizing of personal initiative to attain fortune bestowed by God (*menyempurnakan ikhtiar untuk menjemput rezeki*). This biography of the self-made Muslim resonated with the aspirational piety of upwardly mobile Indonesians and also appealed to corporate managers eager to invest in MQ Training.

Aa Gym also tells his tale (and builds his brand) by conjuring visual symbols of piety and bravery. He devotes a chapter to his most distinguishing visual feature—his turban (*sorban*). Initially worn during the early 1990s to conceal his youthful appearance, Aa Gym's turban eventually became his "*trademark*" (Gymnastiar 2003, 116). In his discussion of Aa Gym as a "spiritual marketer," Hermawan Kartajaya mentions the time when Aa Gym visited his Jakarta office (Kartajaya et al. 2005). Kartajaya's employees were eagerly awaiting Aa Gym's visit, only to be disappointed when he arrived without his turban. Kartajaya uses this example to discuss the emotional and spiritual connections that consumers have with the visual symbols and metanarratives about spiritual brands. Put bluntly, Aa Gym's turban sells. Images of Aa Gym's turban-clad head were plastered on calendars, posters, bumper stickers, and book covers. And prior to public appearances, Aa Gym's assistants always ensured that a prewrapped turban was ready and waiting. Eventually to his own chagrin, donning the turban became part of Yan Abdullah Gymnastiar's ritual of becoming Aa Gym.

Aa Gym not only wears the turban of a revered religious teacher, but he also sports the rugged apparel of an adventurer. The video *qolbugrafi* is full of images of Aa Gym racing go-karts, scuba diving, sky diving, and riding horses. While these activities may be commonplace in the West, these adventure and leisure activities have only recently been associated with middle-class aspirations in Indonesia. In the most recent version, Aa Gym breaks the sound barrier as the copilot of an F5-E Tiger fighter jet. Spiritual tourists at Daarut Tauhiid can even purchase a picture of Aa Gym posing in his flight suit and turban. After the sequence of images fades, his self-help mantra flashes on the screen again: "There is no success without courage." In the marketplace of modernity, Aa Gym's story about himself resonated with the anxieties and desires of Indonesian Muslims who aspired to both piety and prosperity, who embraced tradition and modernity, and who remained loyal to the nation without sacrificing their commitment to Islam.

The narrative arc of his autobiography lends credence to his story of hope and transformation. The chapters follow a chronological narrative, abridged in this discussion, that brings the reader from humble roots to heavenly redemption. Yan Gymnastiar, the son of middle-class parents and the eldest of four children, was born in Bandung, West Java, on January 29, 1962. At that time, Gymnastiar's father, Engkus Kuswara, worked as a physical education teacher and named Gymnastiar (pronounced with a hard "g") after the word "gymnastics." As the story goes, during Gymnastiar's first hajj pilgrimage, the imam of the grand Haram mosque in Mecca bestowed Yan the new name of Abdullah Gymnastiar. When Abdullah Gymnastiar became a celebrated local, regional, and ultimately national preacher, he eschewed the formal title of religious leader, *kyai*, and preferred to be addressed with the less formal, more familiar Sundanese honorific Aa, or "elder brother." This engendered a more relational, less hierarchical preacher-disciple relationship.

Aa Gym has the indefatigable energy and personal charisma of his late father, whom Aa Gym credits with teaching him the importance of respecting and relating to people of both higher and lower social classes (2003, 6). Aa Gym was raised in a household that emphasized strict discipline. When he was four years old, his father joined the military. While growing up, Aa Gym developed his sense of nationalist pride and eventually wanted to join the Indonesian military. However, he was turned down because he was not tall enough. (He did become commander of a quasi-military student organization in college.) This military upbringing would later influence the way he managed Daarut Tauhiid, especially during its early years.

When I began my fieldwork, Aa Gym had the national reputation of a gentle person who managed his emotions and whose soothing voice could placate even the most distraught caller who telephoned his radio show to ask for advice. Thus, I was surprised when a couple of his close friends chuckled with delight as they recalled stories about the Aa Gym of old who often lost his temper. When employees broke with protocol, he even ordered them to do push-ups or to stand for long periods of time as part of their public shaming. Others from his neighborhood were less jovial when they recalled a younger Aa Gym who, according to them, was a delinquent youth who eagerly joined aggressive campaigns to rid the neighborhood of vice (*maksiat*).[5]

Although his approach may be gentler than that of Indonesia's prominent Muslim militants, Aa Gym retains friendly relations with more militaristic Indonesian Muslims such as Habib Rizieq, the leader of the Islamic Defenders Front, and Abu Bakar Bashir, former leader of Jemaah Islamiyah, both of whom have been jailed for orchestrating violence in the name of religion.

In fact, Aa Gym once told me that Rizieq asked for his assistance to encourage a government official to allow two FPI members to be released from jail in order to be with their family during *Idul Fitri* celebrations at the end of Ramadan in 2005. When I asked, Aa Gym would not categorically condemn their violence, especially if it involves defending Christian-majority provinces such as Maluku and North Maluku, where ethnic violence was largely explained at the national level in terms of Christian-Muslim tensions (Duncan 2013). He once told me that their methods were "just a different form of *dakwah*." Whereas discipline and military protocol remain important at Daarut Tauhiid, his close friends report that Aa Gym is no longer quick to anger nor does he support the FPI's anti-vice campaign to forcibly shut down bars and brothels. This stance, however, was as much about marketing as morality. He worried that media images of burning tires, clenched fists, and shouts of "Allahu Akbar" provided fresh fodder for Islamophobes around the world.

Other dimensions of Aa Gym's childhood and adolescence had an even greater impact on the kind of public figure he would become. He began to develop his talents as a performer, songwriter, and actor as early as elementary school. His autobiography also includes images from his adolescent years, when he played guitar, won speech contests, and performed in drama productions. Aa Gym's playful sense of language and song eventually served him well as a television preacher. During sermons, he often assumed the accentuated voice and demeanor of different fictive characters, elaborated in comedic and melodramatic form. One of Aa Gym's favorite character sketches was that of an overly proud mother who would boast about her child's report card while snidely insulting those mothers whose children did not receive high marks. Another character embodied the boastful pride of someone who enjoyed publicizing his good deeds. Breaking with character to emphasize the moral of the story, he admonished the crowd: "Perform good deeds as you would go to the toilet. Do it, but don't talk about it!" Audiences ate it up. He then put the lesson in more overtly Islamic terms with a saying of the Prophet: "The left hand should not know what the right hand gives in charity." This humorous style tethered ethical lessons to everyday life, and its theatrical value appealed to audiences, television producers, and advertising executives.

As recollected in his official autobiography, Aa Gym developed an unrelenting entrepreneurial spirit as early as elementary school when he sold marbles and firecrackers to fellow classmates (2003, 12–20). He writes that, by the time he reached junior high school, he had already shifted his sights to the teachers, whom he referred to as his new "target market." During his college years Aa Gym traveled to various graduation ceremonies to sell camera film. He was quick to realize who had the capital, when they were willing to spend it, and how he could cater to their needs. He was learning more than formal laws of supply and demand. He was gaining an appreciation for the social contours and interpersonal aspects of economic exchange.

Years later this talent would serve him well as a national celebrity trying to forge alliances and leverage patrons. Aa Gym knew that his celebrity status afforded a certain bargaining position, whether with politicians eager for a campaign-season photo-op or wealthy businesspeople looking to invest their money or, for some, to ease their conscience by giving charity to his social welfare foundation. Aa Gym's fame also helped secure several large corporate and government sponsorships to finance his projects, ranging from an eco-friendly Islamic school to his national moral movement, Gema Nusa. To this end, he invited key people into his inner circle. For example, one of the members of Gema Nusa's executive board was Anindya Bakrie, the son of one of Indonesia's richest and most powerful politicians, Aburizal Bakrie. Anindya donated a small percentage of the profit from his wireless telecommunications company in order to finance the operational costs of Gema Nusa. And when Aa Gym sought funding to finance the Gema Nusa 10-K run to promote "the conscience of the nation," he invited then-minister of State-Owned Enterprises, Sugiharto, to sit with him during a fancy fund-raising dinner. A couple of months later, and a few sponsorship dollars lighter, Sugiharto basked in photo-ops with Aa Gym prior to the 10-K run. The title sponsor was the food conglomerate Indomie, who was promoting its brand Mie Sedap (delicious noodles). The real PR coup, though, occurred when Aa Gym leveraged his personal relationship with Indonesian president Susilo Bambang Yudhoyono, who waved the starting flag and jogged beside Gymnastiar. This flow of capital and contracts, however, depended on his celebrity status. Without his fame, Aa Gym would be just another guy selling film at graduation.

Aa Gym earnestly continued his entrepreneurial enterprises during college. Reportedly a good student, Aa Gym nonetheless failed the entrance exam for his college of choice, the prestigious Bandung Institute of Technology. After a year studying accounting at Padjadjaran University in Bandung,

FIGURE I.2. Aa Gym with President Susilo Bambang Yudhoyono at the starting gate for Gema Nusa's 10-K run.

Aa Gym transferred to the Ahmad Yani Technology Academy, where he was elected head of the student senate. He continued to enter (and win) campus-wide contests for singing, poetry, and public speaking. During these years he cultivated a formidable combination of leadership, charisma, and commerce. Years later Aa Gym would direct these personal qualities and entrepreneurial energies into the marketing of Manajemen Qolbu.

Aa Gym's biography describes his personal transformation from selling commodities to marketing "the beauty of Islam." At this time he still lived at home and shared a room with his younger brother, Gun Martin, who suffered from an unspecified medical condition that left him unable to walk. According to Aa Gym, Gun Martin never complained about his affliction, insisting that complaining would not change anything but only increase the burden on others. Gun Martin reminded Aa Gym, who at that time was preoccupied with his entrepreneurial pursuits, that money and popularity would never bring a tranquil heart (Gymnastiar 2003, 22). As Gun Martin reportedly told him, Aa Gym would find inner peace only by becoming closer to God and following the way of the Prophet Muhammad. Some of Aa Gym's closest childhood friends also told me that another reason he turned to religion was to heal a broken heart when a romantic interest chose to marry someone else. This detail does not negate the importance of his deep emotional relationship with his brother. It serves as a reminder that Aa Gym's autobiography, like all others, privileges certain life stories over others. Although the specific details differ about exactly why Aa Gym dove headlong into Islam during this time, by all accounts his relationship with Gun Martin was transformative and certainly became part of Aa Gym's public narrative of repentance and transformation.

Aa Gym's religious awakening led him to seek knowledge in Islam; however, he did not acquire formal religious education and thus lacked the academic pedigree of an Islamic scholar, so he had to stake other claims on religious authority. The nature of Aa Gym's religious knowledge and authority shifted depending on the context and historical moment of his life and career. The degree to which he studied and practiced Islam prior to this point is unclear. In one of the first academic writings about Gymnastiar (and perhaps with more adoration than evidence), Dindin Solahudin reports that Aa Gym had already memorized chapters of the Qur'an by the age of three (1996, 14). In his autobiography, Aa Gym claims that he failed a Qur'anic recitation test in junior high school because the specific passage he was tested on was different from the verse he memorized with all his might (2003, 14). He claims that he consistently fulfilled obligatory prayers but lacked any deeper knowledge about Islam.

During the late 1980s, Aa Gym and several friends (some of whom who would later work as trusted executives in his business) traveled to various Islamic schools in West Java to deepen their religious knowledge. They spent short periods of time studying Sufism with a respected religious teacher, K. H. Choer Affandy, at the Miftahul Huda Islamic school in Manonjaya. Aa Gym never became a permanent student, but Affandy's teachings greatly influenced his later emphasis on Sufi ideas of the heart, the oneness of God (*tauhid*; Arabic, *tawḥīd*), and moral conduct (*akhlaq*; Arabic, *akhlāq*). was originally named Bengkel Akhlaq, which the "workshop for morality." In Indonesian, the e sense of an automobile repair garage (*bengkel hlaq*, then, conveys the sense of a place where ome to improve his or her moral fabric. This appears to be the time period when Aa Gym began to study Sufi esoteric psychology, notably al-Ghazālī's treatises on the heart as well as the *Al-Ḥikam*, the book of aphorisms by Cairene Sufi scholar Ibn 'Aṭā' Allāh al-Iskandarī (d. 1309) that Aa Gym would later use as a textbook for his Monday-morning sermons for Daarut Tauhiid employees.

Aa Gym became especially fervent in his desire to become closer to God during the month of Ramadhan in 1986.[6] According to Aa Gym (2003, 30), the Al-Taqwa mosque across the street became his own "Hira cave" (an allusion to the cave where the Prophet Muhammad first received God's revelation), where he spent long evenings of contemplation and reportedly read the entire Qur'an several times (Solahudin 1996, 18). It was during this time, on the evening of *lailatul qodar*, that Aa Gym is said to have received his religious knowledge directly from God (*ilmu laduni*). Muslims believe that Allah's blessings are a thousandfold on one evening during the final ten nights of Ramadan, but the exact date is unknown. Many of Aa Gym's followers during the early years attribute his divinely transmitted knowledge to his presence in the mosque on this particular evening. That Aa Gym was bestowed with such immediate knowledge was reportedly confirmed by four religious scholars, including Affandy. Many of his followers were also impressed by rumors that circulated about Aa Gym's dreams of praying with the Prophet Muhammad, in which the Prophet directly summoned him to call people back to Islam. Many interpreted this as an auspicious sign that further demonstrates the miraculous blessings and gifts (*ma'unah*) bestowed upon Aa Gym. In the eyes of his admirers, divinely transmitted knowledge and dreams of the Prophet Muhammad compensated for Aa Gym's notable lack of religious education and legitimated his claims to religious authority.

His detractors, however, were not convinced by what they felt were storybook tales. In his aforementioned book, al-Mukaffi (2003) sharply rebuked Aa Gym, arguing that talk of mystically bestowed knowledge and dreams of the Prophet simply proved that Aa Gym was trapped in the "prison of Sufism." Although al-Mukaffi's book did not significantly impact the public popularity of Aa Gym, such a sharp critique influenced how Aa Gym later clarified, perhaps modified, his formal life history as a way to respond to such criticism. Without denying that he received divine knowledge, Aa Gym's autobiography characterizes this interpretation as "less than realistic" (2003, 34). Always careful to deflect criticism, he continued, "I prefer earnestness to learn and to practice improving myself rather than talking about sensitive matters" (35). Aa Gym states that what is more important than the veracity of such claims is the fact that such experiences nurtured his sincere desire to become closer to God.

Similarly, he downplayed, without disavowing, his dreams of the Prophet Muhammad: "Even though there is a hadith that states that a dream of meeting the Prophet must be authentic, what is more important for me is how, after that, I kept learning and trying to follow the Prophet's example" (26). His admirers spread the mystique that legitimated his authority; Aa Gym downplayed its importance; then he somewhat sheepishly mentioned that indeed there was a hadith to that effect. Aa Gym's strategy for legitimating his religious authority (and appeasing his critics) changed over time, especially after he entered the national media limelight. By the time of al-Mukaffi's critiques, Aa Gym was already a national celebrity, and his religious authority relied less on mystical claims of direct knowledge from God than on the public image of him as the embodiment of Islamic virtue and entrepreneurial success.

Aa Gym's wife, Ninih Ghaida Muthmainnah, also played an important role in this public theatrics of Islamic piety. They married after he returned from the hajj pilgrimage in 1987. To provide for his wife and family, Aa Gym continued to pursue several entrepreneurial ventures. In the mornings he sold books in front of the al-Furqon mosque. This business pursuit eventually grew into a bookstore and mini-market. In the afternoons he made and sold handicrafts. Eventually Aa Gym used the knowledge and proceeds from this venture to get into silk-screening and, later, book publishing. He also bought a used sewing machine that Ninih and several female employees used to sew cloth that they bought wholesale. With each venture, Aa Gym sold his products to his local congregation. From the beginning, Aa Gym's followers were also his market. During the early years, however, he was selling tangible commodities and household goods, not religious self-help.[7]

These business endeavors, though on a much smaller scale than Aa Gym's later entrepreneurial ventures, can nonetheless be placed within broader national and transnational forces at that time. The Islamic publishing industry during the 1980s and 1990s was just emerging as a viable business to meet the demands of an emerging middle class eager to use leisure (and study) time to learn more about religion. The Islamic daily newspaper *Republika* was formed shortly after, and in connection with, the founding of ICMI in 1990. In 1983 Haidar Bagir, Ali Abdullah, and Zainal Abidin had formed Mizan Press, which is now one of Indonesia's largest publisher of books on

Islam, especially Islamic self-help (Fadjar 2006). Prior to forming Mizan, Haidar Bagir and Zainal Abidin Bagir served on the editorial board of the journal *Pustaka Salman ITB*, where they were influenced by the training sessions of Imaduddin Abdulrahim, the aforementioned leader of the Islamic campus movement at the Bandung Institute of Technology. Thus, the rise of Aa Gym, his publishing company MQS, and his television company MQTV can be traced to the global Islamic revival (in various forms, places, and spaces), the campus propagation (*dakwah*) movements in Bandung in the 1980s, and the subsequent boom in Islamic print and television media in Indonesia during the 1990s.

As Aa Gym traveled between various Islamic schools in West Java to broaden his understanding of a moral psychology of the heart, his local following in Bandung continued to grow, especially among those college students eager to integrate Islamic ethics into entrepreneurial activities. As Solahudin notes (1996, 35), the very first religious study group founded by Aa Gym and his friends, which between 1987 and 1989 had grown from ten people to approximately four hundred, went by the formal name Group of Muslim Student Entrepreneurs (Kelompok Mahasiswa Islam Wiraswasta). From the beginning, people were seemingly attracted not just by rumors of dreams and divinely inspired knowledge but also by the practical desire to yoke Islamic ethics to entrepreneurship.

This increased interest in Islamic entrepreneurship must also be understood within the national and international contexts of the late 1980s. At that time the Islamic community and business enterprise Darul Arqam was gaining popularity in Malaysia and, increasingly, throughout parts of Sumatra and Java. Founded in 1968, Darul Arqam owned dozens of businesses by the early 1990s, including a supermarket, restaurants, educational facilities, and a tour and travel company—all businesses that Aa Gym would later replicate. Aa Gym and some of his closest friends told me that Darul Arqam became a model for how to combine religious ethics with capitalist enterprise. Unlike the leaders of Darul Arqam, who built the community in a rural area outside Kuala Lumpur, Aa Gym envisioned an Islamic school and business venture that was integrated with the neighborhood and society—what Aa Gym referred to as a "virtual *pesantren* [Islamic school]." I should note, however, that Darul Arqam was perceived as a threat by both the Malaysian and Indonesian governments. Malaysia banned the group in 1994, and Indonesian authorities were wary of its increasing popularity.

Well aware of Suharto's antipathy toward anything that seemed to denote political Islam, Aa Gym was always careful to portray his religious propagation in terms of personal transformation and his "heart-to-heart" ethos.

## Marketing Islam: Gender, Affect, and Authority

Thursday evenings were always lively around Daarut Tauhiid. Typically the first wave of the spiritual tourism and corporate MQ Training groups had already arrived and were getting settled at one of the nearby guest houses that had sprung up to accommodate the thousands of weekly visitors. After dusk prayers, these spiritual tourists and corporate trainees poured out of the mosque in different directions. Some looked for dinner, others dropped by the MQ mini-mart for toiletries, and many others—men and women—crowded the nearby Islamic fashion stores to look for a new outfit for the evening sermon. In less than an hour, they returned to the mosque for the evening prayers, followed by Aa Gym's nationally broadcast Thursday-evening radio sermon.

The theme on this evening was "the beauty of patience" (*indahnya kesabaran*). With microphone in hand, Aa Gym gazed out into the crowd of tourists and trainees: "Wow, looking out at all of your faces, it seems like you have plenty of problems, huh?" After a moment of anxious laughter from the crowd, he continued: "Do you want to know the secret to life's problems?" Then, as with nearly every group that visited, Aa Gym insisted that life's problems were not the real issue; instead, it was our response to life's problems. "The key is whether or not we confront life's difficulties with a pure heart, with the faith and confidence in Allah's pledge to never give us problems too great to overcome, that following every trial is a time of peace, and that there is a path to fortune for every single one of us." Aa Gym's preaching style blended humor with religious lessons:

> Did you ever hear the story about the two salespeople sent to Africa to sell shoes? When the first salesperson noticed that most people didn't even wear shoes, he called his boss in a panic. "Sir, there's no way to succeed here. They don't even wear shoes!" However, when the second salesperson looked at all of these bare feet in Africa, he immediately called his boss: "Sir, almost no one wears shoes—there is a huge untapped market here!"

As the audience laughed, Aa Gym motioned to the sound engineer to increase the reverb on his microphone. With the soothing tone of a therapist, his voice lowered by an octave as he reminded Indonesians that if they clung to their faith and tended to their hearts, then Allah would calm their hearts and souls:

> My brothers and sisters, if we only focus on two things in life, let them be praise [syukur] and patience [sabar]. We must be ready to enjoy the good times but also be patient in those difficult times. We must enjoy not just praise [pujian] but also trials [ujian]. Because people will suffer if they are only prepared to enjoy one of these . . . the key to life's trials and tribulations is patience. This does not mean that we just give up. Rather we wholeheartedly accept the tests that Allah gives us by maximizing our own self-initiative [ikhtiar] in God's path. . . . Know that the tests we are given are in accordance with our ability to overcome them. It is written in the Qur'an: "Allah does not burden one except in accordance with their ability [to overcome the test]." Surely, there is wisdom [hikmah] that can be learned. May Allah always show us the beauty of patience in our hearts. The person who is patient day in, day out will be the person brought close to Allah in accordance with His promise that "he is with those who are patient." . . . A pure heart is a patient heart. Let us cultivate pure hearts.

Even though Aa Gym does not always explicitly say so, this emphasis on praise and patience does draw on the textual authority of the Qur'an and the life, sayings, and examples of the Prophet (sunna). Aa Gym understands his role to be a translator of sorts, a cultural broker who simplifies religious teachings by putting them into everyday language accessible across class (and even religious) boundaries. When he finished his sermon an hour later, the lights dimmed and Aa Gym led the crowd in dzikir recitations in remembrance of God. He tells the audience that only Allah can calm a troubled heart and, thus, the path to a pure heart begins by remembering Allah. After the dzikir, he led a supplication to God, with the audience responding with "Amin" after each plea:

> Ya Allah, we imperfect humans, please grant us patience, please bring peace and solace to our hearts, please let us be an instrument of Your will on earth. Ya Allah, please forgive our sins, all of those times when we are quick to anger, when our hearts are filled not with love and compassion, but with jealousy and spite. Ya Allah, forgive us when we get angry with our family, our children, our wives, our husbands, our parents, ya Allah. Have mercy on us, ya Allah.

Aa Gym sobbed with each supplication, and the weeping of thousands inside the mosque—men and women alike—filled the crisp evening air. When the lights came back on after the sermon, many wiped away their tears, others performed optional ritual prayers, and some lined up to kiss

Aa Gym's hand, as is customary for a revered religious teacher (*kyai*). Even though many, if not most, in attendance do not necessarily self-identify as Sufi, ritual weeping has a long history in Sufi practices of ethical reflection in Indonesia and elsewhere (Gade and Feener 2004). As some participants shared later that evening as we sipped the hot ginger drink *sekoteng*, these were tears of remorse, shame, sadness, and penitence. Yet in those moments of introspection they also prayed for transformation and renewal. Ritual weeping was a staple ending to Aa Gym's sermons, and it played an important role in the emotional preacher-disciple exchange relationship. In the words of one television producer, ritual weeping at the end of sermons was "vintage Aa Gym." A discursive tradition had been transformed into an Islamic brand.

After the sermon I sat with a group of male pilgrims who had traveled hundreds of miles from Pontianak. I remained with them for most of the weekend to learn more about why they traveled such a great distance to learn from Aa Gym. Hanafi, a well-dressed dentist and the founder of MQ Pontianak, led a group of pilgrims to Daarut Tauhiid nearly every month. When I asked him why, he sat back, looked up briefly, and then said solemnly: "Aa touches my heart [*Aa menyentuh qolbu*]. When I come here, I feel inspired and a stillness enters my heart. It cools my heart [*menyejukkan hati*]. Any anger or spite in my heart is subdued." The next morning I spoke with Hanafi's friend Henny over breakfast with other pilgrims:[8]

> I get bored listening to other preachers who only quote from the Qur'an and just talk about Islamic law this and that. And I don't really enjoy those academic types who, in their seminars at five-star hotels, debate religion in their arrogant tone of voice. Aa Gym talks in simple language. He jokes, but his jokes always have a lesson. Being here, listening to his sermons, praying in the mosque, waking during the night for *tahajud* prayers . . . I feel like my battery is recharged. It makes me want to control my anger with my children, to spend time reciting the Qur'an with them, to be a more loving wife, and to not lose my temper at home.

Hundreds of others expressed similar sentiments again and again as I followed Aa Gym around the country and met with pilgrims and trainees who visited Daarut Tauhiid. As most put it, Aa Gym touched their hearts (*menyentuh hati*).

Aa Gym's soothing therapeutics did more than touch hearts. They generated revenue. Indonesia's television producers and advertising executives were eager to capitalize on these tender ties. When I arrived for fieldwork during Ramadan in October 2005, Aa Gym was on television as many as five times a day. You could watch at 2:30 a.m. after waking to eat before the fast, again at 4:00 a.m. before morning prayers, later in the afternoon prior to breaking the fast, and occasionally on two different channels following the evening prayers. In addition to his monthly televised sermon from Istiqlal mosque, Aa Gym was the star of his own reality TV series, *Assalamu'alaikum with Aa Gym,* and also played himself in the program *Voice of the Heart.* Each program had its own logo and catchy jingle.

For Ramadan in 2006, Aa Gym's production company, MQTV, was commissioned to produce short, three- or four-minute "fillers" to be broadcast daily between regular programming. Each filler had a simple message and similar format. The same fictional family experienced various problems. At the precise moment when the conflict escalated, the actors went into freeze-frame and Aa Gym swooped in, smiled to the camera, explained the nature of the conflict at hand, and provided simple tips to resolve the dispute.

In one episode, "The Beauty of Variety in Cooking," a wife serves her husband the same vegetable soup (*sayur lodeh*) for several consecutive days.

FIGURE 1.3. Aa Gym performing his family-mediator role for an MQTV Ramadan production.

The husband enjoys the soup the first day. When his wife serves the soup each subsequent day, however, he becomes increasingly irritated and finally harshly rebukes her in front of their children: "It's always the same: vegetable soup, vegetable soup, vegetable soup! Is that all you can cook?" His wife retorts that she spends her entire days doing work for the family and never receives any praise. At that moment, the actors went into freeze-frame and Aa Gym entered the frame, touched their hearts, and saved the day. Gazing into the camera, he gently observes that variation in cooking is a wonderful gift: "Durian fruit is delicious, but who would ever want to eat durian day in, day out?" Then he admonishes the husband (still frozen in frame) to take a kinder and gentler approach when pointing out his wife's shortcomings. Aa Gym suggests that he praise some of his wife's other dishes as a way to indirectly request a change of menu without openly hurting her feelings. After this, Aa Gym steps offstage, the actors then perform Aa Gym's sage advice, and family harmony is restored. Thus, the term "televangelist" does not really capture the religious psycho-therapeutics that structure this preacher-discipline relationship.

In his classic essay about Javanese concepts of power, Benedict Anderson (1990, 17–77) describes the ideal of a refined (*halus*) ruler capable of emotional restraint (Suharto's reputation as the "smiling general" is a perfect example). The popularity of Aa Gym and Manajemen Qolbu certainly conforms to this ideal; however, to focus solely on emotional restraint would be to miss arguably the most important reason why Aa Gym's public image resonated so deeply with Indonesian women—his ability to express tender feelings of love and longing. Indeed, scholars of femininity in New Order and post–New Order Indonesia have described middle-class Indonesian women's desires for the ideal Muslim man who is gentle, romantic, and emotionally communicative (Brenner 1998; Jones 2004; Smith-Hefner 2009; Suryakusuma 1996). Carla Jones notes that romantic marriage is an important marker of middle-class modernity for many Indonesians and that "emotional labor" and the economy of affect within the family have become a central stressor for middle-class Indonesian women:

> "Caring for a husband and children" meant something very different than simply seeing to it that they had clothes to wear and food to eat. In addition to describing an idealized affective relationship between husband and wife, this phrase was prominent in the advice and self-help literature which women found instructive. (2004, 516)

On the public stage Aa Gym served as the moral exemplar of modern Muslim masculinity, and Manajemen Qolbu provided a religious therapeutics that attended to the desires and anxieties of middle-class women searching for the resources to manage the affective economies of marriage and family. The intersubjective preacher-disciple relationship was marked by the affective tone of a "heart to heart" in which Aa Gym (as master of his own heart) created the hybrid public persona of a preacher-psychologist who promised to soothe modern anxieties about emotional labor and family turmoil.[9]

This was especially apparent in his popular advice columns and morning radio show. On each Friday the popular Islamic newspaper *Republika* featured a special two-page, full color "MQ" section that included Aa Gym's advice column, "MQ Clinic." He also plays the role of therapist in his biweekly publication (*Tabloid MQ*) and his daily radio show (*MQ in the Morning*). In these forums, his followers seek advice on personal problems and Aa Gym provides simple wisdom and sympathetic understanding. I include detailed excerpts to provide a sense of the underlying affective tone of these exchanges and insight into his practical religious wisdom for a happy home:

> *"My Husband Is Expert at Criticism/Finding Fault" (Republika, January 19, 2007)*
> Aa Gym, I am a housewife who has been married sixteen years. During this time my husband frequently hurts [my feelings]. He always criticizes, only caring about my shortcomings. He even frequently insists that I help out with our financial situation. I want to become a wife who deals with this matter wisely. How do I approach this problem so that I am not emotional and so that I have a wise disposition?
>
> *Answer:*
> I salute your fortitude and patience. For sixteen years you have, without complaining, managed to withstand life with a husband who has such characteristics. In fact you even think about how to remain wise. This means that you are a woman who thinks positively.
>
> There is a story about a person whose husband is not yet virtuous. He always demanded, was often really angry, criticized, and rarely gave thanks to his wife. Nevertheless, what did his wife say: "This is my fate from God, to have a husband like this. Every husband does wrong, [and] this is a chance for me to become strong, to not look at [his] behavior. I view this as a means for struggle. When my husband is angry, I must pray for him because, no matter what, he is the father of my children. If I leave him, who else will pray for him? This is a test of my sincerity."

At the same time, she constantly remembered Allah, that Allah is the one who can move the heart of your husband. She continued to be patient by her husband's side. "If I am mindful of Allah, it will feel less burdensome. But if I only look at my husband's wickedness, I will surely be overcome. No matter, this is my good deed," she said.

Nevertheless, if you feel that you are no longer capable of dealing with your husband's overbearing disposition, for example, if he strikes or injures you, then you have a right to defend yourself. What can be done in that case? Resolutely ask Allah for the best. If [the relationship] is to continue, hopefully you will be granted the strength to accept his shortcomings, even as you try to improve them. But if there is another way for you to attain virtue, then just submit to Allah. Submit everything to Him. God willing, by submitting yourself to Allah at the same time as you look for and work toward what is best, every problem can be overcome with ease. May Allah grant both you and your family the best way forward. Amen.

*"Facing Life's Problems" (MQ in the Morning, September 1, 2006)*
Allah does not burden someone except in accordance with her or his ability. . . . In reality, this life is movement from one problem to a different problem. Allah has already promised, what comes back to us is not because of other people's conduct, but because of our own actions.

Remember the principle of the valet parking attendant. He has many cars, but is never arrogant. When those cars are taken one by one, he does not get disappointed. The first wisdom/moral [*hikmah*] is that life is only a stopover. Second, everything is only on loan [to us]. Third, everything we do will come back to us. Occasionally, the form of that which comes back to us from Allah is not according to what we want. Nevertheless it is certainly better and more fitting for us.

My brothers and sisters, never give up on problems. Where is there to run? The moment we run, a new problem will appear. If a problem befalls us, use the formula *HHN: Hadapi, Hayati, Nikmati* [Face it, Get involved, Enjoy]. Whosoever consents to Allah's rules, Allah will bestow blessings upon them. Consent [*ridha*] in the sense of skillfully leading life in a realistic way. The moment we get worried about life's problems, design a solution immediately.

*"The Art of Criticism within the Family" (Tabloid MQ, November 2005)*
In the life of a household, couples will surely meet with discord. There will be things that husbands do not like about their wives, and vice versa. This will usually lead to the desire to criticize their partner. Good criticism is like a map that helps someone understand his or her mistake as well as the perils [of that mistake, flaw in character]. Criticism can also be a way for one to improve on all personal

shortcomings. However, criticism can also have negative effects when offered at an inappropriate time or with hurtful words. In that case the atmosphere of the house becomes unpleasant; wives are afraid to see their husbands; and even husbands are afraid to come home because their wives have become pure critics.

So that criticism can bring about self-transformation, we must take note of a few issues concerning the offering of criticism. First, base [criticism] with a sincere intent. Make the intent that the correction we offer is truly based on a desire to help our partner become aware of his or her mistake. Then round it out with support and motivation so that our partner is moved to improve. Do not feel like you are better. . . . Second, offer criticism at the appropriate moment. . . . Third, the manner must be precise. There are three ways to offer criticism effectively. (1) Don't do it with anger or emotion. . . . (2) Offer criticism with the "my request" method. For example, "Children, Mama likes it better if we can keep the house clean and orderly." Compare that with the "order them" method: "Oh kids, you are all so messy and too lazy to clean." Usually the "order them" method is more hurtful. . . . Fourth, do not criticize in front of others because it can be shameful for the person being criticized. . . . Fifth, be prepared to be refused. . . . Sixth, don't feel meritorious if the person changes based on our criticism. Only Allah has the power to transform a person's heart. . . . Giving advice is an obligation for Muslims. The Prophet, peace be upon him, orders us to proclaim what is right in ways that are wise, soft and gentle, and with integrity. God willing if we give advice to one another with truth and patience, our families will become happy and glorious.

These advice columns, with their simple wisdom and accessible analogies, shed light on how the preacher-discipline relationship is structured by affective exchange within a therapeutic encounter. His sympathetic understanding is rooted in discourses about human psychology and emotion management taken from both Islamic teachings and popular psychology.

Aa Gym relies on biographical narratives as a rhetorical strategy to demonstrate that he has faced, and overcome, the spiritual and material problems of life, family, and career. Michael Lambek (1993) describes a similar pattern in his research on religious knowledge and authority among the Mayotte, in which he describes how one preacher, Yusufi, used self-narrative to claim a particular kind of religious knowledge. Lambek's careful observations and keen insights are worth quoting at length:

> Viewed in practice, Yusufi's knowledge is not as fully objectified and abstract as the textual basis of Islam might lead us to suppose. Rather, as we have seen, Islamic knowledge is embodied in speech acts, ritual, performances, and narra-

tive. It is striking that Yusufi uses narrative as the mode to present and legitimate his argument and that the narrative encompasses aspects of his own life and experience. What Yusufi demonstrates here is less objective knowledge than sympathetic understanding, something that is constitutive of, rather than detached from, his being. Shaped to fit the situation, it thus approximates what Aristotle referred to as *phronesis*, ethical know-how, distinguished from *episteme*, scientific knowledge of what is universal, and *techne*, technical know-how. Neither fully objective nor fully subjective, his understanding mediates these categories. (1993, 178–179)

In Lambek's account, "sympathetic understanding" and "ethical know-how" are forms of religious knowledge that mediate the preacher-disciple relationship and, to some extent, legitimate claims to religious authority. Likewise, Aa Gym claims religious authority through his autobiographical evidence of walking the talk as husband, father, and entrepreneur. The moral of the story is that Aa Gym has already mastered it. And you can, too!

Of central importance is the ideal of Muslim masculinity and its bearing on the fantasy spaces between popular preachers and consuming devotees.[10] Some scholars argue that Indonesia is becoming increasingly patriarchal (Nurmila 2009; van Wichelen 2009) and even on the verge of a crisis of masculinity (Clark 2010). As I have argued elsewhere with respect to Islamic cinema, figures like Aa Gym and moral protagonists in the blockbuster feature films *Verses of Love* and *When Love Is Blessed by God* actually reflect the ideal of a soft (*lembut*) masculinity (Hoesterey and Clark 2012). In the first film, a man marries a second wife, but only with his first wife's sincere permission, and he is dutifully attentive to both. In the latter film, the female protagonist insists on a marital concession that her potential husband will not marry a second wife, and he gladly agrees. Here, we would do well to remember that Aa Gym's success should be understood in the broader context of "aspirational pietism" in Indonesia (Fealy 2008). This is not the objective realm of Islam as it is, but rather the fantasy of Islam as it should be.

Contrary to the ideal world depicted by Islamic melodrama, however, Indonesian women's actual lives often appear less hopeful concerning the possibility of having a soft, sensitive husband. Challenging official gender narratives of men as the masters of their inner worlds, Suzanne Brenner (1995) sheds light on the parallel discourses in which Indonesian men are also widely regarded as incapable of both managing emotion and handling money. In the case of Malaysia, Michael Peletz (1995) has observed a similar trend in alternative gender discourse in which men are widely known to be "neither reasonable nor responsible." In addition to matters of money and emotion, polygamy has long been a controversial topic in Indonesia that connects religion, gender, and politics. In the years that Aa Gym rose to national fame, polygamy became a divisive social issue once again when women's groups protested the owner of a fried-chicken restaurant chain, Puspo Wardoyo, who proudly and publicly flaunted his four wives. Wardoyo named menu items in terms of polygamy and was even a guest of honor at the inaugural "Polygamy Awards."[11]

Indonesian melodrama films such as *Verses of Love* portray a loving and harmonious polygamous household in which sexual passion is *not* the reason for the moral protagonist to marry a second wife. The 2005 Indonesian noir film *Love for Share* (*Berbagi Suami*), decidedly not in the tradition of aspirational melodrama, depicts more difficult gendered experiences with polygamy, poverty, and violence. In that film, the husband cannot provide his wives with either economic or emotional fulfillment, two criteria according to Islamic precepts on polygamy. The film makes clear that polygamy is a distinctively male privilege. This disconnect between women's daily experiences and their fantasy-laden relationship with the image of Aa Gym as loving family man is crucial to understanding exactly why the brand narrative of marital bliss and entrepreneurial success was so popular among women.

## Life and Love on the Public Stage: Everyday Ethics as Exemplary Authority

It was not just Aa Gym's entrepreneurial success, taste for high-velocity thrills, or political protests that cast him as a new celebrity type in Indonesia.[12] He was also admired as a loving father and doting husband. Aa Gym stressed that husbands must truly love and honor their wives. Nearly every female devotee with whom I spoke told me they especially admired how Aa Gym showered his wife with romantic affection. During television sermons, his blushing wife would often sit devotedly in the front row while he serenaded her with the Everly Brothers' hit song "Let It Be Me": "I bless the day I found you / I want to be around you / And so I beg you / Let it be me / Don't take this Heaven from one / If you must cling to someone / Now and forever / Let it be me." Aa Gym sang this Everly Brothers' song frequently, and each time the women in the crowd would coo, giggle, and holler. The fantasy of Aa Gym as the modern and romantic Muslim man thus mediated the preacher-disciple relationship.

During Ramadan in 2005, the newspaper *Seputar Indonesia* published its three-part "Love Story."[13] The article feature used the English words "Love Story" next to a picture of Aa Gym with his arm around Ninih. In Islamic storybook fashion, Yan Gymnastiar and Ninih Ghaida Muthmainnah first met at an event to mark the anniversary of the first revelation of the Qur'an to the Prophet Muhammad (*Nuzulul Qur'an*). Readers are told that Aa Gym and Teh Ninih (elder sister Ninih) were immediately attracted to each other but knew that they must restrain their passion (*nafsu*) prior to marriage. According to Aa Gym, once people fall in love, there is a tendency for one's sense of shame to diminish, at which point sexual passion can seethe. "So, from the beginning," Aa Gym told the reporter, "we really had to control ourselves because we wanted our household to be blessed [*diberkahi*]. We were very serious about learning to control ourselves." In both life and love, Aa Gym portrayed himself as master of his *qolbu*.

The second article in the series describes Aa Gym as a young man and potential candidate for marriage. As the authors attest, "Ninih was not mistaken in placing her hopes on Aa Gym. Ever since he was young, this founder of Manajemen Qolbu was certainly clever in business. As a college student, he had already started a newspaper delivery business." Aa Gym insisted that learning the ropes of business was not easy. "My body was exhausted. But I do not want to complain because my principle is that, if you want success, you have to begin your career from the bottom." The reader learns that Aa Gym himself gained valuable experience in a broad range of entrepreneurial activities where he sold meatball soup, handicrafts, bread, milk, and clothing. Aa Gym's brand narrative of the self-enterprising Muslim man is arguably the success story par excellence of middle-class modernity in post-authoritarian Indonesia.

In the third and final article of the series, Aa Gym shares his secrets for a loving marriage and harmonious household. He tells the readers that spouses must accept each other's strengths and shortcomings as one package. Aa Gym shares insights from his own marriage: "I give thanks for [Ninih's] strengths. As for the shortcomings, my responsibility as a husband is to help in a good way so that [she] can improve. . . . I really want her to become a beautiful woman, both on earth and in heaven. That's what I think about from day to day." For Aa Gym and Ninih, readers are also told, the key to

FIGURE 1.4. Aa Gym and Teh Ninih share stories about their family with trainees and tourists at Daarut Tauhiid, with a large family portrait hanging behind them.

a happy marriage lies in warm, loving, and "two-directional" communication. In this love story, the model family goes public with Aa Gym casting himself as the loving husband, his wife as the pious Muslim woman, and his family as happy and harmonious (*keluarga sakinah*).[14]

This brand narrative solidified Aa Gym's public image among female followers who listened loyally to his sermons, memorized his self-help slogans, and traveled from far-flung corners of Indonesia to meet Aa Gym and Ninih in person. Women's Qur'anic study groups frequently traveled together—often by the busload—to make their pilgrimage to Daarut Tauhiid. Each morning tourists and trainees woke before 4:00 a.m. to perform optional predawn prayers (*salat tahajud*). They listened to Aa Gym's morning radio program in the mosque and joined various training sessions and lectures. As a special treat, each smaller tourist group and training cohort had a more intimate gathering with Aa Gym and Ninih and had their pictures taken with them afterward. As they waited in line (sometimes as long as an hour), these women browsed through Aa Gym's books, DVDs, and cassette sermons, which were carefully arranged on tables along the queue. Indeed, I spent countless hours of fieldwork conducting informal interviews with women as they waited in line. Within minutes of having their pictures taken, they could purchase them just around the corner at MQ Photo. These photographs played a crucial role in Aa Gym's "word-of-mouth" marketing, because people took them home, hung them on their walls, and told stories about meeting Aa Gym. A politician near Banjarmasin, some one thousand miles away, enlarged a photo of himself with Aa Gym to serve as a massive stage backdrop for Aa Gym's sermon in his district.

When I asked women to tell me about the most special moments of their experience, nearly everyone recounted this hour-long visit (*silaturahmi*) with Aa Gym and Ninih. These gatherings were highly choreographed and varied little from week to week. On the morning of November 25, 2006, for example, pilgrims and corporate MQ trainees gathered in the courtyard near Aa Gym's house. First, everyone watched the video biography of Aa Gym that was projected onto a huge screen. Upon learning that Aa Gym

FIGURE 1.5. Women browsing CD and DVD versions of Aa Gym's sermons as they wait in line to have their picture taken with Aa Gym and Teh Ninih.

and Ninih would arrive late, the tour guides asked the audience if they knew the words to Aa Gym's popular song "Take Care of Your Heart" (*Jagalah Hati*). Also printed on the first page of his autobiography, the lyrics are a poetic rendition of a hadith about the heart mentioned in the introduction. Without hesitation, the women's voices soared: "Jagalah hati [Take care of your heart], Jangan kau kotori [Don't tarnish it]; take care of your heart, the lantern of this life; take care of your heart, don't soil it; take care of your heart, the radiance of God." When Aa Gym needed to drink water during a sermon before a stadium crowd, his strategy was to sing the chorus and ask the audience to sing the refrain. Their booming response left little doubt about the importance of this song in the formation of the affective exchange between Aa Gym and his female admirers. Indeed, many women proudly declared that they purchased the song as their ringtone.

All singing came to a halt when the sound of a honking horn announced the grand entrance of Aa Gym and Teh Ninih. They rode in on a tandem bicycle with a personalized license plate. Smiling brightly and waving to the crowd, they circled the courtyard and parked by the stage. Ninih took her seat beside a huge family portrait of Aa Gym, Ninih, and their seven smiling children. "Please forgive me for being so late," Aa Gym pleaded. "In the mornings, my responsibility is to spend time with my kids. I finished my radio show at 6:00 a.m. and came home to a crying child. No matter how busy I am, I must fulfill my duty as a father." The personal played out on the public stage, starring Aa Gym as loving husband and devoted father. His female followers loved it. Then, turning toward the men's section, Aa Gym asked:

> Did you watch [my] James Bond film earlier? Over the years, I've gone scuba diving, sky diving, and was even the copilot of an F5-E Tiger fighter jet. Yeah, the key to everything is training. . . . I am constantly training and learning. It is not our problems that make life difficult, but how we confront those problems. Once, I locked my keys in the car. Without the knowledge [*ilmu*; Arabic, *'ilm*], I couldn't get into that car even after two hours. Then, a man came by who had the *ilmu*. He popped the lock in less than two minutes. After opening the door, he turned to me and said, "I'm sorry, Aa. It was a long time ago. I've already repented."

After allowing a moment for people to get the implicit joke (that the man was once a car thief), Aa Gym continued:

> I use the formula P-T-D: *Paham* [understand], *Terlatih* [practice], *Dzikir* [mindfulness of God]. First, you must understand something. Without knowledge,

FIGURE I.6. Aa Gym, Teh Ninih, and their son Ghaza make a grand entrance to meet with spiritual tourists.

even cooking fried rice is difficult. Next, you must continuously practice to develop yourself. Everything in life is a test. The first time I went sky diving, my knees were buckling, but with practice and determination, I did it. Finally, whatever you do, always remember God. So, just remember P-T-D.

Aa Gym built his brand as a celebrity preacher and self-help guru with humorous stories from his life. According to the brand narrative, he was not only a savvy, hardworking entrepreneur but also a gentle, loving family man. In short, he was the model of Muslim masculinity.

Next, Aa Gym prompted Ninih to share her wisdom with the women to show them how to better control their emotions.[15] Agreeing that this could be difficult for women, Ninih turned to the women and, in the soft (*lembut*) voice so often praised by her husband, she confided in the audience:

> To help me confront life's problems, I use what I call the "Five Nevers": (1) Never panic; (2) Never get emotional; (3) Never make things difficult on yourself; (4) Never overdramatize things; and (5) Never give up.

When Ninih finished explaining each of these points, Aa Gym shuffled a few steps away, turned back to face her, and began a theatrical performance. He lowered his voice an octave and spoke with the tone of a television melodrama actor: "My beautiful wife, mother of my seven children, oh how I admire your virtuous ways. You make me proud to be your husband and the father of your children." Ninih blushed coyly and replied affectionately: "And you, my devoted husband, every day I give praise that God has provided me with a husband so compassionate and forgiving of my shortcomings." A group of women in the front row giggled with delight. Aa Gym then broke character and pronounced playfully, "This is serious, it's *sinetron*" (popular Indonesian genre of televised melodrama). When the keyboardist came in on cue, Aa Gym stretched out an arm to Ninih, gazed deeply into her eyes, and serenaded her with "Let It Be Me." As Aa Gym took his seat after the song, one of the giggling women up front chimed, "Whoa! How very romantic!" (*Wah! Romantis sekaaali nih*). Aa Gym concluded in English, "I love you so much, my darling."

With only minor variations, Aa Gym and Ninih performed this routine of gender, piety, and fantasy every weekend, with every tourism and trainee group, for several years. This public love story, as narrated by Aa Gym and circulated by his admirers, attained mythical status in Indonesia. His female followers turned to Aa Gym to heal their hearts

FIGURE 1.7. Women giggling during Aa Gym's sermon.

because they believed he had already mastered his own. Consequently, the relationship between Aa Gym and Indonesian women was informed by a deeply felt fantasy of Aa Gym as the loving husband of a happy and harmonious family. The faces of Aa Gym's admirers in the photograph (see next page), waving as his motorcade circles the town square, captures this sense of perceived intimacy in this preacher-disciple relationship.

Aa Gym's authority as a celebrity preacher rested on a juxtaposition of public and private produced by a particular preaching style and relationship with devotees. It was not just the style of storytelling and kind of brand narrative that lent legitimacy to Aa Gym's claims to religious authority and ensured his place in the public sphere. It was also the consumption practices and purchasing power of his consuming devotees. Beyond his self-help books and commemorative souvenirs, his female admirers bought the life story—the brand narrative—of Aa Gym as the model husband and manager of his heart. This narrative of Aa Gym mediated the moral, affective, and economic relationships with those who listened to his sermons, bought his books and photographs, attended his training seminars, and made pilgrimages to Daarut

FIGURE 1.8. Aa Gym's admirers waving to his motorcade.

Tauhiid. I would argue that it was precisely through these consumption practices that Aa Gym's devotees legitimated his claims to religious authority. Unlike conventional clerics who relied on orthodox religious education, Aa Gym
garnered religious authority through these exchange relationships that were
at once affective and economic. This marks an important shift toward a marketized form of religious authority in the Indonesian public sphere.

Anthropologist Robert Foster (2007) uses the term "consumer over-
flowing" to describe the way in which consumption helps build the value
of a product (or, in marketing parlance, its brand equity). In his study of
the role of consumer participation in building the value of the Coca-Cola
brand in New Guinea, Foster suggests that "consumer overflowings . . . are
the sources of innovation and competitive advantage for a firm as well as
sources of uncertainty and challenges to expertise and authority" (714). Foster describes how consumption practices can legitimate the authority of a
particular brand. Conversely, the *refusal* to consume can also challenge that
authority. Aa Gym's personal brand as ethical entrepreneur, doting husband,
and devoted family man would prove to be a double-edged sword.

## Conclusion

Television preachers such as Aa Gym can be understood as part of the proliferation of media and the dispersion of religious authority during the global Islamic revival. However, these new figures of religious authority are not simply epiphenomena of new media technologies or neoliberal logics. As I have described, Aa Gym is much more than a television preacher. He rose to national acclaim as a self-help guru, and his authority lies in matters of the heart, not the letter of the law. For his followers, Aa Gym provided "sympathetic understanding" and "ethical know-how" to help them deal with professional anxieties, personal problems, and family turmoil. As such, he carved his niche of authority in the domain of everyday ethics, not Islamic jurisprudence.

Aa Gym acquired a marketized form of religious authority that played out in the psycho-religious marketplace of modernity. I have described how his preacher-disciple relationships with followers were often marked by both affective and economic exchanges. As the enraptured responses of his female audiences attest, many of his followers did not just consume his self-help books. They consumed the public fantasy—the brand narrative—that Aa Gym also embodied the MQ virtues he espoused. Looking to both public performance and the packaging of "Aa Gym," I have argued that this consumption of Aa Gym's religious products, in part, lent legitimacy to his claims to religious authority, and vice versa.

Such an explanation, however, does not exhaust the ways in which Aa Gym garnered religious authority and offered new understandings of what constitutes religious knowledge. In the next chapter, I turn to another way that Aa Gym, and a new generation of Muslim trainers, made claims on religious authority within the wider industry of Islamic self-help. In what follows I elaborate on the public figure of the trainer and explore how both Aa Gym and Muslim trainers transformed psychological knowledge into religious wisdom. In doing so, I continue to develop the argument that Islamic psychology—as both transnational scientific discourse and localized body of religious knowledge and practice—has become an important site of expertise through which personal and political projects are imagined.

CHAPTER 2

# Enchanting Science
Popular Psychology as Religious Wisdom

> We the jury in the case of the Commonwealth of Kentucky vs. John
> Wheeler et al., have carefully considered the points of the case, and
> tested the merits of the several theories advanced, and do hereby
> unanimously decide that the game commonly known as old sledge or
> seven-up is eminently a game of science and not of chance.
>
> —*Mark Twain, "Science vs. Luck"*

> Modern psychology is psychology without soul studying man
> without soul.
>
> —*Malik Badri,* Dilema Psikolog Muslim[1]

Something seemed different about Aa Gym. "Jim, please come inside.
There's something you *must* see." It was more than the exuberance of a
newly returned hajj pilgrim, reinvigorated after a month of ritual introspection in the Holy Land. Aa Gym was sporting a new pair of trendy
ivory-white, thick-framed glasses that added an edge to his look, especially
compared with the boyish and conservative aura of the round, frameless
spectacles he typically wore at that time. "Hey Aa, I like your new glasses—
really trendy. *Gaya funky* [funky style]." I was teasing a bit, linguistically
placing Aa Gym in the same category as the young TV preacher Jefri al-
Buchori, whose self-professed "funky style" was increasingly popular with
the adolescent market.[2] Aa Gym smiled, "Thank you, a gift from a Dutch
friend." Those glasses, the skip in his step, his inability to sit still. He seemed
playful, even giddy. Something was different indeed.

"Speaking of gifts, Jim, I brought you a gift from the Holy Land."
Aa Gym proudly presented a beautiful, dark maroon prayer rug, then
showed me the underside, on which he had autographed a personalized note
in English: "Keep *Dzikir* Forever! Aa Gym." *Dzikir* is the remembrance/

73

mindfulness of God through recitation. As he handed me the rug, he added, "In the hopes that one day you will receive divine revelation [*hidayat*]. In the meantime, remember your *dzikir* recitations and know that only Allah has the power to move somebody's heart. Keep praying to Allah for revelation." I was at once glad to see him again, intrigued by his youthful exuberance, and moved by his generosity, yet nonetheless feeling uneasy about his genuine concern for the state of my soul. "God willing, Aa. Thank you for such a kind gift. I can't imagine you brought this all the way from Mecca, just for me. I am moved by your kindness. May Allah accept your pilgrimage and grant you and your family bountiful blessings."[3] After Aa Gym humbly downplayed the gift, he turned to Ninih, "Ma, could you please bring the *zamzam*?" Ninih brought a tray with a beautiful red pitcher and miniature antique glasses. "Jim, do you know about *zamzam* water from the Holy Land? Every year, millions of Muslims pray at this well. The water can heal, they say. Well, it's Allah who heals, but the water is very special. I was allowed to bring some back with me. Please, try some." Aa Gym poured two glasses and motioned for me to drink.

"Thank you, Aa. Are you sure? Perhaps there are others who are more deserving?" Aa Gym nodded and continued, "You see, the fascinating thing is that water is alive. Water responds to prayer. The water crystals become more refined [*halus*], with six sides to the water crystal, what scientists call *hexagonal*. . . . Zamzam* is some of the purest water in the world. Just imagine, millions of people praying to God at that well." Aa Gym nudged the tray aside, leapt up, and summoned me over to his desk, where he showed me the book *The True Power of Water*. "I just read this book on the plane home. Have you ever heard of Dr. Masaru Emoto? He is a best-selling author in America." Intrigued, I browsed the blurb on the back cover. Aa Gym led me through Dr. Emoto's research by showing images of water crystals from Emoto's book:

> Basically, he's saying that water is alive, that it has a vibration [*vibrasi*]. And we humans can affect the nature of that vibration through our own words. Here, look at this image. In an experiment, he pasted the words "thank you" on this bottle of water. He pasted the word "fool" on the other one. Then, he froze the water and photographed the shape of the water crystals. Look, this is a crystal that formed in the "thank you" bottle. See how refined the shape is? You see, the six-sided crystal is the most refined—what they call *hexagonal*. But now look at the crystal from the bottle labeled "fool." The crystal looks broken. Extraordinary, huh?

Aa Gym showed me several other images of the refined hexagonal water crystals formed from water samples that had received prayers:

> In Islam, we've always known how important water is. It appears in the Qur'an, the stories of the Prophet Muhammad, and our ablutions prior to prayer. But now, through scientific knowledge, we better understand *how* this works. This is fascinating. Our bodies are made of seventy percent water. Just imagine how words can affect the health of our bodies. Just imagine the difference in children whose parents rear them with words of love and compassion versus those who receive negative verbal input, like being called a fool! In Islam, we begin everything by saying *basmalah irrahman irrahim* [In the name of Allah, the Most Merciful and Most Compassionate]. I'm going to preach about this scientific knowledge during tonight's sermon.

Aa Gym preached about the "true power of water" not only on that evening but also on the radio the following morning, during his next television broadcast, and for several months to come. In line with his mantra that "business is *dakwah*," Aa Gym also bought the Indonesian translation rights to Emoto's book. Just months later his publishing company, MQS, flew Masaru Emoto to Jakarta as the honored guest for the launching of the Indonesian translation of *The True Power of Water*.[4] As I will explore in greater detail, translation of Emoto's book involved much more than language. Translation shifted the epistemological, moral, and narrative frames of a pop-science best seller (written by a self-professed Japanese atheist) into a treatise on Islamic psychology about the "True Power of Allah."

Seeking knowledge has long been regarded as a form of religious worship within Islamic education (Hefner 2009). After having explored the figure of Aa Gym, we can now turn our attention outward to Aa Gym's role in the broader socio-religious context of the Islamic self-help industry in Indonesia. I am interested in the social contours, transnational traffic, and points of convergence between science and religion. Taking cues from both Talal Asad (1986, 2003) and studies of postcolonial science and medicine (e.g., Anderson 2008; Pols 2007), I understand science and religion as social, political, and economic projects—not as ahistorical, diametrically opposed givens. I describe how Aa Gym and a new generation of psycho-religious professionals who call themselves *trainers* transform scientific knowledge (*ilmu*) into religious wisdom (*hikmah*).[5] Or, perhaps more aptly put, they demarcate science as squarely within the purview of the "religious." As such, they do not translate science *into* religion inasmuch as they "authenticate" scientific knowledge *as* religious wisdom (Deeb 2006). Barker and Lindquist have commented on the synergies and similarities among the "Muslim Television Preacher" (Hoesterey 2009), "Spiritual Trainer" (Rudnyckyj 2009c), and "Telecommunications and Multimedia Expert" (Strassler 2009b) as "figures of Indonesian modernity":

> These figures, including the [spiritual trainer] and tele-*dai*, seek to mediate among what they believe to be the new sources of power in Indonesian society today—Islam, technology, and capital. They position themselves not as leaders, but as experts, exemplars, and facilitators of a vast enterprise of self-improvement aimed at bringing individuals into line with a notion of what it means to be a good Muslim worker, manager, entrepreneur, and family member. (2009, 71)

Aa Gym and these Muslim trainers carved their own niche of religious authority through an adept ability to market Western scientific knowledge, especially psychology, in terms of practical religious wisdom. Scientific and religious knowledge are not entirely separate bodies of knowledge, one somehow secular and the other religious. Building on Talal Asad's (2003) critique of the secular, I examine how psychological expertise is framed as simultaneously scientific and religious. The perceived scientific nature of psychological knowledge endows it with its techno-scientific gravitas and legitimates the authority of those self-help gurus considered "experts" (*pakar*).

I should note here that expertise and training have a long history in colonial, nationalist, and authoritarian Indonesia (Jones 2010a; Li 2007; Stoler 2009). What is relatively new, however, is the appeal to both Islamic and Western understandings of *psikologi* as a form of scientific expertise that can lead to piety, prosperity, and a national moral order. This chapter explores psychological expertise and the Muslim trainers who wield it. In the first section I describe how Aa Gym imported, repackaged, and subsequently traded on Masaru Emoto's research and scientific expertise.[6] The subsequent ethnographic episodes describe the broader industry of training beyond Aa Gym in order to explore how other Muslim trainers summon Western popular psychology. For example, in 2007 Ahmad Faiz visited Daarut Tauhiid to teach his Islamic healing program, Spiritual Emotional Freedom Technique (SEFT). Aa Gym introduced Faiz as his "young guru." A thirty-something entrepreneur with a master's degree from Malaysia in human resources development, Faiz positioned himself as the fifth generation in a line of experts in "energy psychology." The genealogy of Ahmad Faiz and SEFT does not lead us back to the Middle East through a convenient chain of transmissions of legal rulings or Qur'anic exegesis. Instead, Faiz explicitly presents his work as an Islamic corrective to pop psychology in America. In the final section, we meet Sena Lesmana, a Daarut Tauhiid trainer who designed an Islamic "Firewalking" training seminar based on the neuro-linguistic programming technique promoted by Anthony Robbins, the famous American self-help guru who presented a firewalking seminar in Jakarta. It is important to remember that to speak of hybridity does not assume authentic iterations in the past, pure forms somehow isolated from global forces of psychology and market. We should also note that much of the New Age sciences and self-help circuit popular in the United States during the 1970s–1980s actually claims inspiration (and revelation) from the so-called East. In each ethnographic episode that follows, Aa Gym and Muslim trainers traverse and trade on the interstitial spaces between psychology and success, scientific knowledge and religious authority.

## *The Power of Water, the True Power of Allah*

In the introduction to the Indonesian translation of *The True Power of Water*, Aa Gym explicitly frames Emoto's research within the discursive traditions of Islam:

> *Subhanallah* [Glory be to God] water contains the information given to it. For Muslims this might hark back to what the Prophet Muhammad, peace be upon him, professed about *zamzam* water: "*Zamzam* will carry out the requests and intentions [*niat*] of those who drink from it." Whoever drinks from it to get full, they will become full. Whoever drinks from it to get healthy from sickness, they will become healthy. Is it not true that *zamzam* has already stored the good intentions of the various prayers of millions of people over a thousand years since the time of Abraham? That's the immense, awe-inspiring power of *zamzam*, and Dr. Masaru has already taken photos of *zamzam* that show extraordinarily beautiful crystals. I truly give my appreciation to Dr. Masaru Emoto . . . [whose] findings have opened the door of wisdom [*hikmah*] concerning how we must take care of our water, which comprises 70 percent of our bodies. . . . We *are* water and thus we also respond to the actions toward us.

Emoto advances a concept of vibration energy, what he calls HADO. The English subtitle of Emoto's book transforms this Japanese word into an English self-help acronym: Healing and Discovering Ourselves. Interestingly, in the Indonesian version published by MQS, HADO is translated with an

Indonesian acronym as: *Hikmah Air Dalam Olahjiwa* (The wisdom of water in our soul). Aa Gym reframes scientific knowledge *ilmu* as religious wisdom, *hikmah*. [...] saying by the Prophet Muhammad, he also [...] ward water in terms of the Islamic virtue of [...] For Emoto, science reveals the "true power [...] ms the true power of Allah, the creator of [...] d with damaged water crystals, Aa Gym is [...] rts and conscience, the *qolbu* and *nurani*, [...] nifestations of a spiritual sickness distinct [...] knowledge resonates with, and provides [...] mic teachings. Given these quite differ- [...] , I was looking forward to Aa Gym and E[...] the same stage.

*[handwritten note: legitimates himself as religious authority by "reframing scientific knowledge as religious wisdom."]*

On June 26, 2006, hundreds of people gathered in the ballroom of Jakarta's luxurious Hotel Mulia for what was billed, in English, as an "Inspirational Seminar." The promotional fliers read:

> Thanks to Allah for Creating Water. This astonishing research uncovers the true power of water, complete with spectacular pictures that demonstrate the reactions of water as the biggest determinant of the structures of our bodies and planet. It turns out that, through interactions with water, we can send particles of love and praise [*syukur*] as a form of the strongest emotion to every person on this planet.

Tickets for the daylong seminar cost approximately one hundred dollars and included a welcome drink, a free copy of the book, a training certificate, lunch, two coffee breaks, and samples of Hexagonal water, compliments of the corporate sponsor of the seminar, Artha Bio Tirta. *Training* magazine hosted a promotional booth just outside the ballroom, complete with free magazines and gregarious salespeople. *Training* was a new publication targeting the burgeoning market of spiritual human resources development. The promotional issue given to trainees included an article on American business consultant Edward De Bono's "Six Thinking Hats" as well as a human resources guide for the implementation of Islamic business. This latter training program (Celestial Management) was founded by Riawan Amin, then-CEO of Indonesia's first Islamic Bank and author of the book *Celestial Management* (promoted as an Islamic alternative to the popular American management book *The Corporate Mystic* [1997]).

FIGURE 2.1. Hotel Mulia's grand ballroom for the launching of *The True Power of Water*.

As guests arrived, MQS Publishing employees escorted them to their designated seats among the rows of long tables, adorned with elegant table-cloths, fine place settings, bottles of Hexagonal water, silver candy dishes, and a customized MQS publishing bag including an advance copy of *The True Power of Water*. Upon entering the ballroom, attendees passed by huge, six-foot-tall banners with images of water crystals formed in response to the words "thank you" and "you fool." The elevated stage was set with a podium and fine leather chairs for the speakers. The customized stage back-drop, approximately fifteen feet tall by sixty feet wide, included what were apparently designed to resemble "traditional" Japanese windows, flanked on either side by large-screen televisions, each one encapsulated within a wooden frame in the shape of hexagonal water crystals.

At these kinds of seminars, those who were seated closer to the stage typi-cally either paid more for VIP tickets (which might include lunch at the same table as the guest speakers) or were indeed considered VIPs (and usu-ally were invited free of charge). This seminar was no different. Two rows of cloth-covered ballroom chairs were placed in front of the long rows of tables.

Closest to the stage was a single row of luxurious leather chairs, complete with arm rests. These seats were reserved for Indonesia's most celebrated trainers and self-help gurus: Ary Ginanjar, the founder of ESQ Training; Marwah Daud Ibrahim, the presidium chair of the Association of Indonesian Muslim Intellectuals and founder of the training program Managing Your Life and Planning Your Future; Tung Desem Waringin, ranked by *SWA* business magazine as one of Indonesia's most powerful businesspeople in 2005; Andrie Wongso, the popular Buddhist self-help author and frequent contributor to the Manajemen Qolbu website; and Erbe Sentanu, life coach, radio host, and founder of the Words of the Heart Institute. In the minutes before the seminar began, audience members watched the huge screens onstage broadcasting live images of these trainers and self-help gurus who purportedly embodied the very spiritual and material success espoused in their training.

These industry celebrities frequently appeared as special guests at business and motivational seminars. Their presence lent a sense of prestige to the seminar and, according to several trainees, justified the price of admission. Book publishing companies were always eager to seek their official endorsements and testimonials. For example, Tung Desem Waringin—Indonesia's only officially licensed Robert Kiyosaki and Anthony Robbins trainer—was one of several "experts" (*pakar*) whose endorsements graced the back cover of *The True Power of Water*:

> This book, as convincing science, provides the missing link concerning how positive prayers, thoughts, and words affect a person's health and prosperity. Masaru Emoto scientifically proves that positive prayers and words create good water crystals such that people—who are composed of 70 percent water—can also become good. This book is mandatory for anyone who wants to become amazing and healthy.

Others providing endorsements included John Gray, the American pop psychologist and author of *Men Are from Mars, Women Are from Venus*;[7] Ron Roth, author of the New Age self-help book *Prayer and the Five Stages of Healing*; and Kiril Sokoloff, investment strategist and author of *Personal Transformation: An Executive's Story of Struggle and Spiritual Awakening* (which includes a foreword by His Holiness the Dalai Lama). During my fieldwork, many of these American authors were popular guest speakers on the self-help seminar circuit across Southeast Asia.

Health advocates, scientists, and nationally known doctors also lent scientific gravitas to the "True Power of Water" seminar. The Indonesian minister of health, Dr. Siti Fadilah Supari, delivered a keynote address that commended Aa Gym and stressed the national importance of mental health. The moderator for the seminar, Dr. Lula Kumal, was Indonesia's charismatic celebrity doctor and health product spokesperson. Dr. Tubagus Erwin Kusuma and Tom Suhalim were both invited as experts who would espouse the health benefits and scientific merits of Hexagonal water. Using the techno-savvy allure of "aura imaging technique," Suhalim "proved" that Hexagonal bottled water could make the sick healthy within fifteen minutes. The Hexagonal water advertisement on *The True Power of Water* book cover boldly asserts: "Your Aura Shines Brightly with Hexagonal."

Minister of Health Supari opened the seminar with a story of Aa Gym giving her a gift of *zamzam* water after he returned from the pilgrimage. She spoke of the psychological quality (*kualitas psikologis*) of *zamzam*, how the intentions and prayers of millions of Muslims helped transform it into water capable of changing the dispositions and behaviors of the people. Citing the relevance of this research for the Indonesian nation, she honored Aa Gym for bringing this scientific knowledge to the public's attention and for his efforts to improve the moral fabric of the nation: "We ask your help, Aa . . . to improve the spirit of the nation . . . while we may speak of physical health and sick bodies, perhaps the greater danger are the sick spirits/souls [*sakit rohani*]." Supari advances the idea that health has both physical and spiritual dimensions, and she also positions medical knowledge (and Aa Gym's role as public figure) within the broader context of the perceived decline in public morality in Indonesia (*nurani bangsa, moral bangsa*). With these opening remarks, Supari frames science and mental health in terms of both Islam and the nation.

Emoto's opening remarks, on the other hand, appealed to a different sense of authority—the *New York Times*. One of his introductory Power-Point slides listed the *New York Times* best-seller rankings from July 16, 2005. His previous book, *The Hidden Messages in Water*, ranked number 6, and *The True Power of Water* was ranked number 15. (Other books on that list that were already popular in Indonesia included *Rich Dad, Poor Dad: What the Rich Teach Their Kids about Money That the Poor and Middle Class Do Not!* by American financial guru Robert T. Kiyosaki and *The Seven Habits of Highly Effective People* by American human resources and corporate training guru Stephen Covey). Emoto mentioned that his book *The True Power of Water* had already been translated into more than twenty languages.

He explained the process of photographing water crystals when they reached a certain point in the freezing process. As some attendees later told me, the images from his laboratory—microscopes, petri dishes, and workers in lab coats—helped provide the visual authenticity for his scientific method. He then proceeded to show a series of frozen water crystals taken from around the world: Los Angeles, New Delhi, London, France, Berlin, Bali, and Tokyo. Through an interpreter, Emoto told the audience that tap water in Tokyo was dirty and caused illness among the children. He then showed an image of the water crystal that formed from this water and suggested that one could see faces of sick children. "Where?" asked Aa Gym. The next slide of *zamzam* water, however, assuaged Aa Gym's doubts. Emoto stated that *zamzam* water was so good that it required only a tiny amount to produce crystals. "Subhanallah," whispered Aa Gym as he looked around for others' reactions. Several people chimed in with agreement: "Alhamdulillah" (praise be to God), "Mashallah" (as God has willed).

Emoto spoke about the "law of vibration," explaining to the enraptured audience that all phenomena are made up of the repetition of sound octaves (what he called the "law of octaves"), that vibrations resonate and interact with each other, and that humans are, in a very real sense, conductors for auditory (and emotional) vibrations. The molecular structure of water, he continued, can also transfer vibrations and can even be changed with music. This insight led him to develop a series of "healing CDs" designed to restructure people's physical and emotional HADO. Whereas heavy-metal music supposedly damaged molecular structures in water, Emoto showed pictures of water crystals to demonstrate that the recitation of the Qur'an led to beautifully refined water crystals.

Emoto presented a series of images in his efforts to argue that photographs pasted on a vial of water could affect the structure and shape of water crystals: a picture of dolphins on the vial led to a crystal resembling a dolphin; a heart shape led to a heart-shaped crystal, and so on. While these pictures did not seem to overwhelm the audience, the water crystal image of pilgrims swirling around the Kaaba in Mecca sparked another round of awestruck asides of "glorious is God" and "praise be to God." Just as Aa Gym explained in his office months earlier, Emoto told the audience the story of how the words "you fool" caused poorly formed crystals, whereas the words "thank you" formed a beautiful hexagonal crystal. He presented similar crystal formations for the same combinations in German,

Malay, and Swahili. He then demonstrated the beautiful crystal formation when the positive motivational phrase "let's do it" was pasted on the vial of water. After this slide, he made the point that the words we use with our children can have significant effects on their well-being. "The basic principle is that the world could be peaceful if we didn't use negative words." As he reminded the audience, words change the structure of children's bodies, which are composed of 70 percent water.

Emoto wisely tailored his presentation to address Islam. He told the story of his first encounter with Islam in his scientific research: "When I was presenting my research in Paris, I was approached by two men who wanted me to photograph the water crystals produced by a stack of pictures of Arabic script. I had no idea what they meant; I just agreed to photograph the crystals formed when each was pasted onto a vial of water." The Arabic script turned out to be the ninety-nine names of Allah. This story resonated with Aa Gym, especially because the ninety-nine names of Allah are recited every Monday morning during the employee gathering at Daarut Tauhiid. *Dzikir* plays an important role in Aa Gym's personal practice and public sermons, especially as a way to inculcate a particular emotional disposition. The first photograph Emoto showed was the Arabic script for the twenty-ninth attribute of Allah, "The Just, the Equitable." Emoto presented the related water crystal—a beautifully refined hexagonal structure, with additional crystals emanating from each of the six points of the hexagon. Ary Ginanjar whispered to Aa Gym in the seat in front of me, "Allahu Akbar."

Dr. Emoto screened more crystal formations for the other attributes of Allah: "the Wise, the Loving, the One, the Capable." Finally, he showed the beautiful, kaleidoscopic hexagonal crystal that formed for the phrase *bismillah irrahman irrahim*, "In the Name of God, the Most Compassionate, the Most Merciful." Aa Gym later told me that this particular photo especially resonated with him. As he often reminded his audiences, "Love and compassion are the basis of Islam. That is why nearly every verse of the Qur'an opens with that phrase. And that is why Muslims are supposed to begin every action in the name of Allah, the Most Compassionate, the Most Merciful." The images of Islam and water crystals culminated in a video finale of Emoto's life work, complete with images of a 2004 UN-sponsored "prayer around the world" set to the sound track of John Lennon's "Imagine." In this context, however, the song was not celebrated as an anthem against organized religion, modern nation-states, and the perils of self-righteousness.

Before any of the paying audience members could reach the microphones to ask questions during the Q&A, the get-rich-quick guru Tung Desem Waringin sprang up from his VIP seat and shouted into the microphone that "this seminar was truly amazing.[8] I would just like to provide a *testimony* [he used the English term] that this is true. After I read about this research, I gave a seminar where we tested your experiment with rice. And it was true! The jar of rice that was repeatedly called a 'fool' did indeed turn rotten, whereas the jar that was spoken to with kind words took much longer to spoil. So, that's it. I just wanted to offer that *testimony*."

A woman from one of the back rows related a story about the healing power of *zamzam*. Perhaps a bit nervous in front of the celebrity trainers, she stumbled through her first few words but found her composure: "I found motivation and inspiration from a child who was sixteen years old. Her mouth could not move, and she could not speak. Doctors and clergy could not heal her. Then she expressed her intent [*niat*], 'I will get healthy,' and drank *zamzam. Alhamdulillah,* now she can speak." The room filled with rapturous applause. In response, Emoto related another story about the power of positive thinking, when he suggested to the parents of a stricken child to write "my child is healthy" on the water bottle. And soon thereafter, the child was healed. Or so the story goes.

When it was time for Aa Gym to take the stage, he respectfully thanked Emoto for coming all the way to Jakarta and for allowing MQS to translate his book, which could inspire and transform Indonesians. After these initial pleasantries, Aa Gym was quick to admonish the audience, "Remember that it is Allah who created water. So, if we are astonished by anything today, let us be astonished by the greatness of Allah. We should not be astonished by water itself . . . that's the same as being astonished by a puppet when we must really remember the puppet master [*dalang*]." Aware that Emoto claimed to be an atheist, Aa Gym wanted to be sure that the message of that day was the true power of Allah, not the true power of water.

Aa Gym continued with a saying from the Prophet Muhammad about those who give praise to Allah for their fortunes:

> So the tradition of saying "thank you" is a tradition of giving praise to Allah, of saying "Alhamdulillah." And it is thus written in the Qur'an that everything in the sky and earth is because of Allah. Thus, it's true if this *ilmu* reinforces what is already set forth in the Qur'an. Before, when I was studying at the Islamic school, my religion teacher required that we go out into the forest for twenty-

four hours by ourselves, with nothing to sustain us. He reminded us that, if we get thirsty, we should not place our hopes in water, but rather in the One who created water.

Once again, Aa Gym reframed science within the textual authority of the Qur'an and the Islamic belief in one omnipotent God.

Aa Gym proceeded to entertain the audience with his stock sermon on the "7 keys to healthy living": (1) breathe clean air, (2) drink plenty of water, (3) eat balanced meals, (4) get enough rest, (5) exercise, (6) reduce stress with Manajemen Qolbu, and (7) pray to Allah. He sprinkled his presentation with his usual combination of humor, science, sayings of the Prophet, and passages from the Qur'an. When stressing the importance of drinking plenty of water, he referenced a book titled *Your Body's Many Cries for Water: You Are Not Sick, You Are Thirsty!* (Batmanghelidj 1995). Aa Gym continued, "The Prophet Muhammad, peace be upon him, also knew the importance of drinking enough water. And we know that saying "bismillah" before drinking water helps drive away the spirits [*jinn*]. So, Hexagonal water really makes a difference." Then, with a sheepish grin, he added, "Sorry, just a little promotion, here!" With regard to maintaining a balanced diet, Aa Gym stressed the need to eat leafy greens and minimize meat. Again, he joked:

> Eating greens is good for you. Besides, have you ever heard of a goat that suffered a stroke? . . . And you need plenty of rest! The Prophet Muhammad, peace be upon him, knew about the importance of getting enough sleep. That's why he went to sleep shortly after *Isya* prayers and awoke early for predawn prayers. It's like Mr. Benjamin Franklin says, "Early to bed, early to rise, makes a person healthy, wealthy, and" . . . uhh, what else? Mr. Jim, do you know?

"Wise, Aa, wise," I replied from the second row, to which he replied with a grin, "Yes, *cerdas* [clever]." Aa Gym concluded with a plea for Muslims to remember the primary importance of mercy and compassion in Islam. Once again he summoned the example of the Prophet Muhammad:

> I'm perplexed that Islam is often resented as a violent religion . . . yet nearly every verse of the Qur'an is introduced with the words "mercy" and "compassion," with the words "In the name of Allah, the Most merciful, the Most compassionate." Now, it would be truly amazing were the Muslim community to translate that into actual deeds [*mengamalkannya*]. . . . The Prophet Muhammad, peace be upon him, understood the importance of love and compassion. [Aa Gym raises his fist.] It amazes me when I see Muslims clenching their fists

in anger, yelling out "Allahu Akbar." I've yet to come across the hadith where the Prophet clenches his fists in anger. . . . Instead, we have stories of the Prophet rewarding compassion. For example, there's the story of the prostitute who once gave water to a dog dying of thirst. The Prophet said that her sins would be forgiven. That's the mercy and compassion, the moral conscience of Islam.

The book launching and seminar were a huge success, the first edition of Emoto's book sold out within weeks, and MQ trainers began integrating Emoto's research into their seminar simulations and PowerPoint presentations. The "True Power of Water" seminar, in both form and content, resembled a broad range of seminars offered by those VIP trainers in attendance. Indeed, the "training seminar"—held in hotel ballrooms, not mosques, and led by self-help gurus, not religious scholars—had become an important site of religious learning and practice (Rudnyckyj 2009c). They claim knowledge of how science can be used in the pursuit of success—*sukses*—both in this life and the hereafter. In the process, trainers managed to constitute certain bodies of "expert" knowledge as "Islamic." In what follows I provide more glimpses into Islamic training, the figure of the trainer, and the trainers' formulas for success.

### Persuasions of the Trainer's Craft: Ahmad Faiz and Spiritual Emotional Freedom Technique

On February 26, 2007, Aa Gym told his morning radio show listeners that a "young guru" was teaching him a new strategy for managing his emotions and mental health: the Spiritual Emotional Freedom Technique.[9] Just hours later Aa Gym introduced this guru at the weekly employee gathering at Daarut Tauhiid: "Ahmad Faiz is the fifth generation of psychologists to spread modern psychology [*psikologi modern*]. He modified previous psychological knowledge [*ilmiah*].[10] We will host a two-day training seminar sometime soon, but today Ahmad Faiz is here to give us a brief demonstration of SEFT—Spiritual Emotional Freedom Technique. I have personally experienced the benefits of SEFT, and I hope that today's demonstration will be of benefit to us all."

Faiz took the stage, wearing the *baju koko* shirt typical of self-described pious Muslims and sporting the hands-free microphone that had recently become quite fashionable among young trainers. Faiz's assistant kneeled in the center of the mosque beside the LCD projector and laptop, ready to start the PowerPoint presentation. Faiz first established his education credentials: a bachelor's degree in psychology at Airlangga University in Surabaya and a master's degree in human resources development from the Malaysia University of Technology. He was sure to mention that he had also obtained official training certificates from Gary Craig (founder of Emotional Freedom Technique [EFT]) and Steve Wells (founder of Provocative Energy Therapy [PET]). One of the first slides of Faiz's presentation was a picture of him standing beside Steve Wells in Malaysia, where Wells was hosting PET training sessions. Faiz tried to establish authority by tracing his intellectual lineage to Western pop scientists and self-help gurus, not religious texts or Sufi saints.

Faiz explained that he represented the fifth generation of research on emotional therapy and energy psychology. "SEFT is *ilmiah*; anyone can learn this knowledge." He launched into a well-rehearsed pitch about the benefits of SEFT:

> With SEFT, you will be able to (1) overcome various emotional, physical, and spiritual problems; (2) improve your success and prestige in your business, career, and family; (3) and improve your heart's tranquility and your life's happiness. . . .[11] These are the benefits of SEFT: (1) *Efektif*: The effectiveness of energy psychology has been proven by dozens of research [studies], and has been practiced by one hundred thousand people worldwide; (2) Easy: Everybody, even children, can learn; (3) Quick: Only requires between five and fifty minutes; (4) Safe: No side effects; (5) Cheap: You learn once and can use it forever;[12] (6) Empowering: [You] do not have to rely on therapy; (7) *Universal*: Can be used for almost every emotional, physical, and spiritual problem.

We see in this self-presentation, once again, how Islamic trainers position themselves as dispensers of the practical wisdom that can help Muslims overcome problems in their everyday lives. As part of their powers of persuasion, trainers summon the perceived legitimacy of Western academics and self-help gurus. In a postcolonial twist of irony, these Western corporate trainers and self-help gurus actually appropriate their own fantasies and imaginings of "Eastern" knowledge. Faiz explained:

> SEFT is a *tool for personal development*. It is a spiritual empowerment and harmonization of the body's energy system to improve [your] physical and emotional condition, [your] thoughts and behavior. It is a tool to attain healing, success, and happiness. It actually comes from ancient Chinese and Indian medical knowledge about certain energies in the body. They take advantage of energy flows in the

body, what are called *meridians*, as a path for healing. . . . Then, forty-five years ago modern knowledge from physics proved this bodily energy system.

The accompanying slide was the book cover of William A. Tiller's *Science and Human Transformation: Subtle Energies, Intentionality, and Consciousness*. Faiz continued on the theme of energy flows, meridians, and the first generation of energy psychology:

> William Tiller was a professor of material science at Stanford University in America. He understood the benefits and wisdom of Eastern medicine. He authored five books, 350 scientific articles, and a few patents in *psycho-energetics*. He also invented a tool to detect and measure energy and thought waves, the *Intention Imprinted Electronic Device*. As far as theory goes, his was as radical as Einstein's. . . . Dr. John Diamond was one of the first modern scientists to really pioneer this concept of meridians. Thus, he represents the first generation of energy psychology. He was the past president of the International Academy of Preventative Medicine and author of several books, including *Life Energy: Unlocking the Hidden Power of Your Emotions to Achieve Total Well-Being*.

Faiz praised the newfound science behind this ancient wisdom of energy flows in the body. Regardless of this *longue durée* of science and healing, he tried to establish his authority by positioning himself within a specific, and more recent, intellectual genealogy that aims to connect him with the perceived legitimacy of Western psychologists involved in New Age psychology. The second generation of energy psychology, Faiz tells us, was led in the 1980s by Dr. Roger Callaghan, founder of "Thought Field Therapy" and the "Five Minute Phobia Cure." Callaghan became a celebrity who "even appeared on the Oprah Winfrey show."

In the 1990s Gary Craig ushered in what Faiz described as the third generation of energy psychology. Craig promoted EFT as a simplification of Callaghan's theory. The effectiveness of EFT, Faiz proclaimed, was "tested by thousands of people." Steve Wells became a licensed EFT trainer and eventually hosted EFT training sessions in Australia, the United States, England, and even Malaysia—where he trained Ahmad Faiz. Steve Wells and Dr. David Blake invented a new technique, PET, which purportedly corrected the perceived limitations of EFT. Thus, Wells and Blake constitute the fourth generation of energy psychology. And Faiz, as a student of Wells and Blake, claimed to be the fifth generation of energy psychology. His next slide, titled "The Energy-Psychology Family," includes pictures of Callaghan, Craig, Wells, and himself, complete with his trademark SEFT in the corner of the slide. The lineage was complete, and not a Sufi saint or Islamic school mentioned in the genealogy. Nevertheless Faiz managed to transform SEFT into an Islamic discursive tradition.

This does not mean that SEFT is not authentically "Islamic." Faiz asserted that science reinforces religion. After moving to his slide "The Science of SEFT," Faiz proclaimed, "This is really, truly scientific [*ini benar-benar sientifik*]." Faiz explained that SEFT (much like MQ and ESQ) builds on the perceived weaknesses of secular Western models of psychology. Although Craig and Wells understood the importance of freeing the emotional blockages along the meridian lines, his gurus did not fully appreciate the need for a spiritual component. As Faiz proclaimed, "Adding spirituality is way more effective, God willing." Faiz supported these claims by citing further scientific studies—not from medieval Islamic medicine but from an American pop healer: "According to Dr. Larry Dossey from America, according to the scientific research, prayer and spirituality have been proven [*terbukti*] to possess a power equal to that of medicine." Faiz screened a film clip in which Dossey tells a story about how prayer can actually help heal cancer patients. "And this was a *double-blind* study, people!" Once again, the perceived authority of techno-science served to legitimate religious wisdom.

The next slide was a picture of Dossey's book, *The Healing Words: The Power of Prayer and the Practice of Medicine*. Faiz continued admiringly, "After being published in 1994, this book has become part of the curriculum in over eighty medical schools in America." Faiz cited scientific studies by Dr. Joaquin Andrade that "proved" that prayer can change the structure of blood cells. "See, unlike these blood cells of people who are afraid or sad, prayer causes these other blood cells to radiate [*bercahaya*]. . . . In terms of *ilmiah*, this has already been proven . . . so this is not just nonsense [*omong kosong*]."[13] Just as Aa Gym drew from Masaru Emoto's research, Faiz summoned the perceived science of a New Age psychology of emotion to legitimate an Islamic therapeutics of the self.

Faiz proceeded to demonstrate SEFT. With this therapeutic technique, Faiz mimics the tapping along patients' median lines from EFT, but he adds his own Islamic twist, asking the patient to recite phrases that acknowledge their ailment and assert their submissiveness before Allah (*pasrah, ridho*). Faiz proclaimed this technique could help anyone combat negative emotional energy, overcome phobias, and even quit smoking.[14] Tito, a friend of Aa Gym's who could not walk, heard about SEFT training on the morning

radio show and decided to have someone take him to the mosque immediately to see if he could be healed.[15] As someone who spent years working
with adolescents afflicted with muscular dystrophy, I felt uneasy as Aa Gym
helped Tito scoot to the front of the mosque. Faiz tapped various meridian
points and Tito recited after him: "Ya Allah, even though my body is sick,
I submit this to you."[16] While the audience prayed, Faiz repeated this three
times, tapping the meridian lines on the top of Tito's head, forehead, cheeks,
and chest.[17] "Now, say Alhamdulillah." The audience hushed a few boys
who were giggling. Then Faiz asked Tito if he still felt sick. "No." Everyone clapped loudly, some adding "Alhamdulillah." I am not sure exactly
what may have transpired, but Tito did not walk away on his own accord.
Aa Gym turned to the audience and proclaimed, "This is Allah's science."

For his final demonstration, Faiz was to heal a young boy's phobia of
eating rice. After the boy reluctantly took his seat, Faiz began working his
magic. As he tapped the meridian points, Faiz asked the child to recite after
him: "Ya Allah, even though I do not want to eat rice, I submit to you. I am
*ridho*; I am *pasrah*." After a couple minutes of reciting this mantra, the child
was given a plate of rice. Still he would not eat. Aa Gym chimed in, "You
others pray so that Allah will help." Faiz repeated the tapping, the reciting,
and then tried again. The child put the rice in his hand, brought it closer
to his hand, looked over to his father, and smelled the rice. "Does it smell
good?" asked Faiz. Unimpressed, the child shook his head. Faiz tried again.
Tapping, recitations, tapping, recitations. Finally the child ate one handful
of rice, then another, and then another. Aa Gym pronounced, "At first he
was scared, then he was able to get a little closer, then he could sniff the rice,
and finally he was able to eat the rice. *Alhamdulillah!*"

Let us pause to consider the global chain of events that led to Aa Gym
inviting Ahmad Faiz to present SEFT at Daarut Tauhiid. Pop-culture icon
Oprah Winfrey legitimates an American self-help entrepreneur, whose intellectual offspring proceed to sell training programs to aspiring middle-class
Muslims in Southeast Asia, who then, in turn, repackage the curriculum
within a framework of Islamic ethics and subsequently sell their training program to aspiring middle-class Muslims in Indonesia, Singapore, and Malaysia.

Muslim networks are important, but following them can take us in unexpected directions. My analysis connects contemporary Muslim subjectivities
with more recent genealogies of scientific discourse that do not eventually
lead us back to Muslim scholars in the Middle East but, instead, to psy-

chologists and self-help gurus in the "West." The transnational flows of psychology and self-help between Indonesia and the West might not capture as much media attention or scholarly imagination when compared with the transnational links between the radical fringe of the Middle East and Indonesian Islamist groups such as the Islamic Defenders Front (FPI) and Hizbut Tahrir. Yet transnational traffic of psychological discourses has arguably had more influence on the formation of Muslim modernity and capitalist culture among the aspiring middle classes. As I argue further, American pop psychologists like Daniel Goleman and self-help gurus such as Anthony Robbins have influenced the discursive traditions of far more Indonesian Muslims, albeit a few degrees removed, than any of the Salafist provocateurs with sympathies to Sayyid Qutb or Osama bin Laden.

## *Firewalking the Talk: Transforming Neuro-linguistic Programming into Islamic Self-Help*

In September 2006, Aa Gym was one of three keynote speakers for what was billed as "The Most Incredible Love Seminar of 2006: Mars and Venus at Home & in the Workplace." The promotional flyer read: "Are you serious about achieving success? Are you serious about attaining eternal happiness and love? Then, you must attend this seminar!" Another keynote speaker was John Gray, the American pop psychologist and author of *Men Are from Mars, Women Are from Venus*. At this time, John Gray had begun making the rounds on the Southeast Asia pop psychology, self-help, and corporate training circuit. Tung Desem Waringin, the get-rich-quick guru who offered his testimonial at the *True Power of Water* book launching, organized the seminar and served as the third keynote speaker. Pak Tung, as he was known, was an omnipresent figure on the Indonesian self-help circuit. I will trace the MQ trainers at Daarut Tauhiid, via Pak Tung, to the "Firewalking" training seminars by offered by the famous American self-help guru and author of *Awaken the Giant Within*, Anthony Robbins.

Tung Desem Waringin was a tall man who wore large-rimmed glasses and spoke in a booming, larger-than-life voice. Even though Pak Tung is not Muslim, middle-class Indonesian Muslims paid (or "invested," as Tung preferred to say) approximately one hundred dollars per day for his training. The Indonesian business magazine *SWA* ranked Pak Tung as Indonesia's fifteenth most powerful business leader. With a background in marketing, Pak Tung knew how to sell. And with a keen eye for the needs and anxieties of an aspiring middle class, he also knew *what* to sell: hope and motivation. Pak Tung also traded on the figure of the trainer. Similar to those of Ahmad Faiz, Tung's promotional materials claimed a certain sense of legitimacy by tracing an intellectual genealogy to popular Western self-help gurus. "Learn from the best or die like the rest," Tung once proclaimed. He invested exorbitant amounts of money to become an "officially licensed" trainer for Anthony Robbins. He also paid handsomely for the licensing rights for American financial guru Robert Kiyosaki's Cashflow Quadrant board game and training program (discussed in greater detail in Chapter 4). Daarut Tauhiid trainers were especially keen to integrate the ideas of Kiyosaki and Robbins, via Pak Tung's training sessions, into MQ Training curriculum.

In March 2006 Pak Tung and Anthony Robbins copresented a sold-out training seminar in Jakarta: "Unleash the Power Within: The Real Firewalk Experience." Anthony Robbins, promoted as "The World's #1 Coach," appeared "live via high-def satellite." Robbins originally trained in firewalking with the American New Age guru Tolly Burkan. Interestingly, the corporate firewalking movement, popular in America in the 1980s and 1990s, was itself inspired by romantic ideas about "Eastern" religions (Danforth 1989, 253–288). As recently as March 2008, the morning television show *Good Morning, America* broadcast a live firewalk by Peggy Dylan, Tolly Burkan's former wife, who now directs the Sundoor School of Transpersonal Education and Sundoor Spiritual Adventures. Dylan sells spiritual retreat and travel packages to places like Nepal, which, for many in the New Age crowd, are the quintessence of harmonious spirituality. According to Peggy Dylan's promotional advertisement, "To put foot in the Himalayas guarantees enlightenment."

I mention the transnational imaginary of the American New Age firewalking movement to complicate the idea that Islamic firewalking training in Indonesia is simply the importing of "American" popular psychology. Firewalking training and the broader industry of self-help in America have always been deeply rooted in global flows and fantasies across religious traditions. To add to the complexity, the Indonesian scholar Koentjaraningrat reports that firewalking has long been part of Islamic education in parts of Indonesia. The difference nowadays is that firewalking is being articulated in terms of neuro-linguistic programming.[18] In contemporary Indonesia, firewalking is not being taught by Sufi mystics in rural Java but by gurus and trainers in the ballrooms of Jakarta's five-star hotels.

Three trainers from Daarut Tauhiid attended Tung Desem Waringin and Anthony Robbins's "Firewalking" seminar in Jakarta: MQ Master Trainer Abdurrahman Yuri (Aa Gym's younger brother); Yana Nur Cahyana, director of DT's training division LP2ES; and Sena Lesmana, its marketing director. LP2ES is the Indonesian acronym for one of two training centers at Daarut Tauhiid. On the Monday after the Firewalking Training, Aa Gym invited these MQ trainers to share their experiences with the hundreds of employees gathered for the weekly meeting. One by one, they described what it felt like to be able to walk on fire. The goal of NLP, they asserted, was to create that "magical moment" that would provide the positive thinking necessary to surmount future challenges. As Lesmana put it:

> Sure, I was scared that I would get burned. But, you see, that's just it. You use NLP to overcome your fear. You tell yourself that you will not be burned. Before I walked on the fire, I said "bismillah," and then when I finished, I yelled out, "Alhamdulillah!" See, you can do whatever you set your mind to doing.

FIGURE 2.2. Sena Lesmana with Tunk Desem Waringin during Firewalking Training. Courtesy of Sena Lesmana.

By uttering these words in Arabic, Sena framed his intent in Islamic terms, thereby transforming firewalking into an Islamic technology of self. Building on his "magical moment," Sena subsequently paid fifteen hundred dollars to become a licensed trainer of the Indonesian Firewalker Trainers Association. Shortly thereafter, Sena and Yana were pitching Firewalking Training to Daarut Tauhiid's major clients. When I asked if he thought companies would be willing to invest in the training, Yana replied, "Laaaaaaaaku, Mr. Jim" (Oh, Mr. Jim, this will sell!).

I would like to bring these examples back to the idea of the trainer as a figure of Muslim modernity. Trainers mobilize and market perceived psychological expertise to legitimate religious authority; however, they are certainly not taking over the modes of authority enjoyed by traditional religious scholars. Trainers do claim, however, that the practical knowledge they wield can lead to spiritual and material success. Sena begins every MQ training session with a PowerPoint version of his CV—a series of photographs of Sena posing with Western self-help gurus and their Southeast Asian disciples: psychologist John Gray of "Mars and Venus" fame; John Maisel, the licensed firewalking trainer who traveled to Bali to train Indonesia's inaugural firewalking trainers' association; Earnest Wong, a Hong Kong–based self-help guru who has tapped the Indonesian, Singapore, and Malaysian markets; and his firewalking picture with Tung Desem Waringin. Similar to Ahmad Faiz in his genealogical analysis of energy psychology, Sena claimed authority and legitimacy through his lineage and training with Western self-help gurus, *not* religious scholars or Sufi sheiks.

Training seminars thus provide new voices of authority and new social spaces in which Sena and other Muslims come to articulate and practice Islam. Sena's integration of foreign, techno-science concepts like NLP does not make Sena any less "Muslim." Instead, I would suggest that it is the very foreignness of pop psychology that provides its appeal and authority. Both Sena and Tung told me that training seminars sell much better with English titles like "The Secret of . . . "; "The True Power of . . . "; "The Revolution of . . . ," and so forth. Muslim trainers thus harness the authority of imported, techno-science psychological discourse—without necessarily adopting all of its underlying secular assumptions.[19]

As figures of Muslim modernity, trainers are at play in the interstitial spaces between Islam and the "West," *psikologi* and *sukses*, religious scholars and self-help gurus. Neither *ulama* nor secular psychologist, these figures of Muslim modernity operate in the self-help market niche as human resources consultants. As noted in the Introduction, they garner authority through their knowledge of the practical application of Islamic teachings in everyday life (Volpi and Turner 2007). Trainers also perform a different sort of cultural brokering than Muslim clerics do. MQ Master Trainer Abdurrahman Yuri once explained this difference:

> If you want to know who created water, you might ask a Muslim cleric. However, if you want to learn how to swim, would you ask a cleric or a swimming instructor? You'd ask an instructor, of course. It's like this, *trainers* can explain the *how-to*.

MQ trainer Yana also used the English phrase "how-to" to describe the difference between trainers and religious scholars:

> Jim, we get all of our ethical teachings about the nature of the heart and soul from the Qur'an and sayings of the Prophet Muhammad. But there aren't many specifics about how to implement teachings in our daily lives. So we get the *how-to* from Western self-help and management theories.

Similarly, in the inaugural edition of *Jurnal Psikologi Islami*, Indonesian psychologist Abdul Mujib claims that "the integration of Western theories of psychology is limited to the technical-operational problems not covered in Islam, whereas the essential issues such as the structure of the self are taken from Islamic Psychology" (2005, 28). Unlike the Muslim clerics who rely on an erudite understanding of Islamic law, trainers command a particular kind of authority rooted in their ability to transform scientific knowledge into religious wisdom. Western science is summoned, yet also rejected—summoned for its perceived techno-science legitimacy and rejected for its (supposedly) secular roots. These trainers have not so much encroached on the authority of more conventional clerics as carved out a new niche of psycho-religious knowledge and authority. Trainers have certainly struck a chord with the desires and anxieties of middle-class Muslim modernity in contemporary Indonesia, at least for the moment.

Islamic training evokes an affective tone of something that is "cutting-edge"—not just modern, but hypermodern. Drawing from the Indonesian translation for "cutting-edge" and "the very latest," I use the term *mutakhir* to describe the temporal quality of what might be aptly described as the hypermodern (Hoesterey 2012). The cutting-edge quality of popular Islam has a life cycle of its own and is subject to the market-driven moment. Muslim celebrity gurus and popular trainers do not (indeed cannot) remain on that cutting edge without continually reinventing themselves, their products, and their brands. Despite the ephemeral nature of any single celebrity guru's moment of fame, Islamic popular psychology continues to resonate with the anxieties and aspirations of middle-class Muslims.

## Conclusion

Each example in this chapter describes how Aa Gym and Muslim trainers transformed scientific knowledge into religious wisdom and also repackaged and promoted transnational scientific discourse through print, radio, television, and training sessions. The "true power of water" became the true power of Allah. An atheist Japanese scientist's HADO became a popular Indonesian preacher's *hikmah*.[20] Those celebrity experts who attended the book launching also provided a glimpse into the wider world of Islamic training. Like Aa Gym, they have enchanted science with religion to carve out their respective niches within the self-help industry. This is not to assume such binaries as fact (Asad 2003) but rather to demonstrate how such binaries were imagined and integrated. By redefining what constitutes religious knowledge, these Muslim trainers are able to lay claim to a religious authority based on the practical "how-to" application of Islamic teachings.

I then turned my attention to how Aa Gym incorporated SEFT into the curriculum at Daarut Tauhiid. Ahmad Faiz sought to impress his enraptured audience (and to legitimize his psycho-religious authority) through a PowerPoint genealogy linking him to pop psychologists from the West. However, Western science itself was not held up as the ideal; instead, its secular assumptions were portrayed as problematic, even while its "scientific" merit served to legitimate the authority of the trainer (and justify the price of admission). As cultural brokers, trainers authenticated Western science as Islamic.[21] Much like Aa Gym had done with Emoto's research, Faiz enchanted science with Islamic concepts, especially those related to submission to the will of God (*pasrah*, *ridho*). In doing so, Faiz provided the psychological language with which Indonesian Muslims could articulate new understandings of their faith. Thus, in the case of Islamic self-help in Indonesia, modernization, science, and rationality led to the reenchantment of self and society, not its secularization.

The third section traced yet another Islamic training program that incorporated New Age and psychological sciences from the "West." Like Ahmad Faiz, Daarut Tauhiid trainers also summoned their genealogy to Western self-help gurus. Each of these examples highlights how the Muslim trainer has become a new and important figure of modernity in Indonesia—new in the sense that such trainers are creating novel forms of religious engagement and important in the ways they are redefining what constitutes religious knowledge. As a result, the training session has emerged as a vibrant and popular site for Islamic education for middle-class Muslims who are eager to achieve worldly riches and heavenly salvation. The next two chapters describe how trainers at Daarut Tauhiid designed seminars that tried to cultivate the sensibilities and dispositions necessary to become ethical entrepreneurs and virtuous citizens.

# *Muslim Subjectivity*

CHAPTER 3

# Ethical Entrepreneurs
Islamic Ethics and the Spirit of Capitalism

> Entrepreneurship . . . is coming to be seen as the exemplary
> contemporary way of being a modern, moral Muslim.
>
> —*Filippo Osella and Caroline Osella, "Muslim Entrepreneurs in Islamic Life"*[1]

Roaming through the "applied psychology" aisles of the national bookstore Gramedia, I came across a book-DVD set, *Success Stories: Muslim Business-people in Indonesia*. The book cover shows Aa Gym at the center, surrounded by seven successful Muslim entrepreneurs. The "Bonus DVD" begins with the vintage booming voice of a game-show host: "Who wants to be a Muslim billionaire?!?" What follows is not exactly a game show but a training seminar on Islamic entrepreneurship, featuring some of Indonesia's most successful Muslim entrepreneurs, including M. Reza Syarif, Indonesia's self-proclaimed "#1 Motivator" and founder of the concept of "motivation intelligence." Syarif's motivational seminars attracted huge crowds in Indonesia, including a "Listening Quotient" training seminar at Daarut Tauhiid on April 1, 2006. More than just a trainer, Syarif was also a popular spiritual leader for *umroh* (Arabic, *'umra*) pilgrimage trips to Saudi Arabia. As further evidence of the interstitial spaces occupied by trainers, in the newspaper advertisements for the pilgrimage, Syarif loses the business attire of a trainer and dons the turban of a revered religious teacher. In the entrepreneur seminar featured in the bonus DVD, Syarif invites trainees on a journey: "You have just boarded the plane to success. We are all heading there together." Syarif tries to convince his paying audience that *anybody* can be successful: "See, I'm successful, and I'm just a regular guy. I'm not Superman. You know how you can tell? If I were Superman, I'd wear my underwear on the *outside*. But just look at me. I wear my underwear on the inside—just like everybody else!"

How might we make sense of this rugged individualism, the entrepreneurial bravado that trainers conjure in their seminars? In this chapter I explore the figure of the Muslim entrepreneur and consider how self-help gurus and Islamic training provide religious narratives that frame the relationship between Islam and commerce. Through an analysis of Manajemen Qolbu Entrepreneur Training, I consider how the Islamic self-help industry influences religious experience and Muslim subjectivity, raising these questions: In what ways might the incorporation of popular psychology into middle-class training programs engender an autonomous, neoliberal subject? How commensurate are Islamic ethics of entrepreneurship with individualizing logics of neoliberalism? And how might this renewed emphasis on the enterprising self also recalibrate the prophetic tradition, opening the possibilities for new imaginations of the Prophet Muhammad as the ultimate entrepreneur?

As noted previously, I contend that we should not attribute too much efficacy to the ironclad power of neoliberal logics to forge economic subjectivity. If we take a historical perspective, an Islamic ethics of capitalism has deep roots in Indonesia that precede the privatization and individuation of late capitalism, especially during the democratic era. Islamic entrepreneurship—and the associated discursive traditions of ethical cultivation—was among the central tenets of Indonesia's earliest modern Islamic organizations during Dutch rule in the early twentieth century. Now a century later, the end of authoritarian state rule has brought with it a renewed emphasis on entrepreneurship. Turning to contemporary framings of the history of Islamic entrepreneurship in Indonesia, I suggest that the contemporary emphasis on (and ethical programs for) entrepreneurship is nothing new to Islam in Indonesia. In fact, the social value placed on the Muslim entrepreneur predates the neoliberal economic adjustments initiated during the latter years of Suharto's New Order government. I draw from ethnographic data of MQ Entrepreneur Training to argue that Islamic training seminars, as technologies of self, do indeed forge particular moral and economic subjects. However, I do not reduce their subjectivity to the global spread of neoliberalism.

The very term "neoliberal" has been tossed around so casually within anthropology that it has lost much of its analytic and explanatory value. As Andrew Kipnis has argued, "In using a single, politically and emotionally loaded term to refer to such diverse phenomenon, anthropological analyses of neoliberalism risk a reification that occludes more than it reveals" (2007, 384). This is not to say that structural adjustments and privatization do not have (often dire) consequences. It is to say, however, that we cannot reduce the championing of the enterprising self, as it occurs in Islamic training, to the efficacy of neoliberal logics. Islam plays an important role. Likewise, as Daromir Rudnyckyj observes regarding ESQ Training for the state-owned company Krakatau Steel, "The creation of a spiritual economy in Indonesia in neither a wholesale translation of Weber's spirit of capitalism, nor is it a strict interpretation of Islamic texts and practices. It is an unprecedented assemblage that is as much the Islamization of neoliberalism as it is the neoliberalization of Islam" (2009b, 131). So, how do we make sense of such hybrid formations, what Ong and Collier (2005) have coined "global assemblages"? Using a metaphor of sound, I examine the "resonance" between multiple moral and economic subject positions. I describe how particular neoliberal logics do indeed resonate with an "Islamic Ethic" of entrepreneurship in Indonesia. Such an approach acknowledges the importance of capital accumulation and "techniques of the enterprising self" (Ong 2006) while also allowing for Islamic practices of ethical cultivation that transcend secular models of entrepreneurship.

## Islamic Ethics and the Spirit of Capitalism

"Spirit Ekonomi Santri" (The spirit of santri economics): In big bold letters, these words graced the cover of *Gatra* magazine's end-of-Ramadan edition in 2006. This special issue valorized Islam as a religion of traders and exalted entrepreneurs. The articles could be divided into two general categories. First were academic articles that retraced the historical relationships between business and Islamic reformism in Indonesia. Second were articles that described present-day "success stories" (*kisah sukses*) of Muslim entrepreneurship in Indonesia. The article "Expanding Propagation through Business" features Aa Gym, MQTV, and the twenty-plus businesses under the umbrella of MQ Corporation. The authors praise Aa Gym as having "the entrepreneurial touch."

The idea of an Islamic economy is once again gaining traction in Indonesia, and Indonesian Muslims are looking to both historical legacies and contemporary success stories in their efforts to cultivate an entrepreneurial spirit. The lead article, "The Business Ethos of Muslim People," begins with a quote from the Prophet Muhammad: "Become traders! Ninety per cent of the door to fortune is from business." Muslim entrepreneurs, the reader is told, do not just work for blind profit; rather, they work with their hearts.

In another article, "The Fall of Our *Santri* Entrepreneurs," Indonesian anthropologist and politician Hajriyanto Y. Thohari notes:[2]

> Islam really advocates *entrepreneurship*. Islam is a religion of traders, born in a trading city, and eventually spread throughout the [Indonesian] archipelago by traders. Islam elevated the rank of traders such that this profession first received the honor for paying alms. The first modern Muslim organization was Sarekat Dagang Islam [Muslim Traders Union], founded in Solo at the beginning of the twentieth century. (24)

Entrepreneurship is thus framed within specific discursive traditions of Islam and particular histories of the Indonesian nation. It is not something new per se but rather something being reclaimed.

Another article, "The Fall and Resurgence of a Business Ethos in Kauman," traces the history of the modernist group Muhammadiyah, founded in 1912 in Solo, Central Java. It tells the story of how Muhammadiyah's revered founder, Kiai Haji Ahmad Dahlan, implored members to achieve economic independence to support the reformist cause: "Seek not life from Muhammadiyah; rather seek to give life to Muhammadiyah." During the following decades, donations of land and money (*wakaf*; Arabic, *waqf*) by wealthy entrepreneur members of Muhammadiyah helped fund schools and hospitals across Indonesia. The authors report that in 1916 traders constituted 47 percent of Muhammadiyah's members. Commerce generated wealth. Wealth enabled charity.

Thohari also revisits Geertz's (1963) prediction that reformist Muslims would become an important trader class on the national scene. According to Thohari, Geertz was not necessarily wrong. Rather, Geertz made this assertion a couple of years prior to the beginning of the New Order, during which the bureaucratic *priyai* class—not the pious *santri*—enjoyed state privileges and preferences in matters of business. Thohari argues that this resurgence in *ekonomi santri* must be understood within the post–New Order moment when *priyai* no longer enjoy as much preference. However, as Thohari also notes, Muhammadiyah itself has changed from the trader-dominated organization of the early twentieth century to a bureaucrat-heavy organization. Of particular importance, Thohari notes that Muhammadiyah leaders have decided that "training" is the key to develop the human resources capacity necessary for a return to *ekonomi santri*.

The Muslim Traders Union and Muhammadiyah were not the only modern organizations to espouse the virtues of Islamic entrepreneurship. The article "Awaken the Entrepreneurial Ethos," written by Asrori S. Karni, tells the history of Nahdlatul Ulama (NU).[3] NU was formed in 1926 and is now Indonesia's largest Islamic organization, boasting membership of approximately forty million members. The precursor to NU was the business Al-'Inan, under the organization Nahdlatul Tujjar (NT), the Resurgence of the Merchant Class. According to Karni, in a 1918 speech whose written text is now sanctified at the headquarters of NU, founder K. H. Hasyim Asy'ari offered a plea for NT members: "Sons of this nation who are intelligent and dignified religious teachers, why don't each of you build your own economic enterprises? . . . Each city will have its own unique economic business. . . . [Let us] put an end to the vice that is visible all around us" (18). For both Muhammadiyah and NU, capital accumulation was not simply an end in itself but was understood as a necessary part of living a pious life as a Muslim, of doing good deeds and eradicating moral corruption.

This moral-economic philosophy was not based on some Calvinist anxiety to prove, through worldly success, that one was predestined for the afterlife. Rather, this moral dimension of capital accumulation emphasized the practical necessity of capital in order to fulfill religious obligations of alms giving and improving social welfare. The author notes that NU's founder did not accept that poverty was simply one's destiny. The author Karni observes that Asy'ari, when forming Al-'Inan, tried to "inject the spirit of change by recalling the verse from the Qur'an Al-Ra'd (Q 13:11): 'Verily never will God change the condition of a people until they change it themselves'" (19).[4] This particular passage remains one of the most frequently cited Qur'anic references among Islamic entrepreneur training programs in contemporary Indonesia. As I argue in this and subsequent chapters, the Islamic self-help industry and its trainers do not operate outside the authority of Islamic texts but rather summon particular discursive traditions from the Qur'an and prophetic tradition. Figures such as Aa Gym, we are meant to believe, became successful entrepreneurs because they were willing to change their own condition so that Allah would then decide the fate of their fortune.

## Kisah Sukses *(Success Stories)*

Success stories are important dimensions of the contemporary reawakening of Islamic entrepreneurship in Indonesia. The *Gatra* special edition includes several success stories: the thirty-six-year-old woman Ummu Masmu'ah who sold dolls with Muslim veils; Islamic wedding organizer Nurul Fithrati; and Haidar Bagir, the former student of Imaduddin Abdulrahim and founder of Indonesia's largest publishing company. With his profits from the publishing company, the reader learns, Bagir was able to fund a school and a nonprofit organization.[5] The magazine authors (and editors) also remind readers of the long history of Islamic schools that have sustained themselves through economic enterprise.

Other success stories include those of popular Muslim trainers. One article tells the stories of popular trainers and self-help authors Valentino Dinsi, Jamil Azzaini, and Ary Ginanjar. The article "Work Hard, Work Smart" features a large photo of Valentino Dinsi smiling proudly in his own bookstore. Sporting an oversized khaki sports coat over his tourist Thailand T-shirt, Dinsi clutches the book *Entrepreneur Power: Financial Intelligence*. Dinsi became a national self-help figure following his popular book *Don't Be a Wage Employee for the Rest of Your Life*. The article reconstructs Dinsi's life history. He got his start as the personal assistant to Imaduddin Abdulrahim, the influential reformist figure who led popular "mental training" sessions in Salman mosque at the Bandung Institute of Technology. Before earning an economics degree at the prestigious University of Indonesia, Dinsi worked as a door-to-door salesperson and later became the youngest manager at Garuda Airlines. In 1999 Dinsi "decided to leave Garuda and forge ahead with his own company in the area of *marketing*. . . . In 2002, he founded LET'S GO Indonesia, [which] provided training full of motivation and entrepreneurship." Dinsi is also in the process of founding a LET'S GO Islamic school (*pesantren*) that aims to mentor students in spirituality, motivation, and business. As does any good self-help guru, Dinsi has his own formula for how to succeed in business: "It requires desire, hard work, smart work, along with a trusteeship from God [*amanah*]. . . . As long as everything is a trusteeship, God willing, you will succeed" (62).

For Dinsi and fellow self-help gurus, work is worship. Their success stories are structured around the idea that piety is linked with financial success and personal happiness. Contemporary biographies of Muslim leaders in Indonesia tend to emphasize the entrepreneurial spirit that transformed them into success stories. The public biographies of such figures serve as "proof" that, through hard work and piety, even a pedi-cab driver can achieve worldly riches and heavenly salvation. Aa Gym went from meatball vendor to Muslim millionaire, and you can, too!

## Muhammad SAW: The Super Leader, Super Manager

The importance of the biographies of self-help gurus notwithstanding, the life history of the Prophet Muhammad remains the ultimate success story. And in contemporary Indonesia Muhammad is reimagined as a shrewd businessperson and savvy entrepreneur. Taking a closer look at this world of Islamic pop psychology, where work is worship, I explore how self-help gurus have crafted a life narrative of the Prophet that emphasizes his business acumen. In this section, I build the argument (one that I develop further in later chapters) that the rise in Islamic self-help psychology, especially of the entrepreneurial kind, is significant to Islamic orthopraxy in the ways it revisits the Prophet's life and recalibrates the important ways in which Muslims imagine, and relate to, the Prophet Muhammad. In these histories of the Prophet's life, Muhammad is not just the last Prophet, receiver of divine revelation, and military commander. As Aa Gym's friend Muhammad Syafi'i Antonio puts it in the title of his best-selling book, the Prophet is also *Muhammad SAW: The Super Leader, Super Manager.*

Antonio, who rose to national prominence while still in his thirties, is another important figure (and success story) in the world of Islamic business. Born Nio Gwan Chung, he changed his name when he converted to Islam. He later attended the University of Jordan, studied at Cairo's Al-Azhar University, pursued a master's degree in economics at the International Islamic University (IIU) in Malaysia, and finally earned his doctorate in finance at the University of Melbourne. He went on to found the first Indonesian university that awards degrees in both Western and Islamic finance. Hermawan Kartajaya even asked Antonio to write the introduction for the popular book *Syariah Marketing.* For twenty-five cents a day, Indonesians can also receive his daily text messages on business success, the Islamic way. He also offers seminars at his Prophetic Leadership and Management Center.

The range of public figures who offer praise on the back cover of his book attests to the broad appeal of this particular life history and provides a glimpse into an emerging class of Muslim reformers who hover between religious teacher and human resources consultant. In addition to flowery testimonies from leaders of both of Indonesia's largest Muslim organizations, other public figures of pop culture who endorsed the book included ESQ founder Ary Ginanjar, television preacher and trainer Yusuf Mansur, and even Indonesia's marketing guru and Catholic coauthor of *Syariah Marketing,* Hermawan Kartajaya. In the acknowledgments section, Antonio writes that he "owes a debt of gratitude to those senior *dai* [evangelists] and young *agents of change* like brother Ary Ginanjar Agustian and even K. H. Abdullah Gymnastiar, Ustadz [religious teacher] Muhammad Arifin Ilham, Ustadz Yusuf Mansur and *akhi* Jeffry al-Bukhari who, from time to time, exchange ideas about propagation strategies and hold *events* together" (2007, iv). Once again these public figures of popular Islam—preachers and trainers—appear together in the market niche of Islamic self-help.

The promotional blurb on the front cover of Antonio's book reminds readers that the Prophet Muhammad is the best role model (*teladan*) for business success: "Learn *leadership* and management intelligence from the best role model in *self development*, business and entrepreneurship, family life, propagation, the social and political order, the legal system, education, and military strategy." I limit the present discussion to how Antonio tells the story of the Prophet Muhammad's embodiment of a particular emotional and ethical disposition deemed necessary for self-development, personal leadership, and entrepreneurship. For example, Antonio approaches the story of Muhammad's childhood through these perspectives:

> After Abdul Muthalib passed away Muhammad was cared for by his uncle Abu Thalib. Unfortunately Abu Thalib represented one of Abdul Muthalib's children who had the most simple life, and thus the young Muhammad frequently had to help with his uncle's family finances by doing hard work for the people of Mecca. The experiences of his youth such as this became his psychological capital [*modal psikologis*] for when he became an entrepreneur in the future. (2007, 78–79)

Antonio stresses the importance of this "psychological capital," what he understands as the product of self-discovery. Seen from this perspective, "the essence of *leadership* is *recognizing, discovering*, and identifying one's real self" (2007, 71). He suggests that religious practice and ethical self-discipline can facilitate this process of self-discovery:

> In the teachings of Islam, this can be carried out through meditations on God [*zikir*], recitations of God's names [*zikir asmaul husna*], prayer, contemplative reflection [*tafakkur*], and fasting. The wisdom [*hikmah*] obtained [from these] . . . includes identifying one's total self, calming one's emotions. (2007, 71)

In his "steps to peak performance," prayer, recitation, introspection, and fasting are the necessary first steps of self-discovery and, ultimately, lead people to their peak potential as leaders. And real leadership, Antonio submits, "is a way of *thinking, feeling, and functioning*, a way of life and a way of being that is transformative" (2007, 72).

And leaders, we are told, begin with themselves. To make this point, Antonio quotes an inspirational passage from the website Inspirational Words of Wisdom, written by an unknown twelfth-century monk:

> When I was a young man, I wanted to change the world. I found it was difficult to change the world, so I tried to change my nation. When I found I couldn't change the nation, I began to focus on my town. I couldn't change the town and as an older man, I tried to change my family. Now, as an old man, I realize the only thing I can change is myself, and suddenly I realize that if long ago I had changed myself, I could have made an impact on my family. My family and I could have made an impact on our town. Their impact could have changed the nation and I could indeed have changed the world. (2007, 73)[6]

Antonio then seamlessly summons the Arabic words of the Prophet Muhammad, *Ibda' bi nafsik!* (begin with yourself; Arabic, *ibda' bi-nafsika*). Or, according to Aa Gym's most popular self-help acronym, 3 M: *Mulai* (begin) with yourself; begin with the small things; and begin right now!

Aa Gym reminds Indonesians that the Qur'an tells Muslims to go out and seek their fortune during those times that they are not fulfilling religious obligations. Like his friend Dr. Antonio, Aa Gym has also revisited the life history of the Prophet Muhammad, and in 2007 Aa Gym offered his own assessment of the legacy of the "Entrepreneurship of the Prophet Muhammad."[7] In the excerpts that follow, Aa Gym traces this history to make a broader argument about the nature of "fortune" (*rezeki*) and the ethics of capital accumulation:

> As it turns out, in our studies of the Prophet Muhammad there is an era of his life that we seldom talk about, namely, how Muhammad became a *professional*. The Prophet is proof that when [one] possesses the spirit of an *entrepreneur*, then [that person] will be capable of managing anything.[8]
>
> At the age of six Muhammad was already an orphan, with nothing to rely on. When he was eight years and two months, his relative who raised and educated him died. After that he was under the care of his uncle Abu Thalib, who was not as wealthy as the relative [who had previously cared for him]. It was that moment that the young, small Muhammad tended to/herded his goats, [i.e.,] made his own living.
>
> Imagine, when the Prophet was twelve years old, his uncle invited him along to Syria, which was thousands of kilometers away. When he returned

from that trip, he frequently conducted business. In fact, a young *professional* named Muhammad had become well-known throughout the Arabian peninsula. *Subhanallah* [Glorious God], when he wed Siti Khadijah, he provided in bride wealth as much as twenty camels, or almost one-half billion rupiah.

Let us begin planting the entrepreneurial spirit in our children. Preparing our children also constitutes our responsibility to the future of Muslims. Train your children from when they are small, so that they become independent, free, and brave to take responsibility so they will believe in themselves.

... The Prophet Muhammad, before he ever became a prophet, did not own a thing. After that he was able to become a rich person without any financial capital. The capital that the Prophet possessed was that he was *Al Amin*, or trustworthy. Beginning now we must take steps to become trustworthy throughout our lives.

... All of our fortune has already been decided. Fortune can be divided into three kinds. The first is the fortune that has been guaranteed, that is food. ... The second is the kind of fortune that depends [on us]. In truth Allah will not change a group's fate until that group changes its own fate. Working hard is a physical matter, working smart is a matter of the mind, and working sincerely [*ikhlas*; Arabic, *ikhlāṣ*] is a matter of the heart. Fortune will be reached only when all three are working.

The third kind of fortune is that which has already been promised. With everything we earn, we must immediately provide an allocation for charity. Fortune does not decrease with alms giving; rather, it keeps building and building.

Whatever one desires, the key is honesty. So it was with the disposition of the Prophet Muhammad, peace be upon him. So, do not fear not having money, but rather be afraid that [the money] is not *barokah* [blessings].[9] The Prophet, as it turns out, was adept in his work, and his orientation was to provide satisfaction. The gifts of Allah are not identical with money, rather with dignity/ magnificence at every moment. ...

In Islam, we Muslims consider ourselves fortunate if we succeed at making as many people as possible succeed. Don't measure fortune with money. Don't measure success with money. Success is if we have knowledge [*ilmu*], experience, a good name and become *barokah*. Money is [just] a bonus from God and means little. ... Every time we have money, it should be invested for seeking knowledge, expanding our perceptions, and as money to do good deeds.

... With this tripartite formula, One: honesty and trustworthiness; Two: competence; and Three: satisfying others. So, our choice must be to go forward, forbidden from retreating until the hour of our death comes for us. God Willing.

In Aa Gym's account, Muhammad was not just a prophet. He was a *professional*, an entrepreneur whose trustworthiness and self-initiative (*ikhtiar*) yielded great fortune.[10] The Prophet Muhammad's success, we are told, was due to smart work, hard work, and heart work. As discussed previously, Aa Gym's autobiography portrays Gymnastiar as an entrepreneur whose rags-to-riches journey was the result of courage and unrelenting effort.[11]

At first glance, these success stories and stories of the Prophet's life seem commensurable with an autonomous economic subject, perhaps even the *homo economicus* of neoliberal lore, one who is both capable of and responsible for pulling herself up by the bootstraps. However, a closer look at MQ Entrepreneur Training—both the genealogy of the curriculum and experiences of the trainees—suggests important differences in the formation of moral and economic subjectivity. MQ Entrepreneur Training posits different "techniques of self-engineering and capital accumulation" (to borrow Ong's words [2006]) that have a decidedly different dynamic than the self-governing secular subject of the neoliberal model.

## *Talent Mapping, Cashflow Quadrants, and Ethical Entrepreneurs*

I now explore how MQ Entrepreneur Training incorporates Islamic teachings, popular psychology, and business management theory in order to encourage trainees to cultivate the ethical and disciplinary dispositions deemed necessary to become a Muslim entrepreneur. I begin with an account of the development of the training curriculum to describe how transnational self-help models provide techniques of self-engineering. Then I move to the issue of capital accumulation to sketch out how these training sessions offer multiple, overlapping models of the moral-economic subject. I do not assume radical differences between "Islamic" and "neoliberal" models of the self-enterprising subject; rather, I focus on how Islamic training seminars provide the social spaces, psychological languages, and ethical considerations in which trainees can literally "play" with multiple understandings of capital accumulation and self-knowledge.

Aa Gym's company LP2ES was preparing a bid for a lucrative long-term contract to develop an entrepreneur training program for Bank Mandiri employees who were nearing retirement. In Indonesia the corporate retirement age for such white-collar workers is typically fifty-five, at which point most retirees will need to pursue a second source of income during retirement. LP2ES executives Pak Yana and Pak Sena (who brought Firewalking Training to Daarut Tauhiid) were searching for new and innovative content to make their entrepreneur training curriculum more appealing for the bidding process.

On May 11, 2006, Pak Yana convened several MQ trainers to meet with Abah Rama Royani, president of Lead Pro Management Consulting, whom they had invited to pitch his new "talent-mapping" aptitude questionnaire and software program. Pak Yana met Pak Royani at a human resources fair and hoped to negotiate a deal that would allow LP2ES to incorporate talent mapping into their entrepreneur training classes. Whereas most human resources models try to improve parts of the self deemed lacking, Rama told us, talent mapping takes the reverse approach: identify and strengthen your "God-given talents." Pak Royani, an engineer by training and statistician by hobby, told us that he developed the software formula after tinkering with Gallup statistical measurements for various psychological traits and profiles. After all of us completed his survey, Pak Royani's software program calculated the responses and generated a "talent map" that identified and ranked areas of aptitude and suggested specific career choices commensurate with those strengths.

During his presentation, Pak Royani told us that his model was significantly influenced by American pioneers in "positive psychology," including Donald Clifton (whom Royani referred to as the "Grandfather of Positive Psychology") and Martin Seligman, whose research on happiness is now translated into Indonesian.[12] Royani told me later that he was also inspired by Tony Buzan's idea of "Mind Mapping" as well as Edward de Bono's concept of the "Six Thinking Hats." Both Buzan and de Bono are immensely popular corporate trainers who have licensed their concepts to select corporate trainers (i.e., those willing to pay the requested amount) who have subsequently conducted training seminars in dozens of countries around the world. The "Six Thinking Hats" concept refers to different individual styles of understanding problems and developing solutions. This knowledge, de Bono suggests, is crucial to improving team dynamics and creativity in any corporate setting. The promotional tagline on the de Bono consulting website reads: "Anyone can be creative provided they learn and develop their skills."[13] In other words, what is crucial is that you know your "thinking hat." According to Pak Royani, self-discovery is the process of learning one's talents. Only then can one really be aware of the specific markets and jobs in which one is most likely to succeed and be happy. Royani's PowerPoint slide punctuated this point with an image of a kitty looking into a mirror. The reflection reveals that the kitty is really a lioness.

Pak Royani may have relied on Gallup for the statistical measurements, but he positions the concept of "talent mapping" within the Islamic textual tradition. During his presentation, Royani presented a slide with the Qur'anic verse al-Isra 17:84: "Every single person does good deeds in accordance with his talents/aptitudes and character. Thus, it is God who knows best the right person and correct path that must be taken."[14] When this slide appeared, MQ Master Trainer Abdurrahman Yuri raised his hand and chimed: "That's right. And there's also a hadith that says that 'the person who knows himself will know Allah.'" Once again the process of translation is accompanied by a shift in frames, where psychological expertise becomes religious wisdom.

As this example suggests, Pak Royani consciously tried to find the Islamic textual resources that could support the science. In his words, the science had to be "made Islamic" (*di-Islam-kan*) in order to appeal to the human resources directors in contemporary corporate Indonesia. Pak Royani (and the other trainers considered here) imported Western psychology and management theory, stripped it of its secular garb, and adorned it with Islamic idioms and textual references of self-discovery. Following Royani's presentation, LP2ES trainers added "Talent Mapping" to their entrepreneur curriculum as well as their contract bid for Bank Mandiri. These psychological discourses resonate with particular Islamic discursive traditions of self-discovery and provide the "modern" techno-scientific legitimacy for a "new" way of being a Muslim entrepreneur. Impressed with the Talent Mapping, Bank Mandiri managers eventually awarded LP2ES the contract, and their employees would come to know themselves, and plan their second career, through their own personalized talent map. In that year alone LP2ES trained more than eight cohorts of Bank Mandiri employees, totaling more than two hundred trainees and one hundred thousand dollars in revenue. And Bank Mandiri was only one of many clients.

. . .

I now turn to how MQ Entrepreneur Training frames "capital accumulation" as both economic and ethical pursuit. On February 27, 2006, Tung Desem Waringin and Abdurrahman Yuri copresented a seminar at Daarut Tauhiid: "Entrepreneur Revolution." Pak Waringin's presentation was almost entirely based on Robert Kiyosaki's book (2000), *Rich Dad, Poor Dad: What the Rich Teach Their Kids about Money That the Poor and Middle Class Do Not*.[15] Kiyosaki presents a "Cashflow Quadrant" model to reveal the secrets of capital accumulation. In the quadrant, one could be a salaried employee, self-employed, a business owner, or an investor. Only by becoming investors, Kiyosaki says, can individuals earn passive income, "have their money work for them," and reach financial freedom.

Following this seminar, LP2ES executives added the Cashflow Quadrant board game to their entrepreneur training. By playing the game, participants are supposed to realize that *anyone* can become rich and "get out of the rat race." The game's rules are designed such that even a janitor (my job when I played) is eventually able to get on the "fast track" of capital accumulation and make his dreams come true. Based on the game's glorification of the American dream (or myth) of meritocracy, one *might* conclude that MQ Entrepreneur Training fosters a neoliberal subject who controls her own destiny in terms of capital accumulation. Such a conclusion, however,

FIGURE 3.1. Trainers playing Kiyosaki's board game Cashflow Quadrant.

would assume that the game's logics are somehow uniformly internalized by docile trainees. It would also assume a necessary and neatly demarcated causal link between subjectivity and techniques of self-engineering. My observations of trainees actually playing this game, as well as the debriefing sessions that followed, suggest a different explanation, one that honors how trainers and trainees play with multiple models of capital accumulation and techniques of self-fashioning. Indeed, training brings us into the realm of the ludic, where trainees play with the resonances between the entrepreneurial ethics of Islam and the individualism of Western self-help.

One of the interesting rules of the game is that if players land on a "charity" space, they can donate a percentage of their income for an extra roll of the dice. This would enable them to collect their next paycheck even faster and get a step closer to entering the game's "fast track," where they can purchase their dreams (ranging from a ski house to a beach house). During the debriefing session following the game, the charity dimension was framed in terms of Islamic teachings about charity (*zakat, infaq, waqaf*; Arabic, *zakāh, infāq, waqf*). Trainees were encouraged to discuss occasions when, after giving charity, they actually received fortune that exceeded what they had given. In my group, one of the members mentioned the seminar "The Power of Giving" (led by television preacher Ustad Yusuf Mansur), where people were asked to donate whatever they could and then, in the following days and weeks, experience for themselves Allah's promise that they could increase fortune through charity. As one trainee put it, "I am as certain as certain can be that without Allah's hand, people will not attain riches. . . . The more you donate [to charity], the more you will get in return." A woman at the next table added: "It's true. Once, I was thinking about how I wanted to build a home for orphans—just an intention [*niat*], not yet the actual building. Then, the next week, my husband got a large raise at work." Yet another trainee cautioned, "This is all great, but we should also remember that fortune is not always about money." The trainer concluded the debriefing session by saying that giving charity is an integral part of obtaining fortune, in its many forms, in this life and the hereafter. In other words, capital accumulation is not simply about one's dream house in Aspen; it is about preparing one's home in the hereafter through charitable acts. The game, with its logics of self-enterprise and glorification of individual initiative, was reinscribed with Islamic idioms of fortune, charity, and moral obligation. Piety is thus an integral part of prosperity.

The next session was "The Concept of Business Ethics Based on Manaje-men Qolbu," led by self-proclaimed MQ Master Trainer Abdurrahman Yuri (who goes by Adeda). He differentiated between three eras of business: the secular era, the mixed era, and the era of integration—where business and religion are one. In this third era, Adeda proclaims that piety is an impor-tant factor in determining one's financial success. He discussed the secrets of capital accumulation by summoning Islamic texts that connect piety (*taqwa*) with fortune (*rezeki*).[16] Adeda began to quote from the Qur'an, al-Thalaq [65]:2–3: "And whosoever fears God, He will appoint for him a way out, and He will provide for him from whence he never reckoned."

MQ Training posits three different kinds of fortune. Most central to the present discussion is the kind of fortune that depends on self-initiative, or *ikhtiar*. Trainees are encouraged to maximize their self-initiative (*menyempur-nakan ikhtiar*) in order to "meet up with their fortune" (*menjemput rezeki*). The trainer quoted the Qur'an passage Al-Ra'd (Q 13:11), "God does not change the fate of a people, until they change their own fate" (i.e., God helps those that help themselves). This is exactly the same passage, discussed earlier, that K. H. Hasyim Asy'ari summoned in 1918 when he was trying to mobilize Muslim entrepreneurship. During my fieldwork I would hear Muslim train-ers summon this verse time and time again in a variety of contexts and train-ing programs across Indonesia. This verse was an important source of Islamic textual authority that resonated with Western ideals of the self-enterprising entrepreneurial subject that structure the Cashflow Quadrant game.

This concept of self-initiative, however, does not easily conform to the idea of an unencumbered individual whose efforts alone can guarantee suc-cess. Nor can it be reduced simply to God's will. Rather, fortune is thought to be allocated by Allah, and our task as humans is to exert self-initiative to secure that fortune—not just by chasing after riches but by leading a pious life as a devout Muslim. Aa Gym promotes self-initiative as part of a tripar-tite formula for success in this life and the hereafter: *Dzikir, Fikir, Ikhtiar*. *Dzikir*, mindfulness of Allah; *Fikir*, our cognitive capacity; and *Ikhtiar*, self-initiative. Self-initiative by itself—without remembrance of Allah—ensures neither earthly riches nor heavenly redemption. Trainees are admonished that entrepreneurship is an ethical pursuit, linking self-cultivation and capital accumulation—so that riches can become blessings (*berkah*). Thus, Cashflow Quadrant, when played by trainees in MQ Training, is not merely a secular board game on how to get rich but rather a tool with which to contemplate Islamic teachings on fortune—understood as the result of relations with both fellow humans and God. This marks a crucial distinction between the discursive practices of MQ Training and the neoliberal logics of Western pop psychology and financial self-help gurus. According to its proponents in Indonesian Islamic psychology, then, the cultivation of capital and an enterprising self requires both worldly work and heavenly devotion.

*Praying for Self-Initiative:*
*Some Concluding Thoughts on Pak Barra's Story*

When Pak Barra first visited Daarut Tauhiid in 2002, he was a young and as-of-yet unsuccessful entrepreneur looking for love and riches. Pak Barra lived in a relatively rural area nestled in the Parahyangan Mountains between Jakarta and Bandung. He first became interested in Aa Gym's teachings after watching him on television. Subsequently he visited Daarut Tauhiid every few months for, in his words, a "religious-business retreat." For Pak Barra, business was about managing the heart.

During the following decade—as Indonesia underwent IMF-mandated privatization of state enterprises and emerged from the political-economic distress of the late 1990s—Pak Barra got married, had children, and even built a successful photocopy business with several branch offices. As he recounted his success story to me in 2012, Pak Barra noted that he first came to Daarut Tauhiid for Aa Gym's religious advice about entrepreneurship. For Pak Barra, this was not simply a matter of organizational psychology or entrepreneur board games. He was particularly interested in honing the ethical and enterprising sensibilities of the heart, especially as cultivated during the supererogatory prayers, *solat duha*, that are performed to request God's assistance with worldly pursuits. With respect to *solat duha*, Pak Barra was also influenced by Ustad Yusuf Mansur, the televangelist and trainer who preached about *solat duha* and the importance of charity, *sedekah*. Pak Barra also frequently visited Mansur's Heart Tourism (Wisata Hati) retreat center and training complex. Like Aa Gym, Mansur promoted *solat duha* prayers in his books about the Islamic ethics of capital accumulation. Mansur's signature training seminar ("The Power of Giving") touted the importance of giving charity as one route to acquiring wealth. "When you give *sedekah*," Mansur once told an audience at Daarut Tauhiid, "Allah does not simply take, but He will replenish in ways you had not conceived."

As Pak Barra worked hard to seek his fortune, he cultivated the practices of *solat duha* supererogatory prayers and *sedekah* charity. He described his process of "Islamizing" the corporate culture of his offices to safeguard the moral etiquette of his employees. He also commissioned private sermons with Aa Gym and Yusuf Mansur to educate his employees about the ethics of Islamic entrepreneurship.

Pak Barra's story about his own success is instructive on several levels. First, the discursive traditions of Islamic self-help are not cordoned off from more orthodox practices such as prayer and traditions like giving charity. An important dimension of the enterprising self is the cultivation of a relationship with God through the honing of the heart that is developed during and through supererogatory prayer. Pak Barra's commitment to this otherworldly aspect of the entrepreneurial self is yet another example of how Indonesian Muslims—whether trainer or trainee—are at play with the ethics of entrepreneurship. The discursive traditions generated by Islamic self-help are not easily reducible to any single source or inspiration. Neoliberalism's championing of the individual, especially vis-à-vis state welfare programs, definitely resonates with Pak Barra's conception of the enterprising self. At the same time, however, Pak Barra's embodied practices in such pursuits are explicitly Islamic, and the underlying logic about self-initiative and capital accumulation is informed by the notion that charity and *solat duha* prayers can beget fortune. Islamic ethics thus informs the idea of the enterprising self as well as assumptions about what constitutes fortune, how it is acquired, and how it should be distributed.

In the Introduction I discussed Nikolas Rose's work on "psy-discourses" (1996, 1999) and outlined his argument that psychological discourses, as a Foucauldian form of knowledge/power, were an important part of neoliberal governmentality. In this chapter I returned to the question posed there: Do transnational psychological discourses, when imported and repackaged as part of a renewed emphasis on Islamic entrepreneurship in Indonesia, engender a neoliberal economic subject? I first turned to Indonesian history to argue that, long before neoliberal logics began their serpentine spread around the globe, Islam in Indonesia provided the religious, economic, and psychological basis for understanding the self-enterprising (and self-regulating) economic subject. I demonstrated that the early modernist Islamic organizations were founded on, and infused with, religious principles of entrepreneurship and capital accumulation.

Muslim trainers at Daarut Tauhiid draw from self-help psychology of Western financial gurus, with their talent maps and cashflow quadrants, yet such secrets of success are also reinscribed within Islamic discourses and tenets of ethical entrepreneurship in which sincere piety is believed to bring prosperity. I also stressed how Aa Gym, as a leader and success story of contemporary Islamic entrepreneurship in Indonesia, emphasizes that God commands his followers to exert self-initiative in their quest for wealth. The individual enterprising self also plays an important role, though somewhat different from the one championed by a neoliberal model. Aa Gym and Muslim trainers summon the Qur'anic injunction that states that God helps those who help themselves. Individual effort is necessary but, without piety, insufficient. And the goal of business, as articulated by MQ Entrepreneur Training, is not unbridled capital accumulation for its own sake. Instead, capital is perceived as a prerequisite to fulfill one's religious obligations of almsgiving.

MQ Entrepreneur Training emphasizes particular Islamic teachings that *resonate* with neoliberal tenets of individualism and capital accumulation. Thinking in terms of resonance allows us to acknowledge similarities between multiple models of subjectivity without losing sight of their points of departure. The resonance between transnational psychology and Islamic training helps explain how imported theories of psyche and success can provide the legitimacy for a novel form of Islamic authority (the trainer) without necessarily producing a self-enterprising neoliberal subject. Just as the Protestant ethic apparently has no monopoly on the "spirit of capitalism," the psy-discourses of neoliberalism do not simply produce prepackaged models of subjectivity.

CHAPTER 4

# Prophetic Cosmopolitanism
## The Prophet Muhammad as Psycho-Civic Exemplar

> Only some [Indonesians] have physical illness. . . . Apparently what
> is now spreading throughout our nation is actually an illness of the
> conscience. . . . This requires collective awareness, consensus, and
> earnestness to educate, train, and build every stratum of society.
>
> —*Aa Gym*, Reflections to Build the Conscience of the Nation[1]

On August 18, 2004, Aa Gym went to the Indonesian Film Censor Board to
publicly protest the release of the Indonesian romantic comedy *Hurry Up,
Kiss Me!* (*Buruan Cium Gue*). During the photo-op with reporters, Aa Gym
derided the film as a vulgar affront to national morality (*moral bangsa*). Din
Syamsuddin, influential leader of Muhammadiyah and secretary general of
the Council of Indonesian Ulama (MUI), stood in solidarity next to Aa
Gym. On the other side were celebrity icons of feminine piety, Astri Ivo and
Inneke Koesherawati.[2] Aa Gym lectured the crowd of reporters:

> The title alone. Excuse me, but that is just vulgar. It's bold because it encourages
> kissing outside the context of marriage. Don't we all know for ourselves that is
> not good behavior? . . . Based on what I understand about Islam, kissing outside
> of marriage is one aspect of *perzinahan* [improper sexual relations]. So, actually I
> would say that the title should be "OK, Hurry up and *zinah* me."[3]

Aa Gym claimed that his goal was not to judge but simply to request
further clarification about how the censorship board somehow managed to
approve the film for distribution. From his public pulpit, he urged Indonesians to confront the moral crisis of the country with his formula *3 Semangat*
(spirit): (1) the spirit of family; (2) the spirit of solutions; and (3) the spirit of
success. Shortly thereafter the censorship board retroactively revoked its approval and withdrew the film from theaters. Aa Gym parlayed his celebrity
appeal into political action. He roused a moral debate, summoned the state,
and goaded state officials to act as moral guardian for the nation.

121

Basking in his newfound political capital, Aa Gym decided to build on the momentum of his victory over the censorship board. Less than a month later, from the steps of the national monument and before thousands of supporters and several media outlets, Aa Gym founded his Movement to Raise the Conscience of the Nation (Gerakan Memban-gun Nurani Bangsa, abridged as Gema Nusa).[4] Not only does Aa Gym conceive of conscience in terms of an individual subject, but he also ex-tends this to the nation at large, or the "conscience of the nation" (*nurani bangsa*). Several key public figures stood alongside Aa Gym, including Din Syamsuddin (once again), Hidayat Nur Wahid (then-chair of the People's Consultative Assembly and member of Prosperity and Justice Party, PKS), Islamic finance expert M. Syafi'i Antonio, Islamic television star Inneke Koesherawati, Indonesia's contemporary moral mother figure Neno Waris-man, and young Islamic pop singer Sulis. Aa Gym was adamant that this be a national movement, not an Islamic one. He invited important leaders from each of the major religions, and the formal declaration steered clear of overt Islamic symbolism.

FIGURE 4.1. Aa Gym at the official declaration of Gema Nusa. Courtesy of Daarut Tauhiid.

Aa Gym read the formal declaration point by point:

1. The progress and prestige of the nation are made certain not only by material achievement but also through ethical fortitude, morality, and the character of the people.

2. The building of ethical fortitude, morality, and national character must be carried out in a way that is serious, consistent, and in accordance with each potential and element within the nation.

3. The young generation is a portrait of the future nation. On account of that, [they] must receive the attention, nurturing, and opportunities to flourish as Indonesian people who are intelligent and who possess character and commitment.

4. Our collective efforts to build ethics, morality, and national character for the progress and prestige of the nation must be carried out in ways that are benevolent and wise.

5. To build a pure morality of the nation, we must begin with cultivating the conscience.

Aa Gym reminded Indonesians that the cultivation of the conscience of the nation must begin with their *qolbu*. He marketed MQ as more than the cure for turbulent hearts and the key to becoming one's own *sukses* story. He wanted MQ to provide the model for the moral citizen. Within months of its founding, more than four million Indonesians across the archipelago had signed-up to be Gema Nusa civic "volunteers" (*sukarelawan*).[5]

In this chapter I explore another dimension of Muslim subjectivity in Indonesia—civic virtue—by examining the ways in which Aa Gym promotes Manajemen Qolbu as a form of civic participation in a democratic Indonesia. Tending to the entanglements of psychology and religion, of self and nation, I describe how Aa Gym and Muslim trainers crafted and promoted a psychologized model of moral citizenship. I explore the homologies between the reform of self and society, the purification of heart and nation. Whereas national development programs during Suharto's New Order regime pursued development (*pembangunan*) largely as a project of political and economic reform, Gema Nusa provided an alternative model of moral transformation through the cultivation of a national moral conscience.[6] As Andrea Muehlebach observes in her excellent ethnography of the production of civic virtue in neoliberal Italy, "the focus here is not on calculative rationality but on its corollaries: on other-orientation rather than the fashioning of the self, on affect rather than rationality, on fellow feeling rather than self-interest" (2012, 25). Whether in Catholic Italy or Islamic Indonesia, technologies of self are thus also technologies of community.[7]

I met with hundreds of Gema Nusa volunteers; attended the official declarations of provincial offices in North Sumatra, West Sumatra, Southern Kalimantan, and South Sulawesi; and along the way interviewed people at every level from the executive board members negotiating sponsor funding to the field volunteers providing food and water for earthquake victims. Through these experiences, I became most interested in how Gema Nusa leadership imagined the kinds of knowledge one should possess in order to forge a new generation of pious citizen-believers in a plural, democratic Indonesia. In what follows I examine how Muslim trainers designed Gema Nusa civic training by integrating Islam, transnational psychology, and management theory. Once again, trainers invoked the techno-scientific allure of Western psychology to recalibrate the prophetic tradition in such a way that the Prophet Muhammad is framed as the exemplary model of civic virtue, what I refer to as "prophetic cosmopolitanism."

### Learning to Labor for the Nation

On April 21, 2006, nearly one hundred Gema Nusa leaders from over thirty provinces across the archipelago gathered in Jakarta for the "Training of Trainers" seminar (TOT).[8] The Gema Nusa executive board decided to devote 70 percent of the training curriculum to theories of human resource development (*sumber daya manusia*) and 30 percent to the concept of civic "voluntarism" (*kesukarelawanan*). They chose popular Muslim trainers and human resources consultants—not preachers and clerics—to educate a generation of Gema Nusa trainers who would subsequently provide civic training at the local level across Indonesia.[9] Titles for some of the training sessions include "The Spirit of Struggle"; "A Trainer's Mentality of Success"; "Achieving Greatness"; "A Structural Profile of Gema Nusa"; "Knowing Oneself"; "Work Ethic"; "Managing Training Sessions, A to Z"; "Developing Local Branches"; "Motivation and Team Building"; and "The Spirit of Voluntarism." Before turning to the actual training, I briefly introduce the Gema Nusa trainers whose respective backgrounds and invested interest in Gema Nusa provide a more broad understanding of the trainer as a figure of Muslim modernity.

FIGURE 4.2. Jamil Azzaini training regional Gema Nusa leaders at the "Training of Trainers."

Jamil Azzaini leads corporate training seminars for private companies and state-owned enterprises in every Indonesian province as well as in Malaysia, Singapore, and the Philippines. In the best-selling book *Kubik Leadership,* Azzaini and his coauthors argue for the need to create synergy among the various forms of intelligence—what they refer to as *valensi,* or "valence." Similar to other training programs, he preaches the benefits of spiritual intelligence in the workplace. Azzaini also writes a regular advice column in the Islamic newspaper *Republika,* hosts a corporate radio program on Trijaya FM, and serves on the executive board for the national board of Islamic charity. Azzaini participates in a range of seemingly incongruent political events, from Gema Nusa civic volunteer training to a political rally for Hizbut Tahrir (the transnational organization that seeks to establish a global Islamic caliphate). Azzaini is known more as a motivator and trainer than as a preacher, yet he is frequently invited to preach at mosques and prayer groups and has led pilgrimage tours to Saudi Arabia. Public announcements typically list his educational credentials in terms of social economics and business, "Ir. Jamil Azzaini, M.M.," yet he is occasionally referred to with the title of religious teacher, "Ustad Jamil Azzaini." Once again, the figure of the trainer occupies interstitial space between pop psychologist and religious teacher.

One of Azzaini's colleagues at the SEM Institute, Muhammad Karebet Widjajakusuma, substituted for Azzaini during the second day of training. Widjajakusuma is another popular trainer who integrates popular psychology and Islam for a business audience. The title of his 2007 book, *Be the Best, Not "Be Asa,"* is an Indonesian-English play on words that could be translated as "Be the Best, Not Average." He coauthored his first book (2002), *Designing Islamic Business* (*Menggagas Bisnis Islami*), with M. Ismail Yusanto, the spokesperson for Indonesia's branch of Hizbut Tahrir. Widjajakusuma leads training sessions as part of Hizbut Tahrir's outreach and propagation efforts. When the entire Gema Nusa TOT PowerPoint curriculum was downloaded to CDs for all of the trainees, Widjajakusuma furtively included PowerPoint presentations of Hizbut Tahrir propaganda. One file that was *not* presented at Gema Nusa training summoned Western management theory while proclaiming that Western secular democracy is akin to the "trap of a monitor lizard." I am less concerned with Widjajakusuma's political leanings than the interesting fact that Hizbut Tahrir's recruitment and publishing strategies also draw on the perceived authority of global psychology, trainers, and training sessions. As Katherine Pratt Ewing has observed:

> Under the guise of rejection of certain aspects of Western practice . . . there is actually an incitement within many Islamist and other fundamentalist groups to modernize, through an array of practices that constitute the modern subject, which can be characterized by a reflexive, self-conscious interiority, a sense of rupture with a traditional past, and a global, even cosmopolitan, orientation. (2010, 53)

Thus, Islamic training, the popular psychology on which it is based, and the vision of moral governance to which it aspires are very much part of the modern turn toward a reflexive subject (Giddens 1991) as well as the religious turn in public life (Casanova 1994).

Naufal Mahfudz Ismail, another Gema Nusa trainer who goes by the name Pak Naufal, received his master's degree in human resources in Japan and works as director of human resources for a state-owned company. He also serves on Gema Nusa's executive board, where he advises on issues of human resources, recruitment, and training. Compared with Azzaini and Widjajakusuma, Pak Naufal has more formal training in Western theories of personality, motivation, and organizational psychology. He was not as well known as Azzaini, but he is representative of the figure of the trainer who blends Western psychology with Islamic idioms of self and society. Pak Naufal and I first met at the Gema Nusa executive board meeting in October 2005, when he outlined the human resources strategies of recruitment and management of the volunteers. Subsequently, we met at the "Spiritual Capital" seminar led by Taufik Bahaudin, a business management professor at University of Indonesia and author of the organizational psychology book *Brainware Management.* That seminar featured special guest Danah Zohar, the American coauthor of *Connecting with Our Spiritual Intelligence* and *Spiritual Capital* (Zohar and Marshall 2000, 2004). ESQ Training founder Ary Ginanjar was a special guest of honor at this seminar (once again).[10] An ESQ alumnus, Pak Naufal also earned certificates for other religion, business, and psychology training programs. Pak Naufal told me that, during his training in organizational psychology, he was especially influenced by the motivational theories of renowned Harvard psychologist David McClelland. He also mentioned that he liked the popular management books that acknowledged spiritual dimensions of work, such as *The Corporate Mystic* (Hendricks and Ludeman 1997). As Pak Naufal described it, his "mission and vision" for the Gema Nusa TOT was to teach trainers-in-training how an understanding of organizational and personality psychology could enhance the bureaucratic and human resources aspects necessary to train and mobilize civic volunteers.

Other prominent public figures, not considered trainers per se, presented material for the 30 percent of the training sessions that addressed the concept of voluntarism. Gema Nusa executive chairperson and subsequent CEO of the state-owned *Antara* news agency, Ahmad Mukhlis, led a session about Gema Nusa's bureaucratic structure and five-year plan. Teguh Juwarno, former news anchor and then-adviser to the minister of education, spoke about how local Gema Nusa branches could cooperate with news media to promote their social agenda. And Anas Urbaningrum, a rising star who would eventually become chairperson of President Yudhoyono's Democrat Party, led a discussion about civic voluntarism as a form of national development (*pembangunan*).

Now let me turn to the trainees. Generally, the province-level Gema Nusa leaders who attended the TOT were *not* the provincial executive board members who frequently were chosen by virtue of their status as local political, religious, and business leaders (and thus their ability to secure local public and private patronage for Gema Nusa). Rather, those who attended the TOT represented the grassroots level of civic volunteers. Most were genuinely concerned about what they perceived to be Indonesia's "moral crisis" and were passionate in their efforts to improve society. Many were pleased to be associated with Aa Gym by way of Gema Nusa, but very few stood to gain any significant political or economic advantage from such association. On the other hand, on occasion Gema Nusa board members at the province level also served as regional directors for Aa Gym's direct-marketing company that sold MQ household and cosmetic products.

Of the ninety or so trainees, only 25 percent were women; 75 percent were under the age of forty-five; and approximately 60 percent were under the age of thirty-five. They represented a range of professions, including university professors and graduate students, entrepreneurs, midlevel managers, journalists, college students, high school teachers, and even a self-help author. Most self-identified as conservative Muslims, but they claimed allegiance to a broad range of political parties. They came from families with links to both of Indonesia's largest modern Muslim organizations, NU and Muhammadiyah; however, very few expressed strong allegiances to either organization. There were even a few Christians, but none from any other religious tradition. Such diversity is consistent with new forms of religious mobilization that appear to transcend the conventional fault line between traditionalists and modernists in Indonesia (Howell 2001).

A sense of anticipation and palpable excitement filled the auditorium as trainees arrived, registered, and took their seats for the opening ceremony. Many were already sporting their complimentary Gema Nusa hats and lapel pins. On this day Aa Gym did not wear his trademark turban. Instead, he donned the red-and-white Gema Nusa cap (red and white are the colors of the Indonesian flag). As the son of a military father, he always expressed a solemn reverence for the national anthem. His own political and economic ambitions aside, it seemed to me that Aa Gym felt a sincere angst about the moral fabric of his country. During his opening remarks, titled "The Spirit of Struggle," Aa Gym nostalgically recalled the glory of Indonesia's struggle for independence:

> Indonesia's freedom was won by volunteers who struggled [*para pejuang sukarelawan*] for the freedom we Indonesians now enjoy. . . . Their efforts did not know "office hours"; they did not expect wages or anything in return. Their struggle was sincere. . . . And so now we, too, must take notice, be concerned,

do something, and struggle [*peka, peduli, berbuat, dan berjuang*] to improve the moral crisis in Indonesia.

Turning to the "conscience of the nation," Aa Gym discussed the relationship between microcosm and macrocosm. Moral change can occur, he tells the audience, only through each individual taking the personal initiative to become a good moral example, a *suri teladan*. Aa Gym told the participants that Gema Nusa was not a political movement to critique others' immorality; instead, Gema Nusa was a moral movement to inspire personal transformation. According to the Sufi philosophy that inspired Aa Gym's political strategy, personal transformation at the individual level would engender moral reform at the macrocosm level:

> We must begin with ourselves. In the Qur'an it is written that we must not order others to do something before we have first ordered ourselves. And so it is with national moral reform. Remember 3 M: Begin with your*self*; begin with small things; begin right now. . . . The model is one of setting a good moral example [*keteladanan*]. Volunteers must become a good model of morality. . . . The way to change the nation is to begin by changing individuals . . . and the way to change individuals is through their conscience [*hati nurani*]. . . . So, don't think about others before you first consider and know yourself. . . . We do this through education and training . . . to cultivate our moral character so that we are consistent. . . . Remember the story of the Prophet Muhammad, peace be upon him. Once, when someone had urinated in the mosque and people became angry, the Prophet calmly said, "Fetch water and clean it up." . . . Similarly, volunteers should help, not just judge others. . . . Once I received an angry text message from someone who complained that I was just a self-serving person. I did not reply in anger. Instead, I thanked him for the opportunity to self-reflect on my faults. . . . We must transform antagonistic relations into friendship. . . . Our country has many religions, and Gema Nusa should transcend religious divides. . . . What is important is *khidmat* [faithful service]. . . . We must remember the words of the Prophet Muhammad . . . "the leader of a group must also serve that group."

In this vision of moral and political transformation, trainers were to play an especially important role. After all, the participants were not just learning to be good civic volunteers. They were learning to be trainers. Immediately following the opening ceremonies, Aa Gym departed for an *umroh* pilgrimage to Saudi Arabia, leaving the TOT in the hands of his trusted trainers.

Jamil Azzaini (Pak Jamil) led the first training session, "The Mentality of a Successful Trainer." With background music blaring, he began the "icebreaker"

by inviting the audience to get up and cheer loudly. With all attendees standing attentively, their blood circulating and endorphins firing, Pak Jamil explained the philosophy behind beginning training sessions like this:

> You see, based on research in Australia, people can reduce their stress levels sim-
> ply by shouting and cheering. . . . The goal is also to get people mentally into
> the training, to show them that they can remove the obstructions that prevent
> us from improving. . . . In the words of the Prophet Muhammad, peace be upon
> him, "whoever is better today than yesterday is fortunate; whoever is the same
> today as yesterday loses out [*rugi*]; and whoever is worse today than yesterday
> meets with misfortune [*celaka*]." . . . The key to improvement is that we must
> not be afraid to fail.

The courage to fail, Pak Jamil continued, means that we must be brave
enough to move out of, as he referred to in English, our "comfort zone."
After telling the stories of Helen Keller and Lance Armstrong, Pak Jamil
summoned a historical analogy of the spread of Islam into southern Europe:

> Remember the story of Thoriq bin Ziyad [Țāriq ibn Ziyād d. 720]. He had
> just crossed the Mediterranean and landed at Gibraltar with his seven thousand
> troops. And what did he do? He ordered that the ships be burned. With that
> single act, his troops knew that there was nowhere to run—only sea behind
> them and enemy troops ahead. Outnumbered by an overwhelming margin,
> there was nothing left but to charge ahead in battle. . . . We must emulate the
> bravery of Thoriq bin Ziyad, the willingness to go beyond our comfort zone and
> rid ourselves of the fear of failing.

In a plug for his book *Kubik Leadership*, Pak Jamil told us that leadership
requires a certain synergy between the various forms of intelligence, what
he calls *valensi*.[11] One of the goals of training at the provincial level, Jamil
contended, should be encouraging this synergistic approach to intelligence.
Pak Jamil summoned the expertise of Western science to differentiate cognitive intelligence (IQ), emotional intelligence (EQ), and spiritual intelligence (SQ):

> Based on research from Harvard University and the University of California,
> we know that IQ only accounts for 6 percent of our intelligence. The key to
> "valensi" is to find a way to productively connect each of our intelligences with
> each other. Spiritual intelligence must be part of our lives, at home and at work.
> Prayer and fasting are not enough . . . in fact, EQ and SQ are dominant, so we
> must not leave out God. . . . We must learn empathy . . . and as we know, the
> Prophet Muhammad had extraordinary EQ.

Pak Jamil emphasizes the exemplary affective comportment of the Prophet Muhammad. For Pak Jamil and many others, it does not matter whether or not they are borrowing the phrase "emotional intelligence" made popular by American psychologist Daniel Goleman (1995).[12] In terms of the training session as Islamic education, what really matters is how trainers and trainees cast the Prophet Muhammad as the ultimate exemplar of emotional intelligence. Interestingly, Jamil does not cite specific studies; more important than any specific psychologist is the perceived legitimacy of Western techno-science and its institutions of higher education. The Harvard brand adds intellectual gravitas and scientific legitimacy to religious reform. To borrow the words of Nilufur Göle (2002), the Harvard brand signifies something akin to the "extra-modern." Similarly, Gema Nusa civic training recalibrates the prophetic tradition by portraying Muhammad as the uber-cosmopolitan citizen and civic leader. Science does not lead to the secular; rather, it lends scientific gravitas to the idea of the Prophet Muhammad as the ultimate moral exemplar. As Pak Jamil brought the session to a close, he dimmed the lights and asked trainees to envision themselves meeting with the Prophet Muhammad. What would they tell the Prophet, he asked, about how they had used their various God-given talents? How had they cultivated their EQ? Jamil and the majority of trainees sobbed with each question.

After evening prayers and dinner, everyone reconvened for the session "Profile and Mechanisms of Gema Nusa." Pak Mukhlis led participants through the official Gema Nusa handbook, explaining the goals, organizational structure, and vision for the future of Gema Nusa. He described Aa Gym's vision for Gema Nusa:

> This is a movement of moral examples, not a movement to *do* something. . . . We aim to cultivate a moral conscience as a base for thinking and acting [*nurani sebagai landasan cara berpikir dan bertindak*]. . . . The Indonesian people long for the moral sentiments put forth by Aa Gym. . . . There are 140,000 ESQ alumni for a reason—because people long for spirituality and morality.[13]

Pak Mukhlis conjured the language of moral crisis, and Islamic training would be the remedy. Pak Mukhlis briefed the regional leaders about Gema Nusa's immediate future:

> The next step will be for everyone here to take the TOT training material back to the regional offices and hold subsequent volunteer training sessions. These training sessions will be called *Bina Nurani* [cultivating conscience]. During

these sessions, each region should discuss the pressing moral issues of their respective province, as these will surely vary. We want a decentralized structure where each provincial office can have a certain level of autonomy.

Following Pak Mukhlis's presentation, regional Gema Nusa leaders were given the opportunity to ask questions and to open a dialogue about the future direction of Gema Nusa. As local leaders and field volunteers, many had organizational and logistical concerns. Siti, a journalist from Medan in Sumatra, told the group that her provincial branch was "pleased to report that we have signed-up over seven hundred people who are ready to become Gema Nusa volunteers. Since the launching of that branch, however, volunteers have become restless and are asking us, 'OK, Now what? What's next? What are we going to do?'" Following Siti's comment, several others echoed similar sentiments. Some noted that the initial ease of volunteer recruitment was an effect of Aa Gym's celebrity appeal. Others wondered aloud how this model for a moral movement of volunteers, acting through their own moral example, would actually translate into a viable, enduring movement. The relationship between personal microcosm and political macrocosm, while perhaps rooted in Sufi notions of moral reform, nonetheless appeared as a logistical problem. Later that evening, my roommates, Pak Yatno from central Java and Pak Aslam from South Sulawesi, spent the rest of the evening hours pondering this issue. With no clear answer emerging, we all retired for the evening. In a few short hours we would be awoken by the call to prayer.

### Know Thyself: Civic Virtue, Personality Psychology, and the Prophetic Tradition

Naufal Mahfudz Ismail led the training sessions the next morning. Pak Naufal began by explaining the purpose of this session: "This morning, we are going to learn about ourselves through the insights of a few psychologists. In this first session, we will discuss 'work ethic' [etos kerja]. When we speak of work ethic, one of the first things we Indonesians must talk about is proper time management." To do this, Pak Naufal drew from Japanese and Korean business models of efficiency:

> We Indonesians must learn to value time. When I studied in Japan, I was inspired by the bullet train system. Here in Indonesia, trains operate on "elastic time." But in Japan, the Shinkansen bullet train is a model of efficiency and

punctuality. In Indonesia, we could benefit from the Shinkansen philosophy. . . . In 1985, social psychologist Robert Levine of Cal State in America conducted an interesting study. In this study, Professor Levine measured average walking speeds of people from various countries. Can you guess which country had the highest average walking speed? Which country had the lowest average walking speed? . . . Japan was ranked highest, followed by England, the US, and Italy . . . and Indonesia? Ranked at the bottom! . . . Has anyone read Richard M. Stearns's book *Made in Korea*? It tells the story of how, through hard work, Chung Yu Yung created the Hyundai Empire. . . . We must remember, however, that religion gives us a higher purpose for our work. Only spiritual riches can provide true happiness.

To make his point, Pak Naufal summoned transnational science, psychology, and business management theory. In this case, however, the invocation of transnational science actually reinforces colonial stereotypes of the "lazy native" promulgated by colonial psychiatry (Pols 2007).

Pak Naufal continued his emphasis on self-discipline and hard work with a passage from the Qur'an. His words built to a crescendo, "And, lest we forget what is written in Al-Ra'd (Q 13:11), 'God does not change the condition of a people unless they themselves make the decision to change their own condition.'"[14] Once again, Muslim preachers and trainers summoned this particular passage as part of a broader appeal to foster an Islamic work ethic and, in this case, civic virtue.[15] Similar to what occurs in MQ Entrepreneur Training, Muslim trainers harness the perceived authority of transnational business management and psychological theory at the same time that they "authenticate" civic participation within the moral and discursive traditions of Islam (Deeb 2006). Islam authenticates science, but science also lends techno-scientific legitimacy to Islam. Muslim trainers creatively play with the resonances among multiple models of psychological subjectivity. It is through this conceptual play that trainees forge new ways of being Muslim and of understanding oneself as a citizen-believer.

Pak Naufal began the next session, "Know Thyself," by asking for a volunteer to come up and introduce herself or himself. Rizky Mahendra, a young entrepreneur and self-help author, raised his hand and proceeded to the front of the room.[16] Rizky introduced himself by noting that his name literally means "fortune." At Pak Naufal's nudging, he discussed what he perceived to be his own strengths and weaknesses. Rizky told us that he felt that he was a good people person but had other weaknesses that were keeping him from reaching his "optimal" potential. Pak Naufal stepped in: "No one can be good at everything. Indeed, different people have different sorts of backgrounds, knowledge sets, and skills. Some of these skills are easier to develop than others."

With his introductory hook set, Pak Naufal unveiled a PowerPoint slide of an iceberg. "What we call *hard competencies*," he continued, enunciating the English, "are like the tip of this iceberg. These refer to the knowledge and skills necessary to carry out a project. And, they are easier to learn than what are called *soft competencies*." Pak Arif, an engineer and university rector from Medan, interjected: "Yes, there are *hard skills* and *soft skills*. Soft skills are important indeed. According to a Harvard study, and I forget the exact name of the researcher, 85 percent of one's success depends on soft competency." Pak Naufal built on this statistic, suggesting that each Gema Nusa branch office must be able to identify the various personality strengths and competencies of its leaders and members.

One way to identify these personality strengths, Pak Naufal continued, was to consider people's personality types. Aided by a polished PowerPoint presentation, he briefly explained the history of personality theory in Western psychology. Before long, Pak Naufal introduced the Myers-Briggs personality test:

> Influenced by the famous psychologist Carl Jung, Isabel Myers and Katherine Briggs have identified sixteen personality types/configurations, based on combinations of four axes of personality. It's important to remember that these are not discrete categories; however, they do help us think about different personality types, indicated by a four-letter classification system. After you fill out the questionnaire in a few minutes, you'll know your personality profile.

Pak Naufal tossed in some welcome levity to the serious work of saving Indonesia from moral destruction: "And for Indonesian Muslims, we already know about the category STMJ, *Solat Terus Maksiat Jauh* [Pray Continuously (to keep) Vice at a Distance]." Even Pak Naufal's humor relied on a clever juxtaposition of scientific discourse and Islamic ethics.

After a few courtesy laughs from the audience, Pak Naufal continued by explaining the various personality scales: Extrovert vs. Introvert; Sensing vs. Intuiting; Thinking vs. Feeling; Judging vs. Perceiving. According to the Myers-Briggs test, one's personality profile is the specific combination across these four categories. After the presentation, all trainees completed the Myers-Briggs questionnaire (using an authorized Indonesian translation) and calculated their personality profiles. Pak Naufal emphasized that these categories are indicators of general tendencies and that people could very well fall in the middle of the continuum. Or they might even change during their lifetime:

> For example, the Prophet Muhammad, peace be upon him, over the course of his lifetime shifted from an extrovert toward more of an introvert. The important thing to remember is that, in your local Gema Nusa branches, different personality types can accomplish different things. There must be *synergy* in Gema Nusa. We want to become a *Super Team*, not *Superman*.

Pak Arif raised his hand and chimed in: "It seems that this research is based on Western concepts, not necessarily including Muslims. We should consider the personality profile of the Prophet Muhammad." Pak Naufal replied enthusiastically, "Absolutely. The *ultimate example*," he said, using the English phrase, "is the Prophet Muhammad. If we think about the Prophet Muhammad, peace be upon him, we could say that he best resembles an ESFJ—Extrovert, Sensing, Feeling, Judging." The ESFJ represents the *servant leader*—the leader whose duty is to serve the people. Trainers and trainees played with the meanings and limits of psychology and, in the process, reimagined the Prophet as the exemplar of civic virtue. Once again, Western psychology was reinscribed in terms of Islamic ethics and moral subjectivity. And Muhammad was the measure.

## *Training Trainers: Teaching the Psychology of Citizenship*

That afternoon's sessions were all about learning the tricks of the trade. As previously mentioned, these trainees were to become trainers in their own right, who would return to their respective provinces to wield the psycho-religious authority of the trainer. During the Gema Nusa "Training of Trainers," attendees learned the psychological vocabulary and human resources methods deemed necessary to provide civic education at the local level. M. Karebet Widjajakusuma, the substitute trainer for Azzaini on that day, led "Managing the Training Session" and "Public Presentations, from A to Z." The first session focused on strategies for creating a successful group dynamic. To begin the session, Pak Karebet asked all of the trainees to rise. Similar to each of the previous sessions, trainees shouted the Gema Nusa slogan in unison, complete with hand emblems for each word: "Gema Nusaaaaaa! Peka, Peduli, Berbuat, Berjuang!" (Gema Nusa! Take Notice,

Be Concerned, Do Something, Struggle!). Next, he asked trainees to shout the Gema Nusa motto even louder: "SMS: Sukarelawan Membantu dengan Santun" (Volunteers Courteously Helping). "OK, extraordinary! Please, go ahead and sit down now." Pak Karebet turned to one woman who was especially energetic in her responses:

> Extraordinary! Ibu, I'm sorry, what's your name? Ibu Eva, you really did such a great job. In my own training, I always say that you should always try to "be the best, don't be-*a-sa*" [average].[17] When you begin your training sessions, it's always important to get the audience up and moving around. It helps create a good atmosphere in the room. It's crucial to get the audience to feel comfortable and relaxed before beginning the actual material. Icebreakers [*pencairan suasana*] can also be a very effective means to create a comfortable atmosphere and to introduce your material. Or, as an alternative, you could try a creative introduction by way of a recent event that is relevant to the material or training group. For example, I also could have begun with a recent *Tempo* magazine article about the anti-pornography draft legislation as a way to attract your attention and suggest Gema Nusa as part of the answer to this moral problem confronting Indonesia.

Pak Karebet shared several training tips, including the introductory standing and shouting, selecting a "star" trainee, and possible creative introductions in the form of songs, statistics, or current news stories:

> One of the keys to becoming an excellent trainer is that you really have to know what your goals are. What do you want to convey? Equally important, how will you convey your material? You see, there are three domains each trainer must address: the cognitive, psycho-motor, and affective. We do not learn simply in one way, and each trainee will bring different sorts of intelligence to training. To address the cognitive components, remember to develop and pass out relevant handouts. For the psycho-motor dimensions, simulations are extremely helpful. Remember: we only remember a small percentage of what we read or hear. But we remember 90 percent of what we actually *do*. So, *learning by doing* is essential. . . . It is also important to identify a star trainee [*bintang pelatihan*], whom you can keep coming back to as the model of how to do things correctly.

Ibu Eva blushed, and then Pak Karebet assured her, "But you really did do a great job! Everybody give Ibu Eva and a round of applause! Give yourselves a round of applause!"

In the next session, "Presentations, A to Z," Pak Karebet tried to establish his own authority as trainer through a professed knowledge of *psikologi*. He suggested that the trainer's understanding of proxemics and manipulation of the physical space in the room could drastically enhance their effectiveness: "According to the language of psychology [*bahasa psikologi*], people typically require one meter of personal space." Then he also admonished the trainees to be mindful of their body language:

> For example, you should never address an audience with your hands in your pockets, like this, or by crossing your arms. According to the language of psychology, this can be troublesome. Do you remember the photo of the IMF representative, with his arms crossed, looking from above as Suharto signed the bailout agreement? Such nonverbals give the impression of conceit [*angkuh*].

Indeed, this image was plastered on the front page of Indonesia's newspapers. The neocolonial connotations of Suharto beneath a scowling IMF official with arms crossed became a source of great public embarrassment and loss of face for Suharto. In these excerpts, Pak Karebet invokes the "language of psychology"—not his extensive knowledge of Arabic, the Qur'an, or *sunna*—in order to stake his techno-scientific claim on authority. Once again, trainers claim a particular form of religio-scientific authority through their ability to invoke and demonstrate a command of psychological expertise. Lest we forget, their ability to effectively conjure the perceived techno-scientific legitimacy of psy-discourse matters much more than their actual understanding, often rudimentary, of psychology.

Pak Karebet also tried to establish his authority by invoking the name and method of Indonesia's most famous trainer—Ary Ginanjar of ESQ fame. Karebet claims authority as a trainer by tracing his educational genealogy to, and establishing a sense of fictive kin relations with, Ginanjar:

> As Pak Ary says, from the outset it is important to establish ground rules and agree on a contract with trainees. This puts you *in charge* as a trainer. For example, when you first arrived, each of you agreed to turn off your hand phones. Earlier, I asked each of you to sit properly and really put yourself into the training. . . . In ESQ Training, Pak Ary also asks trainees to write out their ideas, thoughts, feelings, and aspirations at various stages in the training.

By referring to "Pak Ary," Karebet establishes his near-familial closeness to Ginanjar. Trainers have thus created new networks and figures of psycho-religious authority, with Ary Ginanjar and Aa Gym at the top.

Minutes after Karebet "took charge as trainer" by asking everyone to silence their phones, a loud dance-themed ring tone rang out. It would seem that the trainer was not completely in charge. Embarrassed, one of the Gema Nusa executive board members complained with disgust, "You see, even *we* can't implement the 3 Ms. How can we ask Indonesians to change if we can't even '*mulai* [begin] with ourselves' [referring to the first of Aa Gym's acronym 3 M]?" The room was silent. The ashamed trainee averted eye contact while the Gema Nusa board member groaned, "And look at that empty plastic water container on the floor. Didn't we agree to practice T-S-P (one of Aa Gym's acronyms for litter reduction)?" As he continued his plea for Gema Nusa trainees to pursue political reform through ethical self-fashioning, the dusk call to prayers rang out. He stopped midsentence, and the trainees, with the exception of a few Christians, made their way to the prayer room.

Later that night, a few trainees and I stayed awake discussing the future of Gema Nusa. Aslam, a Gema Nusa leader from South Sulawesi, remained enthusiastic despite the late hour: "Just imagine, Gema Nusa could become the next biggest organization—perhaps even bigger than Muhammadiyah or even NU! In Gema Nusa, we can have traditionalists, modernists, Muslims, and non-Muslims—all working toward the hope of a moral Indonesia. Just imagine, no more corruption, no more poverty." Wahyu, a younger trainee from Banten, agreed with this vision for social improvement but wanted to temper Aslam's enthusiasm by wondering whether or not Gema Nusa could become greater than its celebrity founder. He posed the question, "But what happens if Aa Gym should ever fall [as a public figure]? What happens to Gema Nusa? Right now everyone is excited to join Gema Nusa because of Aa Gym. Politicians donate money and get to sit beside him at dinner. It's the same with wealthy businesspeople. But how can we make Gema Nusa more than just Aa Gym?" Without an answer, we retired for the evening.

## Of Self and Nation: Islamic Therapeutics in an Era of Moral and Political Reform

On the final morning of training, Sunday, April 23, there was a collective sense that spiritual summer camp was coming to a close. Trainees exchanged phone numbers and extended invitations to visit. Some reminisced on their favorite moments of training while others discussed ideas for upcoming regional volunteer training. Civic communitas was in the air, and these liminal trainees would soon be reincorporated into Gema Nusa as trainers in their own right. We began the morning with "Teamwork Building," a session designed to get trainees to think about and discuss how to train and motivate local volunteers to carry on the cause of moral reform.

Pak Naufal opened the morning session with a simulation. He gave each group three pictures, asking them to arrange the pictures such that the final image would be a picture of two horses with two jockeys. My group finally figured it out after several minutes of swapping ideas and tediously rearranging the pictures up and down and side to side. When everyone returned to their seats, Pak Naufal asked, "Okay, so what wisdom [*hikmah*] did we gain from that exercise? What did we learn about teamwork?" Trainees chimed one by one:

> "We had to work together, each trying out a different way."
> "Patience. We had to be patient if we were to solve the puzzle."
> "We had to think *outside the box*."
> "We had to be democratic."
> "What was important was the spirit of solving problems."

Naufal wrote the responses on the board, engaged each answer, and added his own final words of wisdom:

> Just as each of you had different perceptions about how to arrange the pictures, Indonesia has an array of individuals with unique individual backgrounds and perceptions. This is the great struggle for Indonesia—different perceptions. But we must work together, honor these differences, and respect differences of opinion. This must also be the spirit of voluntarism in Gema Nusa. And when you return home, you must learn to work together. Now let's try another simulation. For this we have to go outside.

Once again, trainees were divided into groups. Each group was given an envelope with some letters of the alphabet and then instructed to put the letters together into legible words. Like the other groups, my group spread out the letters and began coming up with possible combinations. Ibu Nurbaya, a teacher from eastern Indonesia, took charge: "Okay, let's think of as many possible words as we can. They might even have something to do with Gema Nusa, don't you think?" Rizky chimed in, "True, like this one. We can spell out *nurani* [conscience]." After a couple minutes, Azhar lamented, "Yeah, but what about these extra letters? What can we spell with these?"

Slowly but surely, each group realized that they could form single words, yet they were also left with leftover letters they could not use. Aisha checked in with the other groups to see how they were faring. Group 2 came up with the word *landasan* (foundation), but they were still stuck with extra letters. And Group 3 had just formed the word *berpikir* (to think), but was also having trouble making sense of their remaining letters. Ibu Nurbaya summoned each group leader: "Even though each group is competing to finish first, perhaps we should compare notes and figure out how to make a longer sentence with words from each group." Sure enough, the extra letters from each group that did not make sense alone could be combined to complete a longer sentence. Once each group realized the complete words of the other groups, we were able to guess the final sentence, one of Gema Nusa's slogans: "Make conscience the moral foundation for how [we] think and act" (*menjadikan nurani sebagai landasan moral cara berpikir dan bertindak*). Once all of the letters and words were formed, Naufal took the group picture for the inaugural Gema Nusa "Training of Trainers."

During the debriefing session that followed, trainees once again discussed the wisdom they gained from the simulation, from "learning by doing." Ibu Nurbaya commented on the difference between working together (*kerja*

FIGURE 4.3. Trainees pose after the teamwork exercise.

*sama*) and each person or group working independently (*sama-sama kerja*). Rizky added the importance of being sincere (*ikhlas*) in our efforts: "Without each of us [groups] being sincere in the broader mission, we would not have come together. We would have been too focused on competing to finish first. In the end, none of us could finish without the others." By specifically including the ethical disposition of sincerity, Rizky underscored that developing Islamic virtues was an important part of learning to work together as a team. In doing so, he brought together psychology and civic virtue, Islam and nation.

Pak Naufal complimented the trainees on their insights. In training, he told them, it is important to begin with a simulation and then work backward to the theory:

> Wonderful observations. Now, I'd like to discuss the *teori* [theory] behind team building. This theory will help you once you return to your respective regions to conduct training and to build teamwork among your Gema Nusa volunteers. After we discuss this, each region will break away and develop your respective *action plans*.

Naufal launched into another PowerPoint presentation that invoked theories from human resources and organizational psychology. Team building, according to Naufal, goes through several stages: Forming, Storming, Norming, Performing.[18] One by one, Naufal outlined each stage. He also drew from systems theory to remind trainees, in English, that "the whole is greater than the sum of the parts." Naufal instructed trainees that synergy and togetherness in any group were influenced by situational leadership, the unity of its members, and the attention members gave to the interpersonal processes within the group. "To attain a group that is *solid, efektif, and produktif*," Naufal continued, "a group must demonstrate *trust, openness, self-realization*, and *interdependence*." Once again, a trainer summoned the (English) language of psychology and human resources to forge an ethical model of civic duty.

During the final session, "Voluntarism" (*kesukarelawanan*), this concept of civic duty was framed as both Islamic and pluralist. Prior to introducing the special guest for this session, Gema Nusa board member Pak Rosidin expounded on what it meant to be a volunteer:

> As we look ahead to National Volunteer Day, which we hope will be December 27 of this year,[19] we must reflect on what it means to be a *sukarelawan* [volunteer]. As the word suggests, volunteers are people who do something with a

willing heart [rela hati], not just to follow some movement or because they are obliged to. Rather, a willing heart must derive from a sincere effort to improve society, as a sort of national washing machine for morality [mesin pencuci bagi moral bangsa]. We've invited a special guest to help us think about how to do this, to discuss what it means to have a willing heart and to develop nurani [conscience] so that we might truly live out the al-Fatihah.[20]

That special guest was Anas Urbaningnum, one of the original founders of Gema Nusa and a rising star within the Democrat Party in Indonesia. At the time, he was implementing a nationwide system of direct local elections. He began the discussion about what it meant for nurani to become the moral foundation for the nation:

> Even though the basis of conscience lies in Islamic teachings, [with Gema Nusa] we want to value pluralism in the context of Indonesian-ness and transcend religion, ethnicity, and political organizations. The basis of building morality lies at the level of the individual, but there must also be a collective component. As an example, when the Prophet Muhammad gathered people for prayer, everyone had to be lined up neatly and orderly. Individuals prayed to God, yet they also formed a group. . . . Ideology can be analogous to faith. Islam and the Pancasila [tenets of nationalism] can be analogous. Similarly Islam and Gema Nusa can both strive toward what we Muslims call rahmatan li'l al-amin [a blessing for humankind; Arabic, raḥmatan li-l-ʿālamīn]. Gema Nusa must become a source of mercy and compassion for the growth and development of Indonesia.

At this point, Aa Gym, who had departed on umroh pilgrimage after the opening ceremonies, telephoned from Saudi Arabia to offer parting words of inspiration and motivation. He thanked everyone for traveling and reminded them of the gravity of Indonesia's moral decline:

> Developing the conscience of the nation is as important as ever. We must all join together to improve the moral situation of the nation. We must do so with sincere hearts—not because of Aa Gym and not because we hope for anything in return. This is about our future generations. I'm reminded of the story of the old man who planted a fig tree in his later years. Someone asked snidely, "What good is that? One day soon you'll be dead and won't be able to enjoy the fruits of your labor." But the old man replied, "Yes, you are right. But my children and their children will." This is the wisdom [hikmah] we must follow. May Gema Nusa become our legacy for the next generation. May we carry out the 7 Bs, the 3 Ms, and the 3 As. May our work become part of our good deeds on earth [amal soleh]. Thank you, and may the peace of God be with you.

Aa Gym's emphasis on voluntarism as a form of *amal* (good deeds) served to highlight the commensurability—not the antagonism—between religious practice and civic duty. Civic voluntarism was not cast as a secular moral obligation of this world (*dunia*; Arabic, *dūnyā*). Rather, to lead the life of a good citizen was to sow the moral seeds (*amal*; Arabic, *'amal*) that might be reaped both in this world and in the hereafter (*akhirat*; Arabic, *ākhira*).

Shortly after Aa Gym hung up the phone, Jamil Azzaini led the supplication to God that would mark the official end of the Gema Nusa TOT. With the lights dimmed, Pak Jamil kneeled down, raised his open hands in prayer, and began the supplication:

> My brothers and sisters, I want you to visualize for me. Supposing you were to die in ten years, what *amal soleh* [good/pious deeds] would you bring to Allah? What would you say you did to realize God's vision on earth? What greatest deed will you offer to God? Ya Allah. What sins will you have to account for? If you were to die tomorrow, what deeds would you bring to God? Ya Allah. What shame have we caused our family and ourselves?

FIGURE 4.4. Jamil Azzaini leads the closing supplication to God.

Jamil's voice began to crack, and tears streamed down his face. "Ya Allah, have mercy on us, give us your blessings. Ya Allah, we here want to be like Abu Bakr; we want to be like Umar. Like them, we want to be close to the Prophet Muhammad. We want to serve you, ya Allah. Have mercy on us, ya Allah." Reflections on death and the reckoning day were consciously designed to take place during the emotional climax of training sessions. This imagining of death and the judgment day figured prominently in several Islamic training programs, including MQ Training, Marwah Daud's MHMMD Training, and Ary Ginanjar's ESQ Training (see Rudnyckyj 2010). As a civic practice, volunteer training went beyond any secular model of civic duty to incorporate Islamic moral concepts of the day of reckoning and the possibilities of different fates in the hereafter.

Nearly every trainee sobbed, men and women alike. Occasionally, someone would echo Pak Jamil's pleas by adding "Ya Allah" and "Amin, ya Allah." Once the crying reached a crescendo, Pak Jamil refocused his supplication back toward the trainees. His voice became clearer and his words softer, hinting at the possibility of heavenly redemption through worldly service. "My brothers and sisters, let us imagine what deeds we might offer up [*sumbangkan*] to God. Tell yourselves, I can. And may we all begin with ourselves, and begin this day." The lights were turned on as trainees contemplated these final words and wiped the tears from their faces. Trainees took turns hugging each other, often in groups. Civic communitas was nearing its end, or perhaps preparing for a new beginning. After a few minutes, the organizers asked each trainee to come forward to greet the organizers, receive a training certificate, and say farewell to fellow trainees. The time had come for trainees to become trainers, for each of them to go forth to conduct good deeds—on behalf of both religion and nation, for this world and the hereafter.

## Conclusion

This chapter provides yet another glimpse of how Indonesian trainers summon and mobilize transnational psychology and management theory. The organizers of this "Training of Trainers" decided that knowledge of science and management theory was necessary to develop a particular kind of moral citizenship. In this iteration of the citizen-believer, "knowing thyself" is considered a necessary prerequisite to becoming a virtuous volunteer who can work to eradicate the moral ills of the nation. For this task, they framed psychological knowledge as the religious wisdom deemed necessary to cultivate civic virtue. As evidenced by the creative ways in which trainers and trainees articulate and play with such bodies of knowledge, there was no single, neatly packaged subject position of the moral citizen. Rather, trainers and trainees alike played with a broad range of psychological and management theories as they crafted their senses of self as both Muslim believers and Indonesian citizens.

The study of voluntarism and civic virtue, then, offers a unique glimpse into subject formation, one not easily reduced to rational, self-interested calculus of capitalist modernity. Andrea Muehlebach, in her research on welfare and citizenship in Italy, calls for us to "move toward conceptualizing both liberalism and neoliberalism as entailing subjects that since their inception trafficked in, bartered, and exchanged virtues and passions as much as they did money and commodities" (2012, 26). Likewise, I have argued that Islamic virtues and passions are central to ideas of citizenship. So, too, are the wider discourses of psychology. Trainers believe that Islam, psychology, and management theory possess the insights and values necessary to transform the moral fabric of the nation. Popular psychology and management theory lent trainers a certain amount of social capital. To use the title "MQ Master Trainer," or to drop the name of the most famous Indonesian trainer, Ary Ginanjar, is to summon the newfound psycho-religious authority that is now ascribed to Muslim trainers in Indonesia. Gema Nusa regional leaders were not only learning to be good citizens—they were learning to be trainers. And learning to be a trainer, at least a Gema Nusa trainer, required an education in psychology and management theory.

Psychology was also another lens through which Indonesian Muslims came to imagine the Prophet Muhammad. As argued in Chapter 3, Islamic training recalibrated the prophetic tradition such that the valued attributes of the Prophet Muhammad are framed in terms of his psychological capital and business acumen. In this chapter Gema Nusa trainer Pak Naufal summoned the Prophet as the ultimate model of the Myers-Briggs "ESFJ servant leader." Thus, it is not simply that scientific knowledge is Islamized but that such knowledge transforms the discursive practices, textual references, and contemporary articulations of Islam. Psychological expertise also provides a moral template for what it means to be a citizen-believer.

As I examine in the next chapter, Aa Gym and Gema Nusa volunteers would soon deploy their technologies of the self as a remedy for the purported "moral crisis" of pornography, especially the arrival of *Playboy* magazine. I consider how Aa Gym encouraged state actors to become the moral vanguard of public ethics. As we will see, this moral and affective discipline did not take the form of a condemnation of the state. Instead, it was an invitation—a summons—for state actors to prove their civic virtue by publicly professing their sense of shame.

# Politics of Public Piety

# CHAPTER 5

# Shaming the State
## Pornography and the Moral Psychology of Statecraft

> Whosoever is ashamed before Allah when she or he commits sin, Allah
> will also feel ashamed to torture her or him on judgment day. And
> whosoever does not feel ashamed before Allah when committing sin,
> Allah will not feel ashamed to torture her or him.
>
> —*Imam Ibnul Qoyyim*[1]

> The secular state, like others, is conceived of as a person who can be
> morally threatened.
>
> —*Talal Asad*, Formations of the Secular[2]

In early 2006 the inaugural Indonesian edition of *Playboy* magazine hit
the streets of Indonesia. At that time Indonesia's politicians were drafting
the "anti-pornography and pornographic acts" bill (RUU anti-*pornografi
dan pornoaksi*). The pornography debate was not just a procedural democracy inside congressional chambers but also a theatrics of national morality played out on the public stage. Whereas opponents of the bill worried
that this bill heralded the "Islamization of Indonesia," its proponents fretted about the decay of national morality (*moral bangsa*). The conservative
Islamic magazine *Sabili* featured a cover with the *Playboy* Bunny above the
title "Moral Terror." The foremost Islamic newspaper *Republika* featured
daily front-page articles about the anti-pornography bill in which the word
*pornografi* was crossed out with a red "X." The Islamic Defenders Front ransacked *Playboy*'s Jakarta office and "swept" bookstores that sold this "vulgar"
magazine, which in their view encourages sexual vice (*maksiat*) and is even
part of a Western conspiracy to destroy Islam.

During the anti-pornography imbroglio, Aa Gym parlayed his public pulpit into political voice through the disciplinary speech of shame (*malu*). He
summoned civil society and state actors—including President Yudhoyono—

to appear on his television and radio programs to declare their sense of shame and their support for the legislation. As part of Aa Gym's rhetorical devices and political strategies, he invoked the psycho-political language of moral crisis and shamelessness in order to endow the state with a political affect of shame, what I examine here as the "shaming of the state."

Aa Gym once told me in his Jakarta office that his mission was to create a "culture of shame" in which shame is regarded as a noble emotion that steers one away from immorality and propels one toward God. "Malu itu mulia," he said with a smile. "Shame is noble." *Malu* is more than shame. It also connotes piety and modesty (Lindquist 2009, 59). This focus on shame is more than the sound bites of Islamic psychology. I argue that Aa Gym's mobilization of shame discourse was a conscious political strategy to control the moral terms of public debate and to use affect to discipline state officials. In his critique of the Habermasian notion of the public sphere as a space for rational deliberation, Charles Hirschkind describes an Islamic counter-public concerned with affect and ethics, notably "the disciplining power of ethical speech . . . [these emergent practices] need to be analyzed in terms of a particular articulation of personal and political virtues within contemporary Islamic discourse" (2001a, 4). During the current socio-moral climate of post-authoritarian Indonesia, such "personal and political virtues" are especially evident in the ethical speech about shame and its disciplinary power over state officials. Aa Gym's shaming of the state takes the form of a public demand—a summoning for the state to serve as moral guardian for personal virtue and the common good (Salvatore and Eickelman 2004). In doing so, Aa Gym tries to endow the state—or at least his fantasy of the state—with a particular political affect and moral subjectivity. Asef Bayat describes such strategies to demand reform by the state in terms of the "socialization of the state" (2007, 204). This is a useful way of understanding the agency of Muslim actors and organizations to discipline the state, a process Bayat suggests we understand as the inverse of Foucault's governmentality. However, as I argued previously, socialization of the state in the case of Aa Gym's political maneuvering might be more aptly understood in terms of Althusser's notion of interpellation. As I describe in this chapter, Aa Gym not only disciplines the state. He hails the state, summoning its actors to publicly perform an affective embodiment of shame.

Aa Gym's goal to create a "culture of shame" reflects a style and strategy of political Islam well beyond the ballot box. Whereas some political scientists who focus mostly on electoral politics have argued that political Islam is waning in Indonesia and should be understood in terms of political economy (Mujani and Liddle 2010), I maintain that we must tend to these forms of post-Islamist politics that, though less concerned with "state capture" or the formation of an Islamic state, nevertheless attempt to endow the state with a sense of Islamic public ethics. Recent electoral results in Indonesia suggest that the idea of an Islamic state does not have wide appeal. At the same time, politicians remain anxious about appearing "un-Islamic." For Aa Gym to speak publicly about shame is thus to draw a public line in the sand between those with shame and those who, according to him, are shameless before God and nation.

Aa Gym relied not only on his own charismatic authority and public pulpit but also on strategic relationships with state and civil society actors. In this chapter, I first explain an Islamic ethics of vision—particularly the averted or lowered sexual gaze—that undergirds Aa Gym's focus on shame. Then I examine three ethnographic episodes in which Aa Gym invoked an ethics of shame to rally popular support for the anti-pornography bill: (1) the congressional hearings at which Aa Gym offered testimony; (2) Aa Gym's nationally televised program in which he speaks with then-Indonesian president Susilo Bambang Yudhoyono (SBY) about the anti-pornography legislation; (3) and the public spectacle of Aa Gym's "National Dialogue to Create a Just Anti-pornography and Porno-Action Bill." The shaming of the state is more than a public scolding (as implied in the English sense of to shame another person); rather, Aa Gym summons state and civil society actors to publicly perform their piety and sense of shame.

## Senses of Shame: Al-Ghazālī and an Islamic Ethics of Vision

Anthropologists and historians of religion have offered important insights into the role of the senses in crafting ethical, modern subjects. Leigh Eric Schmidt (2000) questioned assumptions about the primacy of vision in Enlightenment Christianity, and Charles Hirschkind (2006) has described the ethical work of listening to cassette sermons and its relationship with an ethical sensibility of the heart. However, anthropological research concerning what Hirschkind has termed the "pious sensorium" and its relation to the rise of modern subjectivities in Muslim societies (Hirschkind 2006; Meyer and Verrips 2008; Schulz 2012) offers decidedly less insight into the faculty of *seeing* as an ethical and political project. At the same time, anthropological scholarship on Islamic visual culture scholarship has often focused more on public debates about iconoclasm (George 2009) and the politics of portraying the Prophet (Asad et al. 2009) than on vision itself as ethical practice.

I turn now to a combined textual and ethnographic analysis of how an ethics of vision played an important role in the constitution of public piety during Indonesia's pornography debate. I offer two main arguments. First, I emphasize an importance of an ethics of vision itself—not just visuality, visualization, or visual culture—in order to broaden our understandings of visual culture as ethical practice.[3] Second, I argue that the importance of Aa Gym's notion of visual ethics should be understood in terms of what Gade refers to as a "technology of community" (2004, 74). In this reckoning, ethical self-cultivation is not simply about the individual in any Foucauldian or Kantian sense. Instead, technologies of the self aspire toward larger projects of political reform. The concept of the "conscience of the nation" (*nurani bangsa*) is instructive in its linguistic juxtaposition that implies a form of conscience beyond the confines of an individual, and interior, moral self. The key to developing the "conscience of the nation," Aa Gym proclaimed, was to develop a "culture of shame," and he summoned state actors to assist with his grand moral vision. Building on recent scholarship on visual culture, political affect, and the state, I describe how Aa Gym mobilized his media pulpit to endow the state itself with a moral affect of shame.

Aa Gym framed his moral psychology within the discursive fields of the Qur'an and the example of the Prophet Muhammad as well as treatises and aphorisms about the moral psychology of the heart by Al-Ghazālī (d. 1111) and Ibn 'Aṭā' Allāh al-Iskandarī (d. 1309). Manajemen Qolbu Training sessions begin with a PowerPoint slide of a hadith: "Inside the body there is a piece of flesh. If that piece of flesh is pure, so too is the entire body. However, if that flesh is soiled, so too is the entire body. Let it be known that this is the heart." Early in his television career, Aa Gym introduced his sermon about the ethics of vision by quoting a Qur'anic passage that admonishes the ethical perils of the sexual gaze: "Say to the believers to lower the gaze and to guard their carnal desires" (24:30).[4] Next, he recalled the Qur'anic story of Yusuf and Zulaykha (12:23–29) in order to underscore the importance of sexual restraint and lowering the gaze.[5] In Aa Gym's retelling of this story, Yusuf avoided giving in to his sexual temptation by averting his gaze from the lovely Zulaykha. On the other hand, she was unable to restrain her gaze and, as a result, made sexual advances toward Yusuf, even ripping his shirt as he tried to flee.[6] Aa Gym told the audience, "If left unguarded, the gaze becomes a door through which Satan enters and the heart is soiled." To underscore this ethics of vision, he recalled a verse from a popular Indonesian song (and film) "From the Eyes, Down to the Heart" (*Dari Mati, Turun ke Hati*): "Oh, my love. I fell in love with you from the eyes, down to the heart."[7]

In other sermons Aa Gym quoted Al-Ghazālī, who also explains the moral perils of sexual passion in terms of vision and the heart. Aa Gym's book publishing company translated some of Al-Ghazālī's works, and Manajemen Qolbu drew heavily from Al-Ghazālī's treatises about the heart. In Al-Ghazālī's classic *The Revival of the Religious Sciences*, he describes the moral hazard of the gaze as "fornication of the eye." God says: Tell the believers to control their eye sight. The Prophet said: "Everyone has got a share in fornication. His two eyes commit fornication by sight. . . . His heart commits fornication by thought" (3:104). Similarly, in *Alchemy of Happiness*, Al-Ghazālī quotes the Prophet Muhammad:

> "The Messenger said: 'Looking at women is a poisoned arrow from the arrows of the devil. Whoever restrains his eye out of fear of God Most High is given a faith that he perceives in his soul. . . . The eye commits adultery just as the genitals. The adultery of the eye is looking.' Consequently, it is incumbent upon whoever cannot restrain his eye to discipline his sexual craving." (2:491)

As yet another example of this ethics of the averted gaze, consider this television commercial (in Arabic with Indonesian/Malaysian subtitles) in which a man tries to overcome the visual-ethical distraction of an attractive blonde woman passing by.[8] As it turns out, the woman is actually Satan in disguise, but the man seeks refuge in Allah, thus thwarting Satan's efforts. Satan then complains that the man is too God fearing to be tempted. Thus, the moral capacity to avert the gaze is itself a reflection of one's sense of shame before God. This link between ethics and affect, vision and politics, was at the heart of Aa Gym's public campaign to rally support for the anti-pornography bill. In this reckoning, affect can be understood as the product of specific political conditions, not simply as an individualized, interior state of emotion.

This understanding of shame diverges from several important studies of shame in Indonesia and Southeast Asia that focused more on the tensions between inner states and cultural display rules of emotion (Geertz 1973; Heider 1991b; Keeler 1990; Rosaldo 1983). Building on feminist scholarship on the public and private (Gal 2002), I am interested in how the private and personal dimensions of affect are at once public and political. Johan Lindquist also pursues an analysis of shame beyond interior, felt emotions of a private self. He astutely observes that female migrants on the island of Batam often experience shame in terms of a failed nationalist project of migration and economic development:

> It is not shame-embarrassment in other Indonesian languages, such as the Balinese word *lek*—famously translated by Geertz (1973, 402) as "stagefright"—or the Javanese word *isin* that have become key emotional tropes, but rather *malu*. . . . *Malu* thus appears as an emotion (and opens up a space for analysis) that describes the failures to live up to the ideals of the nation. (2009, 14)

Lindquist demonstrates that shame cannot be understood simply in terms of culture-specific models of emotion. Shame is also a product of the cultural politics of public piety and the nation-state. The public performance of piety is not simply the display of an inner state of emotion but part of wider intersubjective relationships. As Carla Jones has also argued, "Rather than direct, exterior expressions of a hermetically sealed 'self' that is ideally unaffected by the tumult of others' feelings or expectations, personhood is in conversation with the social, formed in relation to those with whom one interacts" (2010a, 274; see also Peletz 1996). Rather than mark an interior feeling of an autonomous self, shame is produced in the intersubjective spaces among citizen-believers and can be mobilized as a powerful summons to an imagined audience such as the state. Aa Gym's mission was to valorize the moral cultivation of shame, piety, and modesty—as embodied in the lowered gaze—and to then summon state officials to publicly proclaim their sense of shame.

## Aa Gym Goes to Congress: Embodied Affect and Exemplary Authority on the Political Stage

Aa Gym began his public crusade in the chambers of the Indonesian Legislative Assembly (DPR), where he testified before a congressional special committee responsible for drafting the anti-pornography legislation. For weeks on end, the special committee listened to official testimonies by a revolving door of intellectuals, artists, preachers, and other public figures. On February 8, 2006, it was Aa Gym's turn to give testimony, this time as the spokesperson for his moral movement Gema Nusa. And, as if *Playboy* magazine were not enough to stoke the fires of anti-Western sentiment, this would also be the first occasion on which Aa Gym would make a public commentary on the offensive Danish cartoons of the Prophet Muhammad that had surfaced in Indonesia just days prior.

Two hours before Aa Gym was due to give testimony, some of his closest advisers gathered at Daarut Tauhiid's Jakarta office. Although Aa Gym also consulted *ulama* about the pornography legislation, this particular meeting had the feeling of an executive board meeting of young professionals known for their marketing and public relations savvy, not their religious credentials. As such, it is illustrative of a new network of political and religious elite. His trusted advisers on this day included the wealthy president of an Internet business, the president of a business management consulting firm, a professor of architecture who was a former Fulbright scholar fluent in Arabic with a PhD from Australia, a wealthy lawyer and office building owner, and a renegade entrepreneur. This latter adviser illustrated Aa Gym's tendency to solicit viewpoints well beyond his own sociopolitical comfort zone. This person nonchalantly waltzed into the room a few minutes late, conspicuously plopped his cigarettes down on top of his day planner (Aa Gym is adamantly pro-punctuality and anti-smoking), and proceeded to dismiss the anti-pornography bill as a useless religious intrusion into people's personal lives. Needless to say, Aa Gym's other advisers had greater sway in the end. Within an hour, Aa Gym was dictating a series of seven talking points and an official press release through which he would attempt to establish the moral vocabulary for public debate. "Media are like water buffalos," Aa Gym once told me. "You just have to lead them by the nose ring."

Scholars of Indonesia have long discussed the various streams (*aliran*) of religious politics. In the classic delineation, Clifford Geertz divides these streams into the nationalists, communists, modernist Muslims (Masyumi), and traditionalist Muslims (1959, 37). However, Aa Gym was especially adept at creating a political network that transcended any single stream and, in fact, drew its potency through its network that cut across several organizational streams. Thus, I would argue that we should pay more attention to religio-political networks (*jaringan*) than to a somewhat obsolete notion of "streams." For example, the executive committee for his moral movement transcended conventional modernists versus traditionalists and included, among others, Anindya Bakrie (from one of Southeast Asia's wealthiest families), Yusuf Mukhlis (current CEO of Antara news), Umar Hadi (media and diplomacy director at Ministry for Foreign Affairs), Anas Urbaningrum (rising star in the Democrat Party), and even a PKS member responsible for human resources development). In one sense, Aa Gym's inner circle reflects a long-standing tradition of Muslim leaders seeking patronage from wealthy businesspeople and state actors. At the same time, Aa Gym's private wealth provided greater flexibility to fund his own initiatives whenever necessary.

When we arrived at the DPR, cameras from every major television station and reporters from each major publication were in attendance. As usual, Aa Gym was ushered into the VIP room, but not before a couple of security guards and bystanders asked him to pose for a snapshot taken with their mobile phones. It was no different once we entered the hearing chamber. Awestruck politicians, some even bashful and giddy, requested photographs with Aa Gym. In her introductory remarks, Yoyoh Yusroh from the PKS gushed praise and adoration on Aa Gym as a "public figure" whose religious mission was to spread compassion and to encourage people to cultivate their moral conscience. On behalf of the special committee, she thanked Aa Gym and the others for coming to share their wisdom.

As figures of public piety, the guests invited to provide testimony were a rather motley bunch. Early in her career, Inneke Koesherawati performed in some sensual roles and was widely known as a "sizzling actress" (*artis panas*). After repenting on the public stage, she successfully transformed herself into a public icon of feminine piety and spokeswoman and model for many Islamic businesses. During her testimony, Koesherawati urged the legislature to pass the bill immediately. It was unclear whether she had actually read the bill, but she divulged to the panel that she did not want anyone to follow in the footsteps of her sinful cinematic past. She then thanked her fellow panelist Neno Warisman, or *bunda* as she was reverently addressed, for publicly protesting Koesherawati's errant ways several years earlier.[9] After her testimony Koesherawati politely asked to be excused so as not to miss the taping of her new television series, *A Wife for My Husband* (*Isteri untuk Suamiku*). In this prime-time program, Koesherawati played a pious Muslim woman who, because she cannot give birth, tries to find another woman to provide a child for her husband.

After Neno Warisman offered her support for the bill, the committee invited the commentary of Ratna Sarumpaet, a renowned playwright who had been jailed previously for her political critiques during Suharto's New Order. At the time of her testimony, she was also the director of the esteemed Jakarta arts center at Taman Ismail Marzuki. Sarumpaet finally lost her patience after listening to thirty minutes of glowing testimony about the proclaimed virtues of how the anti-pornography bill would protect women and keep women's bodies from becoming commodities. She sensed religio-political grandstanding and was disturbed by the increasingly real possibility that the bill would become law (as it later did in October 2008). Sarumpaet was furious, and as had happened many times before, she was not going down quietly. She lashed out at the special committee and was then jeered by politicians. As the title of an online report just hours later put it, "Ratna Sarumpaet Blazing with Anger [*nyolot*] at the Members of the Special Committee for the Proposed Anti-pornography Bill."[10] Staring with angry eyes is considered unrefined (*kasar*) and unbecoming of "proper" female behavior in Indonesian society. This characterization of Sarumpaet's way of looking provides yet another example of how ways of seeing and being seen are encoded with ethical and affective registers. Regardless of the headlines, Sarumpaet actually gave rather calm testimony before being interrupted repeatedly by various members of the committee. As she put it bluntly, "Religion these days has become trapped into being a tool for power."

Many in the room were uncomfortable with it being stated so plainly. After all, the committee invited her to join a panel with three of the most iconic figures of Muslim piety in Indonesia. Several committee members interrupted Sarumpaet, while others went "fishing for emotion" (*pancing emosi*). At this point, Sarumpaet became indignant: "I am horrified. It turns out that in this building even speech is restricted. This means that there is no democracy here. If I'm going to be restricted, I'll just leave because I have the feeling that the members of the legislative assembly only want to listen to your own opinions." A few male committee members motioned with their arms, as if inviting her to leave. Another put it more bluntly, "Yeah, fine. Just leave." A nervous tension filled the room as Sarumpaet rose from her seat. The head of the special committee, Balkan Kaplale, urged restraint. When things calmed down, Sarumpaet gave her succinct opinion: "I do not agree that this bill be passed. There's no need for this law. And I do not agree with being invited here as a way to justify the bill." The playwright had been scripted into a political theater not of her making. In an effort to discredit Sarumpaet, proponents of the bill emphasized her blunt and transgressive emotional comportment—not her ideas about the law. Likewise, media portrayals of Sarumpaet's performance focused on her "blazing anger," "sharp tone," and "grumbling complaints." At issue in the politics of public piety was moral comportment (*adab*), not Islamic jurisprudence (*fiqh*).

The committee saved the final word for Aa Gym. He seized the opportunity to embody a different, more refined (*halus*) emotional style. In his soothing and melodic psycho-therapeutic voice, Aa Gym thanked the committee and his fellow panelists in polite, refined Indonesian. Totally dodging any specifics of the legislation, he simply urged Indonesians to approach this debate with wisdom and common sense, pleading that they not be swayed by emotion. As he frequently reminded Indonesians who posed questions about sensitive political issues, "My position is neutral. I am not here to take sides but to urge respectful discussion." Disavowing political motive, however, is itself a political strategy. Aa Gym was well aware that neutrality was often the position least likely to alienate any of his following (and reduce his market share). At the same time, he genuinely understood his public role and specific form of propagation as that of a mediator, as the nation's therapist-in-chief. In his characteristic "heart-to-heart" fashion, Aa Gym offered soothing advice and promoted rational and peaceful civic deliberation. He humorously downplayed the demands of the Islamic right (yet in a way that reasserted the supposed moral authority of conservative Muslims): "It's not that anyone is saying that people can't be naked. It's just that there's a place for it—the shower." After Aa Gym concluded, many in the chamber burst into applause as members of the legislature swarmed around him, anxiously waiting for a photograph. Ratna Sarumpaet quietly left the chamber to share her frustrations with the media outlets waiting outside.

Aa Gym seized the opportunity to make an official statement about the Danish cartoon controversy. Months earlier, on September 30, 2005, the Danish newspaper *Jyllands-Posten* published twelve cartoons portraying Muslims, especially the Prophet Muhammad, as barbaric terrorists bent on jihad. It was only several months later that the cartoons incited condemnation and, occasionally, violent reactions by Muslims.[11] Earlier that morning, I sat beside Aa Gym as he and his advisers viewed the cartoons for the first time. Perhaps the most egregious was the cartoon of Muhammad with a bomb-shaped turban. Much the same way as the anti-pornography bill testimony, Aa Gym sought to embody the cool and calm presence of one not wont to lose control of his heart, even in the hottest of religio-political climates:

> I have seen the cartoons. My heart is crushed and ripped apart [*Hati saya remuk dan tersayat-sayat*]. Our Prophet that we love and exalt was insulted with such pictures that wound our hearts. . . . I feel very sad and wounded. . . . I very much understand the anger of the Muslim community because those pictures really hurt the heart. But at the same time I hope that everything done by those who protest will become a sort of enlightenment/awakening to the world, and that the people of this world will see that the Muslim community really does have virtuous dignity.

With such public comments Aa Gym positioned himself as therapist-in-chief for both religion and nation. He "understands their feelings" (*memahami perasaannya*) but urges restraint. Concerned with the world-wide circulation of images of Muslims clenching their fists, burning tires and flags, and shouting "God is great," Aa Gym often said that he does not want to give any more spices (*bumbu-bumbu*) to Western stereotypes linking Islam with violence. For Aa Gym, politics was a matter of public image, of managing the global brand of Islam.

Shortly after the testimony, Aa Gym asked his assistant to print the on-line news articles about the congressional hearing. Eager to see how the event would play out in the media, Aa Gym browsed two articles as we sat in his luxury van outside the warehouse store Electronic City. The first article was the one about Ratna Sarumpaet "blazing with anger," and the second article was titled "Aa Gym's Heart Was Crushed and Sliced Apart When He Saw the Cartoons of the Prophet Muhammad."[12] In the popular press, at least on that day, Aa Gym was portrayed as embodying a particular kind of ethical affect. And the front-page photo in the national newspaper *Seputar Indonesia* on the following day showed Ratna "blazing with anger" and Aa Gym with his head tilted, listening respectfully.

Aa Gym sensed the growing divisiveness of this legislation, and he was keen to win the media campaign for popular support. He tried to do this, in part, by personal alliances and political networks. Aa Gym invites and embraces key political players into the orbit of his moral polity, what one of his media advisers referred to as a sort of politics that allows him to pull together (*merangkul*) political networks that cut across traditional streams (*aliran*) of religion and politics. And once on the public stage, Aa Gym framed the debate in terms of the ethical affect of shame.

## Summoning the State for a "Heart to Heart"

Just four days after the congressional hearing on the anti-pornography legislation, Aa Gym hosted his monthly televised sermon at the national Istiqlal mosque. Indonesian president Susilo Bambang Yudhoyono (SBY) was the special telephone guest—part of a new program format called "from heart to heart."[13] Aa Gym chose to preach about the dangers of pornography and the ethical necessity for Indonesians to develop a sense of shame. In his rendering, shame is a noble emotion that enables people to fortify themselves from the seductive temptations of sexual passion and other invitations to sin. Aa Gym longs for the day when shame will save the nation from corruption and pornography. The "secret," he tells the audience, lies within our own hearts and conscience. Corruption was just a symptom, not the source of the problem. The real issue was the lack of a shame that would allow people to reel themselves back in when tempted by passion or greed:[14]

> My brothers and sisters, if we want to rise, if we want success, the secret is our-selves. . . . Discipline is a character that we shape, our own self-respect. This also includes shame. A part of this country is morally degenerate because they lack the feeling of shame. . . . Adolescents embracing each other on public transpor-tation. No shame. And their moral dignity suffers—like naughty kids, naughty women. It's the same way with those people who are, excuse me, corruptors. They are corrupt, yet [they still] show off their possessions, show off their house, show off their car—even though they know it's the product of [corruption]. Whoa! They have no shame. . . . Corruptors show off the products of their plundering. . . . [They] grab the poor people's money and don't know shame. . . . My brothers and sisters, according to the Prophet, peace be upon him, "Faith is compiled of seventy branches . . . and shame is one of them." *Alhamdulillah* we are now connected with the President.

In Gymnastiar's reckoning, shame is a moral fortress (*benteng*) that will safe-guard self and nation. When President SBY joined by telephone, Aa Gym invited him to speak about his personal views about the problem of por-nography. SBY was eager to publicize his long-standing friendship with Aa Gym, to cloak himself in the language of Islamic ethics, and even to frame the work of the state in terms of sincere religious duty. I quote the conversation at some length to give a sense of the nature of the exchange and the ways in which both Aa Gym and SBY use the public pulpit for their own purposes.

Aa Gym: *Assalaamu'alaikum Warahmatullahi Wabarakatuh.*

SBY: *Wa'alaikumsalaam Warahmatullahi Wabarakatuh* Aa Gym . . .

Aa Gym: *Alhamdulillah.* How are you?

SBY: *Alhamdulillah.* I'm fine. It's also a pleasure to be able to watch this program that is truly beautful, *The Beauty of Mercy and Compassion.* May the peace of Allah be with our Muslim brothers and sisters today, both those in Istiqlal mosque and those others who are watching this noble program.

Aa Gym: *Alhamdulillah*, thank you, Mr. President, for being willing to share your time. [I'm feeling] nostalgic; do you remember [our times together; presumably a previous occasion in Istiqlal mosque], Mr. President? Are you nostalgic? Now I'm embarrassed; you have now become president.

SBY: I am definitely one of Aa Gym's close friends. I'm only one of many in this country being tested by Allah Subhanahu Wata'ala. [I] have received this trusteeship [*amanah*] from the people, [and] I ask help from the people and from Allah so that I may work as best as I can. . . .

Aa Gym: *Alhamdulillah.* We will pray that you are given strength [by God].

SBY: . . . Day and night I think about the fate of the Indonesian people. Be they farmers, fishermen, laborers, teachers, their future and fate occupies my thoughts. So even though this job is noble [*mulia*], the tests and challenges weigh heavy on my shoulders, Aa Gym. God willing I want to work as hard as my strength allows.

Aa Gym: What is your recipe so that you can confront all of this? . . . Do you have a personal formula? The audience is filled with young prospective presidential candidates!

SBY: Amen. God willing, I will also pray for them. Earlier, you mentioned your principle to always be grateful to God, no matter the situation. . . . You asked us [the audience] to be resolute and resign ourselves to God [*tawakal*]. We cannot whine. How could a president be a crybaby! And also you asked us to take the initiative [*berikhtiar*]. . . . What strengthens my heart, Aa Gym, everything is worship [*ibadah*]. I am really sincere [*ikhlas*], even though [the burden] is heavy, and I am just an ordinary person. But I want to continue to manage this country with mercy and compassion such that there is an inner strength inside myself. *Alhamdulillah.*

Aa Gym summons the state. And President SBY, eager to cloak himself in the Arabic language of Islamic ethics, plays his part in the public theatrics of politics. At this particular moment in his political career, SBY was increasingly critiqued for being too reticent to act. He was also losing support from Islamist political parties, and the pornography debate provided a chance to demonstrate his Islamic credentials. SBY describes his role and the work of the state through carefully chosen words that conjure Islamic idioms of personal and public piety: the presidency was a noble trusteeship, his work was worship, and his heart was sincerely resigned to God's will.

Likewise, Aa Gym was eager to use the occasion to advance his own agenda. Aa Gym believed that the bill needed popular support, and he wanted to mobilize his celebrity status and marketing acumen for just such a cause. Well aware of a good sound bite on the evening news, Aa Gym continued to play with the catchy phrase the "silent majority." He claimed to speak on its behalf and hoped the catchy English phrase would gain media traction. Similar to his strategy with the national film board, Aa Gym also summoned SBY to declare a moral and political position on the imminent arrival of *Playboy* magazine:

> Aa Gym: Earlier, I was speaking with some of the community here. Yeah, you might call this community the *silent majority* who, as they say, do not have much of a voice in the media, cannot write in the newspapers, [and] cannot speak in the legislature building. But their heart moans just the same when they see things that disturb the future of the younger generation. And I believe that you, too, Mr. President, are also disturbed by that, how did someone put it earlier, "obscenity" [referring to *Playboy* magazine]? If you call it "porno," then people like to argue. So, [we'll just say] obscenity. So what do you think, Mr. President?

> SBY: I consider it very dangerous, a big threat to our nation, for future generations. Aa [Gym], for a long while I have stirred up [discussion] and declared war on things like this: pornography, *pornoaksi*, sadism, mystical programming that goes too far, drugs and other such things. . . . Because of this, at the recent meeting of the Association of Indonesian Journalists, Aa [Gym] you also attended, I asked the press and mass media to help, to not add to the vice in this country. Isn't that the spirit of *Amar ma'ruf nahi munkar* [enjoining the good, forbidding the wrong], to battle against vice? Everyone, not just the president, not just Aa Gym, not just cabinet members, governors, but every party/side must join in safeguarding the nation. This nation will wage war [on pornography]. God-willing, it will succeed.[15]

Aa Gym waxed nostalgic about the "silent majority," and President Yudhoyono pandered to the conservative Muslim constituency by summoning the Islamic language of enjoining the good and forbidding the wrong. The president, who referred to Aa Gym as his "dear friend," was well aware of the political value of a cozy public appearance with Aa Gym. Just a few months earlier, on October 28, 2005, *Republika* newspaper featured a photo of the president driving Aa Gym around the national monument in a golf cart. They were chummy, but in a political way. Aa Gym was not oblivious to the political motivations behind campaign-season photo-ops. But his conscious "positioning" in the public sphere required that he remain politically neutral, never claiming affiliation to any party or candidate. He did not enter the terrain of *fiqh* guarded by the *ulama*. And he did not make official forays into electoral politics. However, Aa Gym was keenly aware of his ability to use his celebrity status to make particular moral and political ideas go public. Bringing Manajemen Qolbu into the political arena, Aa Gym framed the debate in terms of ethics and affect.

> Aa Gym: Ladies, gentlemen, those viewing from home, surely those with conscience do not willingly watch as the morality of this nation is destroyed, the next generations buried. So, who could it be that would not like this law? How could it be that some protest?
> SBY: It's like this, Aa Gym. Some people mistranslate freedom. Or human rights. In this grand world, no freedoms are absolute, without limits. . . . Take the Danish cartoon example. . . . Freedom [along with a free press] is not allowed to destroy religious values, morality, peace, and order. And so it is that we embrace this legislation. . . . I believe [chasing profits and ruining morals through pornography] is something that is not praised by our religion.

Before bidding Aa Gym and the audience adieu, SBY reminded them that love and compassion could guide Indonesia and that all of his efforts are worship (*ibadah*). Toward the end of the program, Aa Gym finally addresses *Playboy* magazine directly, though never by name, as part of his efforts to demonstrate the link between faith and shame:

> Thank you, Mr. President . . . for joining us in solidarity, for greeting our audience. God willing, sometime soon you will have more input for us. And we will pray that you are a just leader whom, with your trusteeship, can take responsibility for leadership in this world, and later before Allah. Amin. Yaa Rabbal 'Alamin.
> Okay, audience, now where were we. Ah, yes, why don't so many people have shame anymore? . . . I am saddened by the decline of how people dress nowadays. Oh sure, some men are happy in terms of their *nafsu* [sexual passion] because *nafsu* is happy when it consumes further *nafsu*. But in terms of faith

[*iman*] this is dangerous. If the eyes frequently look at shameful things, then the heart has a tendency to harden, sexual stimulation burns, and the mind always tries to find a way to satisfy *nafsu*. . . . And if pornography spreads, and porno-action ruins morals, *na'ūdh bi-llāh min dhālik* [I seek refuge in Allah from such an awful thing]. National morality fades away.

I hear a magazine is coming. Tick-tock, tick-tock. This country is currently sick, [stuck] in a moral crisis. In no way does it need a magazine like that. We need a magazine that educates, that gives the people spirit, motivation, ethics, and dignity. Those who like [pornography] are only those who are enslaved by their sexual passion, and those against implementing regulations are only those business people that carry on with their obscene business. But we know that shame is a part of faith. *Al-aḥyā' min al-imān..* Shame is a part of faith. . . . [commercial break] My brothers and sisters in the audience and at home, we must begin to judge our level of faith by [the presence of] the emotion shame. . . . The good kind of shame is that which makes us obedient to God and steer clear of vice. This is the key to shame. So, my family, those mothers, please help your children increase their shame because, excuse me [for saying so], if their shame is lacking, their faith will also be lacking. Shame and faith go together. The more shameful, the more faithful [*makin malu, makin kuat iman*]. God Willing. [cut to commercial]

Although Aa Gym's sermons were typically more extemporaneous and free flowing, during this program he was deliberate with both content and style. He carefully crafted his theological argument about shame and faith, situated it within the diverse moral problems confronting the nation, and leveraged his personal relationship with President SBY in order to propel a moral psychology into the realm of national politics. And for his psycho-political finale, "the more shameful, the more faithful." I would never claim that Aa Gym successfully implants this model of moral psychology into the minds of his audience (or even some of his own patrons). What I would like to underscore here, however, is how Aa Gym framed the public debate in terms of an ethical vision and a sense of shame. This is the cultural politics of Islamic psychology. Shame is not just an interiorized, felt experience of inner subjectivity. Shame became the measure of an emotional economy of moral reform for both self and nation. Or, to borrow from Ann Stoler, we could say that Aa Gym used his public pulpit and political allegiances to "intervene in shaping which feelings mattered, who had a right to them, and how they were politically framed" (2009, 68–69).

The affect that mattered was shame, those who had a right to profess their shame were those who supported the anti-pornography bill (or so his story goes), and the public expression of shame was framed in terms of vision and virtue. Employing shame to discipline the state, he invited President SBY to proclaim his sense of shame on behalf of the state itself. Thus, Aa Gym summoned the political affect of shame as a way to forge the "subjective life of this formation we call the state" (Aretxaga 2003).

### Marketing the Moral Majority: or, How Piety Goes Public

With the inaugural edition of *Playboy* still looming in early 2006, activist groups across the political spectrum began to mobilize their media campaigns to either support or protest its publication. For Aa Gym, the moral righteousness of his position was never in question. What mattered was the ability to market his message in such as way as to attract the media limelight. Aa Gym envisioned a Gema Nusa rally to support the passage of the bill, except Aa Gym and his allies would not promote it as such. Instead, they would call it "The National Dialogue to Create a Just Anti-pornography and Porno-Action Bill."

Aa Gym invited some of the most famous religious, civil society, and state leaders with whom he had cultivated political, and occasionally financial, ties: Agung Laksono, head of DPR; Marwah Daud Ibrahim, head of ICMI; Din Syamsuddin, national chair of both the reformist organization Muhammadiyah and MUI; Hidayat Nur Wahid, head of MPR;[16] Dada Rosada, then-mayor of Bandung; M. Syafi'i Antonio, expert on Islamic finance and one of the original founders of Gema Nusa; Sulis, young Muslim pop singer and poet; Yoyoh Yusroh, the PKS representative pushing the bill in the special committee; and many more, including leaders from the Christian, Hindu, and Buddhist faiths. They expected over ten thousand people, including one thousand Gema Nusa volunteers. Those who disagreed with the bill, however, were apparently not invited to the "dialogue."

The "National Dialogue" was officially a Gema Nusa event, but the planning committee included MQTV producers responsible for staging and sound, as well as representatives from Aa Gym's security team, who dealt with city officials to work out street closings, escorts of government VIPs, and so on. Aa Gym was adamant that the planning committee should produce a complete schedule with every last detail, including a minute-by-minute breakdown of the event. They would need to invite national leaders (*tokoh nasional*), find sponsors, write press releases, purchase advertising, set up staging and sound, work out traffic control, set up tents for the press conference, order meals and drinks for the special guests, and carry out other necessary arrangements of the event. As discussed previously, religious propagation (*dakwah*) assumed a corporate form in which writing compelling press releases, securing corporate sponsors, and marketing the message were integral elements. To put it in terms of Aa Gym's concept of *dakwah* and marketing, the anti-pornography legislation was a "ripe durian fruit." Now they just needed to sell it to the public.

Aa Gym and his advisers discussed the public accusations that this bill signaled the "Islamization" of Indonesia. During one of the first meetings he was adamant that they position pornography as a national issue, the moral crisis of *nurani bangsa*—not as the political pet project of conservative Muslims who secretly aspire to an Islamic state. As he made clear, they would wave the red-and-white Indonesian flag, not the green banner of Islam. They mapped out key sectors of society from which they had to invite certain experts (*pakar*) and prominent leaders of the people (*tokoh masyarakat*). To position this bill as an interreligious plan to "protect the people," Aa Gym also reached out to Christian, Hindu, and Buddhist leaders to solicit their ideas and to invite them to appear on the same stage.

The choosing of particular prominent figures (*tokoh*) was also motivated by the desire to combat the argument that this bill would impinge on artistic creativity and freedom. To address this issue, Aa Gym invited his old friend Deddy Mizwar. If Aa Gym is Indonesia's "elder brother," Mizwar is the "sage grandfather." Among other television roles, Mizwar played the wise, moral protagonist in the popular series *Judgment Day Is Near*. Mizwar is a popular actor and, especially during Ramadan, promotes products ranging from Yamaha motorcycles to beef jerky. In early 2009, over a dozen political parties rallied behind Mizwar for the presidency. Despite his unsuccessful bid for president, in 2013 he campaigned largely on his moral credentials during a successful bid for vice-governor of West Java. To appeal to the younger crowd, Aa Gym also invited the young pop singer Sulis, whose hit song "Love the Prophet" was especially popular among Muslim youth at that time.

In addition to these national leaders, Aa Gym and the planning committee created a separate list of public "experts" (*pakar*). As Karen Strassler (2009b) has argued, the "expert" has emerged as an important figure of modernity, whose authority in the cultural imagination derives, in part, from increased anxieties about political authenticity in post-authoritarian Indonesia. The planning committee selected each public figure, or *publik figur* as they referred to them with the common English-Indonesian phrase, in order to target particular socioeconomic groups and to counter specific criticisms of the bill. As ringmaster, Gymnastiar would remain neutral, acknowledge people's feelings, and encourage Indonesians to maintain respectful dialogue, whatever the outcome.

Aa Gym knew that this debate would be settled as much on the public stage as in the legislative chamber. With so many prominent figures gathered, media attention would not be a problem. Why pay for media when you don't have to? The press release conjured folksy, nationalist sentiments about the "silent majority"—those pious people across the archipelago who, according to Aa Gym, may not have material wealth or political voice but who nonetheless have maintained their moral compass of shame. During his meeting with advisers prior to testifying before congress, Aa Gym decided on the English phrase and quipped proudly, "*Silent majority.* Hey, I like the sound of that!" By this point, several weeks and sermons after his congressional testimony, Aa Gym was even more enamored by the phrase. The press release read:

> Everywhere the people are anxious about this problem [pornography]. They do not have access [to the media] and are confused about where to direct their anxious complaints. Gema Nusa wants to help channel their aspirations as the "extension of the voice" of that silent majority. This silent majority does not yet have the opportunity to come to the legislative assembly to offer its opinion, write in the media, or get time in front of the camera.

This press release consciously evokes the populist language that Soekarno, Indonesia's first president, once conjured when he described himself as the extension of the people's voice (*penyambung lidah rakyat*). The "silent majority" became the new sound bite.

The day before the rally, Aa Gym gathered the planning committee in the lower level of the mosque to hammer out final details. On this day Aa Gym had a skip in his step, as if proudly observing the public spectacle he was engineering. He would be the master of his hometown (*tuan rumah*), and he felt deeply that he was speaking on behalf of the moral majority. As always, Aa Gym prided himself in his ability to create a theatrical and energetic atmosphere that would both move and motivate the audience. Ever the showman, Aa Gym was aware that a string of consecutive speeches in the hot sun would eventually bore the audience. He also understood that simple sound bites would not convey the desired sense of widespread popular support. Aa Gym wanted to incorporate the images and excitement of "the people" (*rakyat*), something that could bind the experts and leaders with the silent majority on whose behalf they claimed to speak.

In their initial marketing efforts to create "brand awareness" in 2004, Gema Nusa leaders decided the organization needed slogans and even a song. As noted previously, they invented the slogan *Peka, Peduli, Berbuat, Berjuang!* (Take notice, Care about [a moral problem], Do something, Struggle!). Aa Gym wanted to transform the slogan into a public battle cry of sorts, something that would energize the audience and add to the rally's production value. He envisioned thousands of people shouting the slogan in unison. He also suggested they add hand gestures to go along with each word of the slogan. So, in the hours before one of the biggest anti-pornography rallies in Indonesia, a celebrity preacher sat with his advisers, trying to decide which hand gestures should go with which words. One person suggested that they finish the last word "struggle" with clenched fists raised high in the air. Cognizant of the perils of being branded as "angry Muslims," Aa Gym cautioned otherwise: "There is no hadith where Muhammad raises his fist up in the air. Nothing about a clenched fist conveys a sense of compassion and mercy." After more discussion, they decided that they could have a clenched fist as long as it was not the final gesture.

With the combination of slogans and gestures now decided, next they discussed how they might train the audience in the call and response, beginning with those from Daarut Tauhiid. The planning committee had already decided that hundreds of Gema Nusa volunteers, part of the DT training program Muslims Ready to Be of Use, would attend as a show of support.[17] To add to the dramatic effect, on the afternoon before the rally these volunteers would make the "long march" to a mosque near the rally site, where they would sleep that evening. Following the morning prayers, the volunteers gathered at the rally site for a brief training rehearsal of the Gema Nusa call and response. Aa Gym would shout "Gema Nusaaaa!," at which time they would shout in unison: "Peka, Peduli, Berbuat, Berjuang!"

The crowd amounted to only half of the early estimate of ten thousand people but still managed to fill the main area around the Lautan Api monument in Bandung's Tegallega Park. This monument commemorated the intentional burning of the south side of Bandung in 1946 by Indonesian soldiers as an act of defiance against British troops who were seeking to assist the Dutch to reestablish colonial rule. As discussed previously, Aa Gym frequently compared Gema Nusa volunteers to those who freely gave of their time, energies, and resources during Indonesia's independence movement.

Gema Nusa volunteers filled the first few rows of both the men's and women's sections. Behind them were thousands of ordinary citizens, mothers, fathers, sisters, and brothers who wanted to publicly express their moral and political solidarity. Some waved Indonesian flags, while others held posters and banners. One woman held a poster showing the midsection of a woman in a cut-off shirt. A hand pointed to the exposed belly button and accentuated breasts. The text read "Irreligious Woman" and "Infidel." Another poster took a more humorous tone with a picture of Bugs Bunny behind a shower curtain. Referring to the parts of the body that are expected to remain covered, the poster read: "Exhibiting *aurat* is not entertainment. Stop pornography and *pornoaksi.*" Yet another banner read, "A woman's body is not a commodity! Return women's dignity." As the special guests arrived and took their seats on the main platform, live Islamic music (*nasyid*; Arabic, *nashīd*) revved up the crowd. Two bands performed covers of Aa Gym's songs, "Take Care of Your Heart" and "The 3 Ms."[18] With the audience clapping to the beat and Aa Gym mingling with the guests on the platform above, the singers sang the final chorus, "Mulailah dengan diri sendiri, ia!" (Begin with yourself, oh yeah!).

As the last note rang out, an MQTV producer handed a wireless microphone to Aa Gym, who came in on cue at exactly 7:00 a.m. He looked out over the crowd, turned to acknowledge his esteemed guests on the stage behind him, and then turned back towards the crowd and called out, "Gema Nusaaaaaaaa!" The loud response pierced the morning air: "Peka, Peduli, Berbuat, Berjuang!"

Pleased with the dramatic effect of the call and response, Aa Gym offered his warm gratitude to those who arrived early in the morning on a hot, sunny day in the hopes of saving what he described as the deteriorating conscience of the nation. He urged Indonesians, both those for and against the bill, to use their "common sense" (*akal sehat*): "We understand [opponents' views], but we are not allowed to become angry, we are not allowed to become emotional, and we must not hurt others when dealing with this draft legislation." Aa Gym understood his role—as both as citizen and believer—to be a voice of reason, a soothing force that could calm the tensions and anxieties of the nation.

FIGURE 5.1. Gema Nusa volunteers performing the call and response.

This emphasis on restraining emotion, however, is a bit misleading. Aa Gym wanted to conjure an image of the everyday virtuous people, the *rakyat*, who still understood the moral importance of feelings like shame (or so the story goes). They were the silent majority for whom he presumed to speak: "And to those who oppose [the bill], we appeal to you to listen to the voices of the people who cannot speak in the mainstream media . . . like those millions of teachers, those tens of millions of housewives who are restless and anxious about pornography and *pornoaksi*." Aa Gym invoked this silent majority as a moral demographic, the bearers of the nation's conscience.

Aa Gym kept his formal comments brief. He relished his role as master of ceremonies for an event that included some of Indonesia's most influential political, moral, and cultural power brokers. When he introduced each guest, Aa Gym also introduced the Gema Nusa volunteers. "Gema Nusaaaaaa!" He smiled with satisfaction with each response that seemed to get louder and louder, "Peka, Peduli, Berbuat, Berjuang!" After this initial call and response, the guest would also try the call and response.

"Gema Nusa!" One by one, each of the guests spoke from their position of "expertise"—politics, entertainment, law, economics, journalism, and several religious traditions—to counter specific public critiques against the bill. Agung Laksono, head of the DPR, acknowledged differences of opinion as beneficial for Indonesia's democratic government but urged legislation that would respond to the people's anxieties concerning increased pornography. Deddy Mizwar, the actor who plays the moral protagonist in Islamic films and television melodramas, dismissed the public complaint that this law would limit artistic creativity: "This legislation will not destroy the film industry. It will actually give birth to actors and entertainers who are creative. Entertainment and art do not mean showing off a woman's body. Those who exploit the beauty of the body are not artists; they are peddlers of art." Mizwar proclaimed that a new generation of artists must possess pure and sincere hearts capable of developing moral stories. Next, attorney Humphrey Djemat tried to assuage anxieties that the bill would violate human rights or freedom of expression. Islamic economics expert Dr. Syafi'i Antonio countered the arguments that the bill would bring financial ruin to tourist destinations. He assured the audience that there has never been a case in the "history of humanity" when an increase in pornography has spurred economic growth. Marwah Daud Ibrahim, chair of ICMI, who also had aspirations for national political office, proclaimed her support for Aa Gym, Gema Nusa, and the passage of the bill with a fanciful sound bite: "If last week was national immunization week to eradicate polio, then now Indonesian people must also be immunized from pornography!"

As each guest spoke on his stage, Aa Gym appeared more and more satisfied. A few months earlier, Marwah Daud Ibrahim had invited Aa Gym to serve on the executive board of advisers for ICMI and to give the sermon for ICMI's annual meeting. During our drive back to Bandung following that sermon, Aa Gym shared with me his simultaneous sense of surprise and triumph—surprise because Muslim intellectuals seldom took him seriously and triumph on account of the circles of religious and political elite in which he now circulated. He had carefully cultivated relationships across traditional religious and political cleavages in Indonesian society in the hopes that someday he might be in a position to mobilize this network to help achieve his moral vision for the nation.

At the anti-pornography rally, Aa Gym was noticeably pleased with his capacity to acquire legitimacy and authority through his personal affiliation with politicians and public figures. When it was his turn to offer concluding thoughts, he motioned to his employees to cue the audio recording of his televised conversation with President Yudhoyono. When confronted with technical difficulties, Aa Gym opted to just read from a prepared transcript of the conversation so as not to lose the momentum of the moment. Once again, shame was at the forefront of the discourse: "the more shameful, the more faithful."

Aa Gym's sense of triumph returned when the rally ended and he was center stage, surrounded by his special guests. After the closing Gema Nusa theme song and a final call and response to the cheering audience, the special guests filed into the luxury bus and followed the police-escorted motorcade back to Daarut Tauhiid, where Aa Gym gave everyone a personal tour. On the bus, one of Aa Gym's close friends leaned over and whispered in my ear, "You know, Jim. It's not easy to herd all of these big elephants." The fact that such influential cultural and political power brokers accepted Aa Gym's invitation to appear on that day (for whatever moral, personal, or political reasons) was a testament to his standing as a public figure. Aa Gym man-

FIGURE 5.2. Aa Gym stands in moral solidarity with guests at the end of the rally.

aged to summon some of Indonesia's most prominent religious and political leaders. If only for a moment, he was at the center of an impressive network (*jaringan*) of political actors.

Aa Gym basked in this personal triumph. Whether the bill passed or not, Aa Gym had hosted some of the country's most famous Muslim voices on his stage, in his hometown, on behalf of his moral movement. He had honed his skills to parlay celebrity status into political capital. He was not content with representing a new stream (*aliran*) of politics. His strategy was to embrace several streams of politics that would help summon state actors to proclaim their sense of shame and fulfill their duty to serve as moral vanguards of the nation. In this sense, Aa Gym was not just interpellating the state. He was also surveilling the state, reminding state actors in post-authoritarian Indonesia that they were being watched and would be held accountable to fulfill their moral obligations.[19] Aa Gym had not won the moral battle against pornography with a single rally, but he had successfully managed to make shame and the silent majority go public.

President Yudhoyono signed the Anti-pornography Bill into law in late 2008. Whereas some have described the law as a watered-down version of the original bill, article nineteen of the enforcement clause ambiguously cedes authority to nonstate actors to help enforce public morality. One might interpret this as a moral victory for Aa Gym, evidence that he successfully managed to rouse state actors into performing the subjective life of shame. Such countersurveillance and moral socialization of the state can be effective only when the one dishing out the moral discipline is believed to embody that very virtue she or he espouses. When Aa Gym preached about shame as virtue, he was at the top of his religious, economic, and political game. However, ethnographic research often takes unexpected turns. Two years before the bill was finally signed into law in 2008, Aa Gym suffered a dramatic fall from public grace. In the process, he lost the public pulpit, celebrity appeal, and moral authority with which to summon the state. And his MQ empire began to crumble.

CHAPTER 6

# Sincerity and Scandal
## The Moral and Market Logics of Religious Authority

> Semakin tinggi pohon, semakin kencang angin.
> The taller the tree grows, the harder the wind blows.
>
> —*Aa Gym*

Every Thursday evening shortly before Isya prayers, Aa Gym walked the short distance from his house, up to the main road, and over to the mosque, where he delivered his weekly radio sermon, "Knowing God" (*Ma'arifatullah*; Arabic, *Ma'rifat Allāh*). Always one for detail, Aa Gym figured out exactly how many steps and seconds the walk required. Others—friends, journalists, and the occasional anthropologist—knew that this was the moment that one could ask Aa Gym a quick question. On the evening of November 30, 2006, shortly after he left his home, journalist Erna Mardiana of *Detik News* confronted Aa Gym to ask if it was true that he had secretly married a second wife. As it turned out, Aa Gym had indeed married a second wife several months earlier. He was well aware that his public image, his brand narrative, was on the line. Immediately after his sermon that evening, Aa Gym worked behind the scenes to persuade several news agencies to wait before publishing the news, pleading with editors and producers that he needed time to "get his team ready." Aa Gym frantically tried to control many of the same media moguls and mechanisms that launched him into the national limelight. Despite his pleas, Erdiana broke the news the following morning. Within hours, journalists from nearly every national media outlet descended on Daarut Tauhiid, swarming the complex in search of gossip, visuals, and sound bites.

Aa Gym's female devotees were outraged and heartbroken when they learned that he had furtively married a second wife. Over the course of approximately two hundred interviews, these women consistently reported feeling anger, betrayal, disappointment, sadness, and even heartache (*sakit hati*). Among these feelings, the sense of betrayal was perhaps most poignant, injurious, and infuriating. Many former admirers took to the streets to shred pictures of Aa Gym, denounce his polygamy, and urge Indonesian women to boycott his programs and products. In the immediate aftermath of the news, thousands of women canceled upcoming trips to Daarut Tauhiid, President SBY instructed the minister for women's empowerment and the vice-minister of religious affairs to review the national polygamy law, and TV executives refused to extend Aa Gym's contracts. The television cameras ate it up, and for several weeks the scandal became fodder for popular gossip magazines and television programs. Seemingly overnight Daarut Tauhiid turned into a ghost town.

This celebrity scandal and the public backlash bring the cultural politics of public piety and religious authority into sharp relief. Whereas several scholars of Islam have noted the marked rise of such popular preachers and its implications for the nature of religious authority, none has described such a dramatic fall from public grace. As I argued in Chapter 1, Aa Gym's popularity was not merely an epiphenomenon of media technologies; Aa Gym

FIGURE 6.1. Dozens of kiosks and food stalls once filled this area of Daarut Tauhiid.

garnered a form of exemplary authority based on the brand narrative that he embodied and the virtues he preached. This became even clearer with his downfall. The harsh words and emotional tone of the following text message is representative of the many public statements by former devotees:

> Thank you President SBY for quickly reacting out of concern for women, children, and the people on account of the news about Aa Gym, whose words are inconsistent with his actions. Does he consider himself a prophet? Because only God and the prophets can be just. Why should we listen to this hypocrite anymore? Let us act on behalf of wives, women, and children so that men who cannot control their sexual passion do not justify Aa Gym's *poligami*. Please circulate this widely.

In this chapter I explore the cultural politics of scandal and sincerity, resentment and reparation. I examine the polygamy debacle at three levels to provide different glimpses into the religious biography of Aa Gym. First, I describe the social work of reparation with his immediate community at Daarut Tauhiid—employees, family, and financiers from whom, in most cases, Aa Gym hid the truth for months. For some, this episode became a test of faith and loyalty. For a few others, it was a dilemma of conscience that could be resolved only by departing Daarut Tauhiid and denouncing Aa Gym. Next, I consider Aa Gym's personal path of introspection and describe how he turned to Islamic self-help psychology to cope with the anguish of abandonment and to make room in his heart for the possibility of redemption. Finally, I examine Aa Gym's efforts to reach out to his followers and to rebrand his public image. Extending my previous argument that Aa Gym garnered authority based on his image as the ideal family man, I suggest that the sharp reaction against Aa Gym reflects a deeper politics of authenticity and sincerity in post-authoritarian Indonesia. Like his rise to fame, the scandal and reparation associated with Aa Gym's fall from grace must be understood in terms of economic and affective exchange relationships between a preacher-producer, corporate consumers, and fickle devotees.

## Moral Reparation at Daarut Tauhiid

Aa Gym's second marriage turned into tabloid fodder, and the public scandal rekindled a long-standing polygamy (*poligami*) debate in Indonesia.[1] For several years, each weekend at Daarut Tauhiid had the crowded, energetic atmosphere of a festival. Now the only ones dining in the nearby food stalls were local college students and scores of tabloid reporters. On the day after the news broke, I dropped by Aa Gym's front office to find people stunned and dumbfounded. Aa Gym's driver was slouched on the front stoop. Others looked gloomy, moved slowly, and murmured quietly. His secretary fielded phone calls from tourist groups who were already canceling their trips to Daarut Tauhiid. As I meandered from office to office that day, I sensed the same feeling of disbelief and despair. Neighbors gossiped about polygamy, employees fretted about their fate, and one executive even bemoaned, "The entire enterprise hinged on Aa Gym's personal brand. We were afraid of this day."

Initially, Aa Gym told reporters that he would explain everything only after he returned from the pilgrimage the following month. This made the story seemingly more scandalous. Only after the urging by his media advisers did he schedule the press conference in the hopes of damage control. Dozens of cameras and journalists packed into the front lobby of Aa Gym's Jakarta office. In well-rehearsed fashion, Aa Gym wondered how it came to be that polygamy, a practice permitted in the Qur'an, had such a negative connotation in Indonesia. Sounding a somewhat different note, he then proclaimed that God allowed polygamy as an "emergency exit."[2] When it was Teh Ninih's turn, she told the crowd of reporters that her approval was sincere (*ikhlas*). As she uttered these words, tears streamed down her cheeks. Indonesian women believed the tears, not the words. For days on end, national newscasts and popular tabloid TV programs bombarded viewers with dramatic slow-motion images of Ninih's tears, set to a melodramatic sound track, while commentators deciphered the alleged insincerity of her smile. This became arguably *the* defining moment in how the story of scandal and insincerity played out in the public sphere. The personal became political, and Aa Gym's authority and authenticity hung in the balance.

Just weeks into my research, Aa Gym spoke with me about polygamy when I joined his family vacation at the end of Ramadan. As we traveled along the West Java coast on our way back from visiting Teh Ninih's relatives, Aa Gym leaned back in the captain seat of his luxury van, glanced toward Ninih, and then confessed that he had been tempted to marry a second wife. Ninih repositioned herself and stared out the window, as if trying to escape. Aa Gym continued, "I have some friends who have two wives. But they say it's only great for about six months. Then it's just a hassle. . . . But understand, there are many men who come to me wanting me to marry their beautiful daughters." During my fieldwork, young women who knew I was traveling with his entourage occasionally asked me to give their phone numbers and glossy photos to Aa Gym. Even though I was aware of these temptations, I also knew that Aa Gym had been adamant that his assistants never leave him alone with a woman so as to avoid even the hint of impropriety. I also thought the pragmatist in Aa Gym would heed his closest advisers' admonishments to avoid the two things that could lead to his demise in the public eye, what they touted as the 2 Ps: politics and polygamy. Their advice proved sage.

Aa Gym occasionally cautioned his employees that there would come a day when Daarut Tauhiid would not be able to lean on the figure of Aa Gym. He was angered by the fact that attendance at the mandatory Monday employee gathering fell dramatically when employees knew he would not attend. Executives at MQ Corporation worried that everything hinged on the image of Aa Gym. As one insider put it, "The personal brand of Aa Gym was too closely aligned with the corporate brand MQ. We knew this and had already tried to address it so that Daarut Tauhiid and MQ Corporation could still succeed if anything were to happen to Aa Gym, God forbid." None imagined it like this, though. Aa Gym's inner circle was in shock, and Daarut Tauhiid's more than seven hundred employees were nervous about the potential fallout. Some disagreed with Aa Gym and said so publicly. Others held steadfast to the theological permissibility of polygamy, while still others argued that the Qur'an emphasizes the impossibility of a man actually living up to the stipulations of fairness and the fulfillment of a husband's material, emotional, and sexual obligations toward multiple wives. Many projected their resentment onto the second wife, their fellow employee Rini, whom they felt had maliciously broken up a happy family. Many employees—especially those processing the cancellations—began to calculate the revenue losses if the clients of MQTV and MQ Training refused to extend their contracts. The marked drop in visitors during the first few weekends felt like a harbinger of doom.

At the Monday-morning gathering the day after the press conference Aa Gym formally addressed his anxious employees for the first time since this scandal erupted. The nervous energy was palpable as hundreds of employees filed into the mosque, Aa Gym was not standing outside the entrance, where he typically received the kisses on the hand that disciples offered their *kyai* (religious teacher). Some employees performed supererogatory prayers, some fidgeted with prayer beads, and others murmured in hushed tones. They did not yet know, but many suspected, that the majority of them would soon be laid off (or in the refined language that MQ executives would employ several months later, "They were being channeled to new forms of trusteeship bestowed by God").

After the opening passage from the Qur'an and *dzikir* recitation of the ninety-nine attributes of Allah, Gymnastiar entered from the private entrance behind the pulpit. He sat down and asked one of the religious teachers to read from the weekly textbook of aphorisms written by the thirteenth-century Sufi scholar Ibn 'Aṭā' Allāh al-Iskandarī, *Al-Ḥikam*, number 142. The second paragraph read: "The key to having every good deed accepted by Allah is devout, heartfelt sincerity [*ikhlas*] to Allah. But humans are tested by arrogance; the feeling that one has already done enough good deeds is made even more wicked when done for outward show [*riya*; Arabic, *riyā'*], in the hopes of receiving praise on account of such good deeds." As they had done so many times before, Aa Gym's sermons narrated the blurry boundaries of his public and private selves. For the next several months (years, in fact), his sermons became thinly veiled treatises of self-critique, marking a departure from his previous rhetorical style that expounded his exemplary authority.

Aa Gym was beginning to understand the scandal in terms of Allah making his shortcomings known to the public. He was worried that he placed praise before piety, the adoration of the masses before the blessings of Allah. He even described himself as being "drunk with popularity."[3] Expounding on the content of the passage from *Al-Ḥikam*, Aa Gym admonished his employees:

> People think someone is virtuous [*saleh*] only because Allah covers up his or her shortcomings and disgraceful ways. . . . So don't chase after people's praise; rather seek Allah's praise. . . . People don't have a single thing. Don't fear the verbal railings of humans; fear the verbal abuse of Allah. . . . Focus on whether or not what we do is right, whether or not there is a prophetic example.

Aa Gym was looking to Islamic teachings to deal with the public backlash and to help his employees confront this ordeal.

Following this introduction, Aa Gym's close friend and longtime patron Pak Palgunadi asked to speak. Pak Pal, as he is known at Daarut Tauhiid, was a protégé of former president B. J. Habibie, former director of a multinational company (Astra International), and a guest speaker during MQ Entrepreneur Training. Pak Pal pledged continued support for Aa Gym but then suggested that the prophetic tradition they should reference is not polygamy but the Prophet Muhammad's love for his first wife, Khadijah: "As long as his first true love was still alive, the Prophet, peace be upon him, did not marry another wife. We support both of you, Aa, but especially Ninih."[4] Aa Gym had not planned on launching directly into the polygamy issue, preferring instead to first speak indirectly through the aphorisms of *Al-Ḥikam* as a way to set up the inevitable polygamy discussion. After Pak Pal's comments, he could wait no longer. Aa Gym paused, straightened his posture, scanned the audience, and, as if on cue, lowered his voice into the soothing, therapeutic tone that had cooled so many hearts before:[5]

> *Assalamu'alaikum Wr. Wb. Alhamdulillah,* this is the moment we have all been waiting for. I am about to convey something very, very important. . . . I offer my greatest apologies to those Daarut Tauhiid employees, in the event that this decision I have made has caused any unease. First, feelings of unease due to a lack of information; second, unease because it [the decision] might go against some of your convictions; and third, because this will impact Daarut Tauhiid and MQ Corporation. . . . Why take a risk as big as this? First, we see that, among a large portion of Indonesians, the word *polygamy* is still considered something awful. . . . In the text messages I received, women are so angry, so much so that they want to spit [on me], hit me if they see me; they ripped apart [my] books and do not want to look at pictures [of Aa Gym]. This is not something that should make us emotional; rather, this is a sort of map/guide showing us that not everyone is capable of hearing the word *polygamy*. Here are my thoughts. Prayer, they do it. Fasting, they do it. The pilgrimage [*haj*], *umroh*, they do it . . . but once they hear the word *poligami*, they feel stung. They get angry . . . and even gossip, as if the law of Allah were wrong. I understand . . . that it is very difficult for women to hear this word, and that's only human. But [when] it causes them to be uncertain of the truth [*tidak yakin kepada kebenaran*], especially this particular one, [when] they berate [me] and become hostile . . . this is what we must help to improve.

In this version, Aa Gym begins with the *Al-Ḥikam* passage that seemingly might lead to his reflections on his own shortcomings. Then, after being publicly critiqued by Pak Palgunadi, his formal tone seemed to change. Rather than explain the specifics of his personal reflections, he turned the ordeal into a social issue in which his ultimate point is that most Indonesian Muslims—especially those women who are angry with him—do not really accept the word of God. In the coming days, he would try on other explanations as well. In some, polygamy was natural because men's "hardware" was somehow wired differently than women's, and, therefore, men were more sexually active. When advancing that particular explanation, Aa Gym claimed that God the "Most Just" permitted polygamy as an "emergency exit." Depending on the audience, he drew more or less from textual sources. On this morning he continued in much the same scripted, point-by-point style as during his press conference:

> My brothers and sisters, after concentrated contemplation for nearly a year . . .
> I chose to go through with it. Why only now has it been made public? It's like
> with soccer, because it requires a tough team. I had to wait until the moment the
> team was strong . . . Teh Ninih, my children, and my parents. I really hoped that
> Allah would open up the [correct] time. *Alhamdulillah* with the help of God,
> the [right] time opened up a few days ago.

In fact, the secret had slowly leaked out to an ever-widening group of Aa Gym's inner circle over the previous weeks. During the Monday gatherings over the previous few weeks, Aa Gym occasionally offered what seemed at the time, at least to me, to be cryptic messages to the select few with privileged information (which did not include me), proclaiming indignantly that "it is not lying when you do not tell someone something that they do not have the right to know." Discontent was slowly building among some employees, especially with respect to the secretive nature of Aa Gym's marriage and the suspicions about his sincerity and authenticity.

The issue of sincerity was also important to Aa Gym's reparation with himself. He wondered publicly whether he was a sincere preacher or perhaps a charlatan who craved popularity and adoration. In his speech to employees, Aa Gym considered the wisdom he learned from this ordeal. He looked inward in search of the sins that may have led Allah to permit such a public catastrophe. Aa Gym spoke in terms of lessons learned:

> First . . . wisdom for me personally. This is the ideal moment to test whether
> all this time I [just] enjoyed praise, awards, popularity, [and] respect; or did I
> struggle because I wanted something I was certain [*yakin*] was true? . . . The
> second lesson: This is a chance for the Indonesian people. I want to know, has
> my propagation [*dakwah*] all this time invited people to commit to Allah's law,
> Allah's rules? Or have [they] only committed to liking Abdullah Gymnastiar?
> If they commit to the law, that would mean there is no problem. This is some-
> thing that is permitted [*halal*] . . . and the Prophet did not forbid it; his friends
> did it . . . this is *HALAL!* . . . Apparently my preaching has not yet succeeded
> in making people more certain of truths from Allah, only as far as the public

figure of Aa Gym. . . . The lesson, then, is to become more earnest in depend-ing on Allah. To whom else other than Allah? Most holy Allah, hopefully in the future one of your blessings will appear, namely, how can we get serious about relying only on you? . . . I notice that followers oriented [*berkiblat*] themselves too much toward me. This is not healthy.

The word *berkiblat*, indicating the direction toward Mecca for prayer, in-sinuates a sort of dangerous religious orientation to an idol other than God (*shirk*). The polygamy ordeal allowed Aa Gym to contemplate an issue that had long bothered him—not just disproportionate adoration from his fans but the possibility that he had become seduced by fame, caught up in his celebrity status, and had lost himself in the process.

In the context of the pending financial fallout for MQ Corporation, once again he admonished employees to depend only on Allah, not Aa Gym. Ever since my first week at Daarut Tauhiid, Aa Gym had been irritated by complaints that, when he was away from Bandung, employees were more lax and local vendors did not earn as much revenue. He felt trapped by the pressure to financially support seven hundred employees and the weight of a neighborhood whose livelihood depended on his popularity. He translated this frustration into a religious lesson:

> I believe in Allah's assistance, that Allah is not going to neglect Daarut Tauhiid. This is the moment for you, my brothers and sisters, to depend more on Allah instead of Abdullah Gymnastiar. Perhaps there will be a decline in visitors that come here, trainees, customers. . . . If you rely on Abdullah Gymnastiar, this is the moment you will feel disappointed. The one who distributes fortune is not me but Allah the all-powerful. We've already said frequently, "At some point you will no longer be able to rely on Aa." This is that moment. Some who made reservations with MQ Travel have already canceled. *No problem, good! They must straighten their intent [meluruskan niatnya].* Not because of Aa Gym, but it *must be because of Allah!!.* . . . Guests will cancel. That's good! They cannot come because of a human; they must come because they want to seek knowledge, to search for truth.

Aa Gym was especially keen to discuss the impact on his family. Here, it is important to remember that Ninih was a beloved figure at the Islamic school and served as director of the new Muslimah Center for Women. As Siti, a Daarut Tauhiid employee and mother of three, shared with me, "Ninih is virtuous, beautiful, and dedicated to Allah. How could anyone want any-thing else?"[6] Such sentiments were widespread at Daarut Tauhiid and added fuel to the argument that Aa Gym could not avert his own gaze and had simply given in to the sexual passions of the lower self (*nafsu*). Aa Gym was trying to convince himself, and others, with a different sort of explanation:

> The lesson for my wife: Some have asked, "Aa Gym, what is Ninih lacking? She is good, intelligent, virtuous, and beautiful." It's hard to express this in language. . . . This is a sign of my love for my wife. I know my wife is very good, and I want her to become even better. I long to see her become an angel in paradise someday . . . and I know . . . I am an obstacle that prevents her from loving Allah with all her heart. . . . I know that my wife will be hurt. . . . I want her to only love Allah rather than loving me. This is the truth.

When he spoke of Ninih's pain, Aa Gym began to weep. When Aa Gym was unable to continue, his friend Pak Pal stood up, embraced him, and wept with him. Many others followed suit. It was as if this scandal, and its repercussions for all that Aa Gym and others like Pak Pal had meticulously built over fifteen years, was only now hitting Aa Gym. Although Aa Gym might view it differently, it seemed to me that the carefully rehearsed script became less believable, perhaps even less palpable, to its author. My interpretation, corroborated by some, was that Aa Gym fell in love with someone outside marriage, feared Allah's wrath for adultery, and opted for polygamy. However, as Aa Gym was fond of saying to employees who offered reasons for arriving late, "An excuse only clarifies one's wrongdoing." His challenge was trying to make the explanation fit simultaneously into a particular theological worldview, national context, and affective preacher-disciple relationship.

That he wanted his wife to love Allah more than himself was just one of Aa Gym's several explanations. This particular explanation did not play out well in the national press, with women's advocacy groups, and even among many at Daarut Tauhiid. In the days and weeks following the initial news reports, Aa Gym tried to address the anxieties of his female followers and employees. He frequently asked women what exactly made them angry, and listened earnestly to some women's fears that their own husbands would take a second wife. However, Aa Gym also used religious teachings to try to shame women for their alleged inclination to gossip. Although men and women alike gossiped about him, he reserved his theological wrath for the women:

> For the Muslim women [at DT], those who fear their husband will marry again, those who suddenly hated Teh Rini [his new wife] . . . Teh Rini is just a person who was destined by Allah to become part of this. . . . Are you, my sisters, going

to hate a fellow woman, be spiteful to the point that, as Pak Miftah Farid has re-marked,[7] will make you sadistic. As we know from the Qur'an [49:12], "You shall not backbite or gossip, for this is as abominable as a person who eats the carcass of their dead relative." This is a test of faith for you women. And for the men . . . this is also a test of faith. Are you going to suddenly do the same thing, even though you don't have the knowledge? And for the Muslim people, this is the moment to test whether what they have sought all this time is just something gratifying, in accordance with their pleasure, or is what they seek what is right by Allah. Why are they so angry with me? Because [my polygamy] is inconsistent with their hopes. It should be the case that Muslims wish to be in accordance with Allah's hopes, not their own . . . but I believe every heart is in the grasp of God. Now they may hate me, but that doesn't mean they will hate me tomorrow . . . because it is not our scheming that instills love. Rather, only Allah can plant love.

For Aa Gym, his speech had initiated the healing process at Daarut Tauhiid. However, his show opened to mixed reviews. Some adamantly de-fended Aa Gym. Others believed this was a sign that their guru had lost his charisma and the blessing of God. Still others worried about the rumors of pending financial collapse and began to look elsewhere for employment. Aa Gym likened this latter group to those on a sinking ship who imme-diately run for the lifejackets rather than try to help fix the leak. During the Monday-morning gathering the following week, on December 11, 2006, he also referred to a saying of the Prophet: "Say good things, or be quiet." Displeased that employees had granted interviews with various media out-lets (many of whom were actually men), he suggested that Teh Ninih teach a course for women in how to refrain from gossiping. Aa Gym had a differ-ent strategy for shaming reporters. When several journalists were huddled outside his house, waiting for an interview or photo, he came out briefly to scold them. He inquired who among them were Muslim and then asked how they could buy rice with wages earned from ruining someone's good name. The rice they bought with such wages, he admonished, would be-come poison for them and their families.

Shortly thereafter Aa Gym departed for the hajj pilgrimage. However, the anxious rumors and gossip about Daarut Tauhiid's demise only increased. When Aa Gym returned in mid-January 2007, his Monday-morning ser-mon addressed the increasing anxiety that Daarut Tauhiid faced imminent financial disaster. Perhaps more than anyone, Aa Gym was all too aware that the success of nearly all of his businesses hinged on his personal brand. And his vertical integration model of business succeeds only when people actually consume his products and visit Daarut Tauhiid. Also weighing heavily on Aa Gym's mind was the approximately $1.3 million that he owed an investment fund for the construction of a new environmentally friendly Islamic school on the northern slopes of Bandung. That kind of money was once all in a month's work on TV. But that oasis had dried up, and now Aa Gym had to devise a new path to fortune. Whereas he once championed individual effort, persistence, and self-initiative (*ikhtiar*), now Aa Gym offered a somewhat different path to fortune.

After returning from the pilgrimage, Aa Gym opened the weekly employee meeting on January 22, 2007, by reading from *Al-Ḥikam*. During his interpretation and extrapolation on lesson number 148, he repeated one particular passage: "The only obligation is Allah, whereas those others, leave them to the compassion of Allah." Next Aa Gym asked one of the religion instructors to read Qur'anic passage 35:2, about fortune: "What God out of His Mercy doth bestow on mankind there is none can withhold: What He doth withhold, there is none can grant, Apart from Him: And He is the Exalted, In Power, Full of Wisdom" (Ali 1983). As business contracts were canceled and administrative costs piled up, Aa Gym tried to grapple with this monumental reversal of fortune.

Aa Gym's idea of *ikhtiar* began to shift from a worldly, business sense toward one defined by obedience to Allah: "Daarut Tauhiid was too focused on *ikhtiar* that we forgot about *dzikir* [remembrance of God]." He continued with a passage from the Qur'an (65:2–3): "And for those who fear God, He (ever) prepares a way out, And He provides for him from (sources) he never could imagine" (Ali 1983). Aa Gym frequently summoned these passages, but now each seemed to have a new meaning for him. Similar to the time he immersed himself in Islam after a marriage prospect broke his heart, Aa Gym's reaction was to find inspiration in the concept of *tauhid* (the oneness of God). He wanted to remind himself that nothing happens without God's approval. Therefore, he believed that he had to repent because there must be reasons that God was withholding his fortune. As Aa Gym described it, his new mission was to focus on eliciting God's help through unfailing obedience to His word.

Some found inspiration in Aa Gym's newfound zeal, while others responded less than enthusiastically to what had turned into Monday-morning pep rallies at which Aa Gym tried, often unsuccessfully, to instill spirit and confidence in hundreds of downtrodden and sluggish employees.

With a tone of excitement that tried to mask his nervousness, Aa Gym frequently asked his employees, "Do you now have spirit or not?" (*Semangat nih, tidak?*). The desired response was hundreds of voices shouting in resounding chorus, "Semangat!" However, the lackluster volume of the actual response betrayed deeper doubts and anxieties. It had already been several weeks since the news of Aa Gym's marriage. With each passing week, fewer and fewer tourists and trainees visited Daarut Tauhiid. Rumors of impending layoffs continued to haunt employees.

Low employee morale went beyond financial anxieties. For some, Aa Gym had lost his charisma (*kehilangan karisma*). As one employee put it, "It's just not the same anymore. When I was an adolescent in the Islamic school, we were always so very close to the *kyai*, but now it's just not the same with Aa Gym." Arif,[8] a recent graduate from Paramadina University, also lamented what he perceived to be Aa Gym's shift toward fatalism. "Jim, do you know about the concepts of *Qodariya* (Arabic, *qadarīya*) and *Jabariyah* (Arabic, *jabarīya*) in Islamic thought?" he continued, referencing a debate within Islamic thought about the extent to which humans control the outcomes in their lives. "What attracted me to this place was Aa Gym's emphasis that through hard work and human agency we can succeed. But now it seems like Aa is running from the problem. He's gone to the fatalist *Jabariyah* extreme." Disillusioned, Arif resigned soon thereafter.

### Reparations with Self, Reparations with God

Aa Gym was also coming to terms with the remarkable extent of the public backlash against him—the emotional fervor of his former admirers, the cold market calculations of television producers, and the former friends, investors, and politicians who abandoned him. His face was plastered on the tabloids. His children were embarrassed at school. And he received over two thousand spiteful text messages. To put it mildly, the MQ guru was struggling to manage his *qolbu*. In public and among his advisers and staff, Aa Gym worked hard to maintain a calm, cool presence to show that he was confident, that he was convinced (*yakin*; Arabic, *yakīn*) that this humiliating hullabaloo was God's will, that by increasing his own God-fearing piety (*taqwa*) he would invite God's help, and that eventually he would enjoy God's blessings once again.

Aa Gym's anxieties were not so easily masked. Shortly after his first address to Daarut Tauhiid employees, Aa Gym was scheduled to record a commercial advertisement for the company that promoted his daily inspirational text messages, *Al Qur'an Seluler*. Typically he could seamlessly record commercial after commercial with grace, humor, and unfailing oratory. But on this morning Aa Gym kept faltering, stuttering, and losing his train of thought. Take one. Cut . . . Take two . . . Cut . . . Take three . . . Cut. Even when he led prayer during this time, he occasionally (and embarrassingly) stumbled over the imam's verses. On more than one occasion his assistant in line behind him had to correct his Arabic to ensure that the prayers would be complete.

Aa Gym had entered a difficult period of introspection about his own shortcomings. He spent each Thursday night quietly reflecting in the mosque (*i'tikaf*; Arabic, *i'tikāf*). Even his sermons assumed a self-reflexive, therapeutic tone as he sorted through his vices that, he believed, caused God to allow such misfortune. He preached about the dangers of arrogance, attachment to worldly things, placing idols before God, and putting on a show for others (*riya*). He admitted feeling pangs of shame every time he saw his image plastered on banners throughout Daarut Tauhiid. He even opted to forgo his luxury van and entourage for a simpler way of travel.

Aa Gym once remarked that it was difficult, even burdensome, to have such power over an audience. He worried that he had become too enamored with his own power to move an audience. Even before the polygamy scandal, he preached about how arrogance causes people to stray from God. He loved to tell the story about a particular *muezzin* (the person who calls people to prayer) who had an astonishingly beautiful voice. As Aa Gym told the story, this *muezzin* would even pause during the call to prayer to admire the beauty of his call to prayer. So enamored with his own voice, the *muezzin* forgot that he was calling people to submit to God. After listening to this stock sermon several times after the public backlash, it became increasingly clear to me that Aa Gym was the *muezzin* of his own story.

. . .

On January 29, 2006, I rode together from Bandung to Jakarta with Aa Gym and his second wife, Teh Rini. He was scheduled to preach at the monthly Majelis MQ, a gathering of upper-middle-class professionals who routinely met each month at Jakarta's Al-Azhar mosque. However, after the polygamy ordeal and the subsequent displeasure of the power brokers at Al-Azhar, the gathering moved to the mosque at the Bank Indonesia building in central Jakarta. On this day one of Aa Gym's assistants was driving; however, before we left Bandung, Aa Gym instructed his assistant to return to Daarut Tauhiid. At that point I asked if Aa Gym would prefer to travel alone with Teh Rini, but they both encouraged me to ride along with them. Teh Rini rode in the passenger seat, thumbing through a new book that chronicled Indonesian women's reactions to Aa Gym's second marriage (Mustika 2007). "Anything positive [in the book]?" Aa Gym prodded with a gentle tone. She closed the book and sighed sadly, "No." Aa Gym tried to console her: "No need to read that stuff. Just think about getting closer to Allah." Aa Gym knew all too well that more books would be appearing soon. Just that morning, his advisers provided an update on the publication of another book, *Poligami itu Selingkuh* (Polygyny is an extra-marital affair) (Baswardono 2007),[9] which, at their prodding, was temporarily pulled from the shelves for unlawfully using the likenesses of Aa Gym, Ninih, and Rini on the cover. And before getting in the car that afternoon, Aa Gym's longtime friend and media consultant Achmad Setiyaji gave Aa Gym's assistant a folder of recent newspaper and tabloid clippings about the polygamy scandal.[10]

As Aa Gym gazed out the window at the tranquility of the terraced rice fields and the beauty of the Parahyangan Mountains that stretch between Bandung and Jakarta, he told me about the toll this trial (*ujian*) had taken on him personally:

> Yes, of course this has been hard for me. It's not easy to hear those kinds of things said about me, to read those text messages, to have people say such things, even when I have done nothing wrong, violated no religious law. . . . But, what can I do? I can only focus on my obedience to God. It is God, not me, who is capable of moving [*menggerakkan*] the hearts of humans.

Shortly thereafter, Aa Gym pulled over at a rest stop to switch to the passenger seat so that he could rest while Rini drove the rest of the way to Jakarta. Fatigued and seemingly depressed, he rested his head on the window and fell soundly asleep.

Aa Gym awoke when we were on the outskirts of Jakarta. Now rested, he tried to sound upbeat. "Jim, this is very good for your research. You get to see firsthand how I try to manage a situation like this." Not exactly sure how to reply, I simply said, "Aa, I appreciate your speaking so openly with me, but I wish it was not under these circumstances." Next, he tried to convince me (and perhaps himself) of his own optimism: "This has already been decreed by God. Now what matters is how I approach the problem, whether I have a sincere heart. What do you think; can I come back from this?" Now

FIGURE 6.2. Aa Gym devoted himself to intense introspection after his fall.

definitely unsure what to say, I replied diplomatically, "Aa, twenty years ago would you have ever imagined that you would preach to crowds of twenty thousand, that the president of Indonesia would invite you to the palace to speak with world leaders, and that you would own over twenty companies? Who am I to predict anything? Perhaps only God knows our fate."

Aa Gym was still trying to come to terms with his fall from public grace. He was concerned not only with orchestrating his comeback campaign but also with dealing with his own feelings toward those friends, admirers, and investors who had abandoned him. Despite his outward appearance and public optimism, Aa Gym was having a hard time managing his turbulent heart. His first wife, Ninih, cried often, and her psychological distress was the subject of national tabloid stories. And his second wife, Rini, also felt increasingly agitated by the paparazzi and depressed by the public condemnation and onslaught of hurtful text messages. During the drive, Aa Gym described his own sadness, bewilderment, and resentment. His children were hurt and confused. Some of his former employees criticized him publicly. His neighbors gossiped about him. His former admirers cursed him on television. Aa Gym was trying to find a way to manage his heart.

A few weeks later, at the end of his morning radio show, Aa Gym told his listeners across Indonesia that he had recently begun studying with a young guru to learn how to cope with the public backlash. As he recounted to his listeners, he was learning to surrender his worries to Allah (*belajar rela*). As it turned out, that young guru was Ahmad Faiz Zainuddin, the self-proclaimed fifth generation of energy psychology and creator of the Spiritual Emotional Freedom Technique. Four days later, Ahmad Faiz Zainuddin presented the SEFT demonstration and training session at the weekly employee gathering at Daarut Tauhiid.

Before introducing Pak Ahmad, Aa Gym shared his own experiences with SEFT. He stressed the importance of submission to the will of God: "I'm learning to recite to myself, 'Even though I've been affronted [*dihina*] and slandered [*difitnah*], I resign myself [*rela*]; I submit/surrender [*pasrah*].[11] I surrender everything to Allah.'" Looking out at the hundreds of employees (many still wondering whether or not Aa Gym could rise again), Aa Gym confessed the emotional toll the polygamy scandal had taken on him:

> The year 2007 is one of learning for Aa. . . . After I was befallen with this incident, I was truly taken aback and I felt very anxious/dismayed [*cemas*]. . . . SEFT is a form of guidance from Allah. Someone recommended Pak Ahmad, and

now I am learning how to deal with these negative emotions, to give them up to Allah. . . . Allah has entrusted so much knowledge to his servants.

Following Ahmad's presentation and live simulation on energy psychology, Aa Gym turned the discussion back to the polygamy debacle:

> May this become a virtuous deed [*amal soleh*] [for Ahmad]. . . . I am as convinced, as convinced as possible, that the energy in this room is transferable and can have an influence. What is important is that we become a community who always wants to learn. . . . Following the earthquake-like rumblings [*goncang-gancing*] a couple months ago [the polygamy ordeal], Allah has already bestowed so many gifts [*karunia Allah*] upon me. After all that, here comes this *anti-stress* method. . . . Glorious is Allah.

Much like his former devotees, Aa Gym now found himself turning to *Psikologi Islami* to overcome personal heartache, acquire worldly riches, and seek heavenly salvation.

## Reparations and Rebranding: Sincerity and Authenticity in the Public Sphere

The issue of polygamy has a long history in Indonesia. Muslim women all along the socio-religious spectrum have advanced diverse theological arguments debating the meaning of specific Qur'anic passages regarding polygamy, especially in sura An-Nisa. Some argue that Islam encourages polygamy, others suggest that it permits but discourages it, and still others maintain that Islam implicitly forbids it. Whereas some scholars of Islam and gender note an emerging patriarchy structuring Islamic belief and practice in contemporary Indonesia (Nurmila 2009; van Wichelen 2009), I suggest that we must also attend to a parallel pattern in which public icons of Muslim masculinity, such as televangelists and moral protagonists in Islamic cinema, actually endorse and valorize soft (*lembut*) and loving forms of Muslim masculinity. It was this very ideal of the loyal, doting husband that Aa Gym's polygamy had shattered.

The vast majority of public outrage against Aa Gym did not take the form of theological arguments. Although polygamy is generally frowned upon and runs counter to contemporary ideas about romantic love in Indonesia, the vast majority of the roughly two hundred people I interviewed (mostly women) believed in the permissibility of polygamy in Islamic texts and traditions. For most of his female followers who felt hurt by his second marriage, the problem was not polygamy per se, rather *Aa Gym's* polygamy. As one widely circulated text message vented, "Apparently the man who preached about heart management only really cared about lust management."[12] On YouTube another woman posted her parody of Aa Gym's hit song "Take Care of Your Heart." With a harsh voice and out-of-tune guitar, she exposed what she perceived as his insincerity. Rather than the introductory line, "Take care of your heart, don't tarnish it," she crooned: "Cruel Aa, took a young wife / Cruel Aa, took a young wife."[13] The visual caption for the song was a picture of Aa Gym with first wife, Ninih, digitally altered so that most of the image appeared scratched out with an eraser. In another example of parody, a figure known as "Aa Jimmy," who became popular as a sketch comedian during the prior Ramadan television season, dressed like Aa Gym and spoke in self-help slogans. The polygamy debacle gave Aa Jimmy plenty of material, and viewers ate it up. With unfortunate irony, Aa Gym had become a caricature of himself.

In post-authoritarian Indonesia, expertise purports to assuage anxieties and uncertainties. Yet such expertise, and those who wield it, is also subject to accusations of inauthenticity and insincerity. For women in particular, the issue was less about theology than the credibility of his personal brand. Aa Gym marketed himself as the ideal husband, and he was judged accordingly. As I argue in Chapter 1, this brand narrative mediated the relationship between preacher and disciple, affect and economy, commodity and consumption. His female admirers did not have a relationship with Abdullah Gymnastiar. They had an economic and emotional attachment to the idea— the branded fantasy—of Aa Gym. The moral and affective basis for this form of exchange was an implicit trust in the authenticity of the story. Aa Gym shattered that trust, so they shredded his pictures. The problem was one of sincerity, or perhaps more aptly put, insincerity. In the case of Aa Gym, his followers were not wary of the marketized preacher-disciple relationship or the commodification of humans or religion (see Keane 2007, 197–222). Instead, they felt betrayed by the insincerity of Aa Gym's personal brand.

Aa Gym's form of exemplary authority was thus subject to a particular moral and affective economy of exchange. This is not to reduce religious authority to rational market logics or formulaic renderings of commoditization and consumption. On the contrary, the backlash against Aa Gym suggests that economic ties that bind preacher and disciple were done and

undone by the public life of affect, fantasy, and scandal, not the mystified logics of a religious marketplace. During the present moment of late
capitalist modernity in Indonesia, Aa Gym's religious authority was created
through a different kind of preacher-disciple relationship, and his authenticity was mediated by the commoditization and consumption of his personal brand.

This language of branding and rebranding also emerged in popular discourse about Aa Gym's downfall. A special edition of *Marketing* magazine
("Erasing the Sins of Brands") described the fate of several fallen brands.
The article about Aa Gym's fall from grace ("Repositioning Aa Gym") delib-
erated whether or not Aa Gym could ever rebrand himself and, if so, would
his followers, advertisers, and investors return.[14] Old marketing habits die
hard. As part of his own psychological efforts to dust himself off, Aa Gym
tried to convince himself and others that he could turn the tide of public
sentiment. Just as marketing strategy played a pivotal role in Aa Gym's rise,
it would also shape his comeback campaign.

The idea of rebranding weighed heavily on the minds of employees at
MQ Productions, the company that produced the cassette sermons and
video autobiography that originally transformed Aa Gym into a brand
name. The article "Repositioning Aa Gym" hung next to the entryway of
MQ Productions as a constant reminder of the task at hand. This article also
circulated widely among Daarut Tauhiid employees in other divisions. With
clients refusing to renew contracts and spiritual tourists canceling weekend
trips, anxieties of "rebranding" (they used the English phrase) structured
most corporate conversations in the weeks and months following the polygamy ordeal.

Employee morale was low, and dissent was in the ranks. Nevertheless, Aa
Gym wanted to forge ahead by circulating images and messages of a harmonious family. Unfortunately for Aa Gym, rebranding got off to a bad start.
On the day of his first televised Sunday sermon following the news about
polygamy (the final sermon under that TV contract with TPI), Aa Gym
and Ninih arrived through a private rear entrance of Istiqlal mosque. His
second wife, Rini, arrived separately through the public entrance. Rini was
among the first people at Daarut Tauhiid to befriend my wife and me, but
I had not spoken with her since the debacle began (our car ride to Jakarta
with Aa Gym would be the following month). Camera crews from the gossip and entertainment television programs were combing the mosque trying

to film Rini and her son (from a previous marriage). When I coincidentally bumped into her in the upper atrium of the mosque, she seemed glad to finally see a friendly face. She was unsure whether she should, or even could, go backstage with Aa Gym and Ninih, and she did not know where to go to escape the cameras. When the media finally converged on her near the entrance, she politely excused herself and fled in a panic. Moments later, the camera crews filmed as Rini and her young son abruptly fled Istiqlal mosque in a taxi before Aa Gym even had a chance to begin the rebranding. It was this image that made the evening news, not the display of spousal solidarity between Aa Gym and Ninih. Aa Gym's desires to rebrand polygamy in terms of fairness and harmony were not off to a good start. Embarrassed, Aa Gym now required his staff to arrange Rini's transportation to and from every event.

Despite this early stumble, Ninih and Rini came to play important public roles in Aa Gym's quest to convince Indonesians (and perhaps himself) that even polygamous families could be harmonious. Ninih, a television preacher in her own right, was a cherished figure whose face frequently adorned the covers of women's magazines. Ninih hosted her own television program on MQTV during which she counseled women on personal problems. Many Indonesian women identified with Ninih, and some fretted that one day they might share a similar fate. Well aware of the public outcry following her tearful acceptance of polygamy, Ninih publicly discussed her emotional turmoil: "Of course I struggle with jealousy. That's natural. But I ask for your prayers that I might confront this with sincerity [*ikhlas*] and become closer to God. Sincerity is a process." To my knowledge Ninih has never publicly condemned polygamy. During the first few years, she continued to support Aa Gym publicly and even tried her best to perform the elder sister role toward Rini.

Aa Gym was keen to promote the idea that all was quiet on the polygamy front. Following the monthly "MQ Gathering" in Jakarta on January 29, 2007 (the day we drove from Bandung with Rini), he summoned a group of women in the parking lot: "Here, I have something to show you." Aa Gym took out his mobile phone and played a video recording of Ninih and Rini sitting side by side, pleasantly exchanging gifts. "Look! Rini gave her a beautiful watch. Don't they look happy? They didn't even know I was recording this. . . . This is different from what you imagine or hear in the media, huh?" Just weeks later Aa Gym showed the very same video to Sulistyo, a reporter for the popular magazine *Gatra*. In the feature article, "Seven Days of Dividing Love," Sulistyo quoted Aa Gym as saying, "Neither of them knew I was recording this. . . . Until now, that watch has remained on Ninih's hand."[15] As with his rise, Aa Gym's comeback relied on making the personal public in an attempt to portray the image of a harmonious family.

Aa Gym waited patiently for the right moment to appear in public with both wives. On June 23, 2007—over six months after the news broke— visitors to Daarut Tauhiid could finally have their pictures taken with Aa Gym and both wives. Despite his deliberate calculations in other arenas, this particular photo-op occurred spontaneously when Teh Rini arrived and sat in the audience during a tourist visiting session with Aa Gym and Teh Ninih. A visibly nervous Aa Gym described this as a "test run" to determine if the public was ready to accept them together. A couple hundred visitors anxiously lined up for photographs. Aa Gym's assistants had prepared two drinks on a nearby table. When a staff member realized that there should be three drinks, he hurriedly whisked away the two drinks and soon returned with three. Despite the public image being projected, apparently everyone at Daarut Tauhiid was still getting accustomed to the new arrangement.

For Aa Gym, rebranding was not just about reclaiming celebrity fame. He wanted to chart a new path of propagation and, if necessary, find a new audience that was willing to heed his message. In uncharacteristic fashion, Aa Gym drew a theological line in the sand. You were either for him or against him, but God, he claimed, was on his side. Aa Gym spoke indirectly about this shift in *dakwah* by reflecting on the Prophet Muhammad's life during his radio broadcast:

> On account of his reputation as an honest businessman, the Prophet Muhammad, peace be upon him, was bestowed the title *al-amin* [the trustworthy; Arabic, *al-amīn*]. But apparently ethics [*ahlak*; Arabic, *akhlāq*] was not enough. When the word of God was revealed to him, people did not believe him. Yet this is the very word of God that we Muslims now hold dear.

Aa Gym pronounced that, as long as his followers loved him only as a celebrity but did not believe the words of God that permitted polygamy, his twenty years of preaching universal ethics apparently had no real meaning. When he returned from the hajj pilgrimage, just over a month after the ordeal began, Aa Gym vowed to shift from his previous preaching about universal ethics (*akhlak*) toward an unabashed focus on Islamic articles of faith

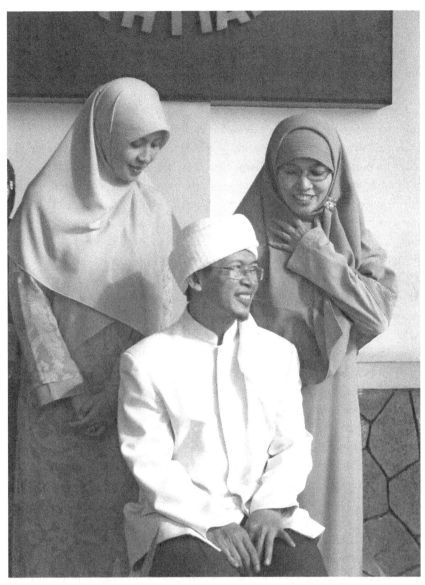

FIGURE 6.3. Left to right: Teh Rini, Aa Gym, and Teh Ninih.

(*aqidah*; Arabic, '*aqīda*). On January 15, 2007, he shared this strategy with Daarut Tauhiid managers: "Now we are going to carry the flag of *aqidah*. . . . Previously we carried universal colors. Now, let us not be afraid to show our green [color associated with Islam]."

During this meeting they also entertained the possibility that Aa Gym's fall from public grace might actually be punishment from God for their collective moral failures. As one of his closest advisers suggested, "Aa, perhaps this disaster is our penance [*kaffarah*]." Aa Gym then reflected on what he perceived to be his own mistakes: "Before, we wondered how to get people to like us, to come to us. Perhaps we were too focused on the business side. There were times when the first thing I'd ask was, OK, what's our gross revenue? . . . The other day, I felt so uneasy seeing my image everywhere." Aa Gym confessed that he had forgotten who he was. "Now," he said, "we must focus on how to attain God's blessings again." Aa Gym then declared 2007 a year of learning. He began a regimented program of Arabic language training and worked with a private tutor to deepen his knowledge of the Qur'an and example of the Prophet Muhammad (*sunna*). After losing legitimacy in matters of ethical comportment (*adab*), it appeared he would try to reclaim religious authority the old-fashioned way— through jurisprudence (*fiqh*).

On August 12, 2007, Aa Gym spoke at a political rally organized by the Islamist organization Hizbut Tahrir to promote their agenda for an international caliphate. This openly conservative repositioning did not necessarily indicate Aa Gym's support for an Islamic state. As one of his close advisers told me, his attendance at the rally was "to show that he is still a religious leader who wields religious authority and can summon the Indonesian masses." When I later asked a former Daarut Tauhiid employee about this claim, he replied with a healthy dose of skepticism, "Mr. Jim, that's just sales-speak" (*bahasa jualan aja*). While that may indeed be true, I prefer a different explanation for why Aa Gym would support Hizbut Tahrir, despite the evidence that he does not share their utopian vision for an international caliphate. Abandoned by former friends and financiers who now considered him a liability (including President SBY), Aa Gym wanted to stand in solidarity on that day with those also in attendance, such as Hidayat Nur Wahid and Din Syamsuddin, who adamantly expressed their public support for his polygamy. It was less clear whether ordinary Indonesians would buy the idea that a polygamous family could be a harmonious family.

## Sincerity and the Performance of Redemption

By mid-2007, visitors to Daarut Tauhiid were still down approximately 80 percent and showed little sign for optimism. The souvenir store that once enjoyed the prime location near Aa Gym's house was forced to close. It reopened several months later as a shoe store. And Aa Gym's conspicuous absence from television during Ramadan in 2007 seemed to suggest that the gatekeepers of television would rather market new idols than rebrand old icons.[16] One of these young tele-*dai* on the rise, Ustad Yusuf Mansur, was even chosen to preach about harmonious families (*keluarga sakinah*) at the Sharia Expo (October 24–28, 2007). Aa Gym, down but not out, was invited to lead an expo seminar about Sharia economics with his friend and loyal ally Hidayat Nur Wahid (from the Islamist political party PKS). Indeed the expo theme that year was "Sharia Business and Entrepreneurial Spirit." Still unable to play the head of a harmonious family, Aa Gym returned to the public narrative of the self-made man. The Sharia Expo also provided a glimpse into the public image of Aa Gym as a Muslim self-help guru. Whereas MQ Training had once been the market leader of the Islamic self-help industry, one of the highlights of the expo was Ary Ginanjar's ESQ alumni reunion, featuring several prominent Muslim leaders who delivered testimonials about how ESQ could solve the nation's moral crisis.[17] The Sharia Expo thus marked a subtle shift in who could speak for which aspect of Islam. However, it did not necessarily forecast Aa Gym's demise.

Over a year after the scandal first broke, on December 6, 2007, Aa Gym finally returned to television as a guest on the popular Metro TV talk show *Kick Andy*. The public relations department at Daarut Tauhiid's Jakarta office launched a massive e-mail campaign urging people to watch: "Aa Gym answers! Invite your friends, family and colleagues to watch together. Don't let this chance pass you by!" The e-mail read like a sales pitch. Contrary to this billing, Aa Gym dodged questions about *why* he took a second wife. Instead, he used the platform to perform humility, sincerely recount his life story, and describe the wisdom he had obtained from the polygamy ordeal. A teary-eyed Aa Gym praised God for stopping the "machine" that had made him famous at great cost to his personal happiness. He felt unjustly slandered by the media. He said that his task was not to cast blame but to manage his *qolbu* and to improve himself every day. As the closing credits rolled, Aa Gym sang the former fan favorite, "Take Care of Your Heart," while audience members received two complimentary books: *Aa Gym: Just as He Is* and *Aa Gym: A Spiritual Marketer*. Once again, Aa Gym marketed his life story as part of his bid to claim legitimacy.

Building on the perceived success of the *Kick Andy* show, Aa Gym next appeared on the Jak TV program *Beyond Marketing*, hosted by his friend and marketing guru Hermawan Kartajaya.[18] Once again Aa Gym told his life story. This time he identified four phases of his life, the last being the polygamy ordeal. In the following excerpts, Aa Gym explains this episode in terms of *dakwah* and marketing.

> HK: Why were Indonesian women so very angry with you?
>
> Aa: I can't really look at others' faults . . . but I can look at my own mistakes in my *dakwah* style, which was too focused on the figure of Aa Gym. . . .
>
> HK: Could you tell us about the effect on your businesses?
>
> Aa: . . . The problem was that everything depended on my personal brand. . . . Certainly we had to "say good-bye" to some [businesses] because they were not professionally managed. They relied too much on my name . . . my direct marketing company, for example. . . . Others are doing just fine . . . because from the beginning they did not sell my name. . . . The difference now is that we've strengthened our commitment to *tauhiid* [the unity/omnipotence of God]. Only One can provide fortune and that's God. . . . We don't pursue fortune. We pursue the One who distributes fortune.
>
> HK: You are a national asset. We need you because your appeal transcends religious divides. . . . Don't stay in this fourth episode too long. When does the fifth begin?
>
> Aa: This program is the beginning.

And so began the next chapter in Aa Gym's *qolbugrafi*—his brand narrative. Television executives were not yet ready to offer new contracts, but 112 radio stations across Indonesia continue to broadcast his daily program. His female admirers seldom make the pilgrimage to Daarut Tauhiid to meet Aa Gym the fantasy family man, but thousands still travel to Istiqlal mosque each month to listen to Aa Gym the healer of hearts. Seminar organizers seldom invited Aa Gym to preach about harmonious families, but they did ask him to speak about Muslim entrepreneurship. This latter market segment of Islamic business (*ekonomi santri*) appears to be the arena of contemporary religious life in Indonesia where Aa Gym's *qolbugrafi* remains credible and valued. It remained unclear to what extent his former female devotees would forgive him and whether they might, once again, seek his heart-to-heart advice to soothe their turbulent hearts.

## New Brand in an Old Bottle?

When I returned to Indonesia for follow-up research a year later (2008), Aa Gym's brother, Aa Deda, insisted on picking me up at the Bandung train station. Over the course of two years at Daarut Tauhiid, it became increasingly clear to me that Aa Deda played an important, yet often un-recognized, role in creating some of Aa Gym's self-help slogans. Every time I dropped by his office at MQ Corporation, Aa Deda would proudly show me a new stack of business management books on his desk. As "figures of modernity" go, Aa Gym was the tele-*dai* and Aa Deda more the trainer. Whereas Aa Gym liked the energy of a stadium crowd, Aa Deda preferred the intimacy of the corporate seminar. Indeed, Aa Deda could move a small audience to laughter and tears in ways that rival his brother's command of the stadium crowd.

I kept abreast of developments at Daarut Tauhiid through online and social media. Rumor had it that neither Aa Gym's family life nor his busi-nesses were faring too well. Aa Deda had recently been removed from his role as chair of MQ Corporation, but he still provided contractual services (and earned a lucrative living) as an MQ trainer. "Great to see you again. Wow, Jim, you have received bountiful blessings [*banyak rezeki*] since we last met." This was the MQ way of saying that I had put on a few pounds during the prior year of sitting idly at my desk, thumbing through field notes. As we drove through the winding and crowded streets from the train station northward toward Daarut Tauhiid, Aa Deda spoke excitedly about his new training seminars. "I recently returned from MQ in-house train-ing in Pontianak, where I tested out some new material. My new focus is how to have a 'positive heart.' Trainers have talked about positive thinking, but not positive hearts." Aa Deda was positioning his training curriculum within the increasingly competitive market of Islamic training. "The key to a positive heart is sincerity." As we approached Daarut Tauhiid, I was inter-ested to see whether it would be as desolate as it was in July 2007 when I completed the bulk of my fieldwork. We parked in front of what had once been the local distribution center for MQ household products sold by Aa Gym's direct-marketing company, MQ Blessings (MQ Baroqah). Aa Gym's followers boycotted these products, and their collective actions had material consequences. MQ Blessings was now defunct.

As we walked inside, Aa Deda described how he converted the ware-house space into an open-air food court, a joint collaboration based on a profit-sharing model between Aa Deda and local food vendors. His comparative advantage: free Wi-Fi. Food courts were increasingly popular with the thousands of digitally connected university students who lived in that area of Bandung. They sat together in groups, snacking on fried foods and surfing the Internet. With his distinctive salesperson tone of voice, Aa Deda explained: "We offer a clean environment, free Wi-Fi access, and reasonably priced food. I named it the '5-Mu Food Court.'" (Of all the self-help slogans I had learned, I could never seem to remember the 5-Mu). Aa Deda graciously reminded me: *Mutu* (quality); *Murah* (cheap); *Mudah* (convenient/easy); *Mutakhir* (trendy); *Multimanfaat* (multiuse). As we took our seats at one of the tables, Aa Deda picked up a cigarette butt from the ground and threw it in the trash. "Cleanliness is part of faith," Aa Deda reminded me. Areas associated with Daarut Tauhiid had always been no-smoking zones. Yet the tables at the "5-Mu Food Court" had ashtrays. Things around Daarut Tauhiid had changed indeed.

Keeping this observation to myself, I reached into my bag of souvenirs (*oleh-oleh*). In Indonesia, someone who returns from a trip is supposed to bring back a small gift characteristic of the area visited, perhaps a small food item, key chain, or something similar. When I was scouring the souvenir shops of Charlottesville, Virginia (where I was living at that time), I came across what I thought would be a perfect gift for Aa Deda: "Thomas Jefferson's Ten Rules," outlined by a simple wooden frame. Each of the rules was written in beautiful calligraphy. I translated the ten rules, sure to note the similarity between Jefferson's ideas and the principles of Islam and Manajemen Qolbu. "See, here, the tenth rule, 'When angry, count to ten before you speak. If very angry, count to one hundred.'"

As I read off the rules, I could tell that Aa Deda's mind was not exactly focused on the merits of what I described as Jeffersonian *hikmah* (wisdom). Aa Deda picked up the list of rules, inspected the calligraphy, and opened the multiple layers of matting that formed a dark green border around the rules. "This is amazing, Jim." All too pleased with myself, I replied, "*Alhamdulillah*. I'm glad you like the gift. I know you are always looking for new quotes to incorporate into your training seminars." Politely brushing aside my misinterpretation, Aa Deda continued, "Yes, but this has really got me thinking about something else. This is relatively simple to make and would be inexpensive to mass-produce. I could *sell* these. There's a market for things like this!" Back in Bandung for less than an hour, I was reminded once again about the relationship between commoditized religion, the self-help industry, and an Islamic ethic of entrepreneurship.

After our conversation, Aa Deda dropped me off at my guest house inside Daarut Tauhiid. After settling in, I strolled around the complex to get a sense of the atmosphere during the afternoon hours prior to Aa Gym's Thursday-night sermon. It was certainly not the vibrant atmosphere of prepolygamy Daarut Tauhiid, but neither was it the ghost town of the previous year. The streets were not filled with thousands of "spiritual tourists," yet dozens of corporate MQ trainees made their way from the MQ Guest House to the mosque for afternoon prayers. Only a couple of souvenir stores managed to stay open. And the MQ mini-mart was losing business to a new Alpha Mart that had opened one hundred meters down the road.

I was on my way to check out what was supposed to be a renovated TV studio, guest house, and hajj pilgrimage training center when a voice called out from behind. "Aa Jim." I turned around to see one of the camerapersons from MQTV who had been generous with his time and allowed me to participate in a range of meetings and set locations with MQTV. Over the course of two years we often discussed mutual interests in documentary film, so I told him I was in Indonesia this time primarily to work on a BBC documentary in West Papua. "Any chance I can join? I would just do it for the experience and networking. Maybe you have not heard yet, but MQTV went bankrupt." The public backlash against Aa Gym happened just months after he invested in satellite transmission for a local MQTV channel. Despite a brand-new production studio, MQTV simply could not sell enough advertising to pay the bills. And the producers of the major private networks were still reticent to promote Aa Gym, preferring instead a new generation of hip and younger television preachers. Aa Gym's close friend and fellow televangelist Ustad Yusuf Mansur reportedly agreed to purchase the MQTV properties until MQ Corporation was on more stable financial ground.

The audience for Aa Gym's Thursday-evening sermon (still broadcast live on national radio) filled the entire mosque, and dozens more spread out on the steps and street outside. Afterward Aa Gym joined me for a warm cup of the Sundanese ginger drink *sekoteng*. "Jim, do you notice anything different here at Daarut Tauhiid?" A few souvenir shops had managed to survive, and the food vendors and restaurant owners nearby seemed to be doing well. Other than that, though, I did not notice a radical transformation in his message or popularity. Based on several e-interviews during the prior year, my sense was that some employees were disillusioned that Daarut Tauhiid power brokers pushed out those employees who did not fit the DT mold. And from what I could glean while observing a meeting with DT leaders earlier that day, Aa Gym continued to surround himself with young male leaders eager to win his praise, perhaps at the expense of sound advice. I had learned to move slowly with such inquiries, so I replied by repeating what he discussed in his sermon, "Aa, you must feel good that the mosque is full once again for your Thursday-evening sermon. Perhaps nowadays those who come are more motivated by the religious wisdom rather than the figure of Aa Gym?" He gazed slowly around the complex and replied, "Can you feel how much stronger the sense of *tauhid* [oneness, omnipotence of God] is now? We're getting back to the basics. In everything, only for Allah. For Allah. Allah."

He then took a small amount of pleasure in turning the conversation, "And how about things in the US? I hear your economy is crashing? And Mr. Bush's war in Iraq? As I wrote years ago in my letter to Mr. Bush, violence will not change a thing. It doesn't matter how cutting edge the weaponry technology. Only love and compassion." We talked briefly about when, in 2003, Aa Gym organized the die-in to protest the impending war in Iraq. Just five years earlier, he was Indonesia's new hope in an uncertain time. Shortly thereafter, Aa Gym excused himself. "Thank you for the drink, Jim. I'm going to *iktikaf* [introspection] in the mosque this evening. Feel free to join in the mosque later, or we can talk more tomorrow." Three nights with one wife, three nights with another, and a night by himself in the mosque. He occasionally joked that the night in the mosque was always his most peaceful. "Okay, Aa, it's good to see you again."

Sliding back into my former fieldwork schedule, I joined the LP2ES entrepreneur weekend training program with yet another cohort from Bank Mandiri. Their trainees were scheduled to meet with Aa Gym. From the airport in Saudi Arabia earlier that month, Aa Gym confessed to a reporter with the infotainment tabloid *Cek & Ricek* that he had become "drunken with popularity" (*mabuk popularitas*), but now he considers himself stronger in his faith than ever before. When he arrived a few minute late, he apologized to the trainees: "Please forgive me. On Friday and Saturday I am responsible for dropping my children off at school." The narrative was remarkably similar, but his wife Ninih was no longer part of the routine. He continued as so many occasions before, "As I look out at all of you, I see a crowd with a lot of problems. Yes? . . . Don't fear the issues of this world. For example, that *badai* [sudden storm] I experienced before [referring to the polygamy scandal]. Now my sermons are more deeply felt in my soul [*terjiwai*]. I asked my employees to take down all of the signs in Daarut Tauhiid that feature my face." He looked self-consciously to his left and then apologized for the LP2ES training banner next to him that still featured a blown-up image of his turban-clad image. "There are two traits of someone who loves worldly things: they seek praise and they are afraid to be slandered. We must remember the philosophy of the valet parker. He drives luxurious cars but is never arrogant. And when cars are taken from him, he never has a soiled heart." As usual, Aa Gym opened the floor to questions. "This morning you talked about *riya* [pretending to be virtuous; putting on a show]. What are some ways to avoid becoming *riya*?" Once again, Aa Gym narrated religious wisdom through his personal life story:

> I have also been wondering, after twenty years of giving sermons, has my *dakwah* [propagation] really just been about myself? Or was it about Allah? So, now I'm in the midst of a program of repentance, and I spend a lot of my time in the mosque. I'm more focused on being a *mujahaddah* as part of an earnest struggle for Islam. I developed the "5 Nevers" [5 *Jangan*] [for doing good deeds]: One, never seek attention; two, never wish to be seen; three, never wish to be praised. Before I was praised all the time, but that praise did not mean a thing. Allah changed my fate—one of the blessings of polygamy. Seeking praise makes us forget who we really are. . . . And one's own outward humility should not be one of [furtive] arrogance. . . . Four, never wish to be respected; and five, never give while seeking something in return.

After repeating these "5 Nevers" (a different version from the original "5 Nevers"), trainees gathered to have their pictures taken with Aa Gym. No long lines, no fluttering hearts, no Ninih, no Rini.

On the following day Gema Nusa held a "National Gathering" (*Silaturahmi Nasional*). Representatives arrived from over twenty provincial offices, including many of those civic volunteers who attended the "Gema Nusa Training of Trainers" in April 2006. For Gema Nusa, it had been a sluggish eighteen months of lackluster progress and widespread uncertainty in its regional offices. Prior to the opening ceremony, I shared a coffee with Pak Mukhlis, Aa Gym's friend and marketing strategist who served as chair of Gema Nusa's board and, in 2008, had recently become the CEO for the

206 POLITICS OF PUBLIC PIETY

state-owned news agency, Antara. Pak Mukhlis knew better than anyone the financial, logistical, and motivational obstacles necessary to make Gema Nusa an effective civic organization after the fall of its celebrity leader. Nonetheless, Pak Mukhlis had genuine convictions about the virtues of working toward a more just and pious Indonesia. No stranger to the lingo of transnational pop psychology and management theory, he told me in English, "It's like Steven Covey says. It's about leaving a legacy. To do that you must articulate your inner voice, your *suara hati* [voice of the heart; conscience]." The work of Gema Nusa, he said, would be to encourage the cultivation of this inner voice in Indonesia, this "conscience of a nation" (*nurani bangsa*) that would transform the moral fabric of the nation, its leaders, and its citizens.

When Pak Mukhlis and I arrived at the opening ceremony, a couple hundred people gathered in the Daarul Hajj training building awaited the arrival of Aa Gym, Hidayat Nur Wahid (head of MPR), and Marwah Daud Ibrahim (head of ICMI). The ceremony began with a reading from the Qur'an in Arabic and translated into Indonesian. The last verse read, "Verily, never will God change the condition of a people until they change it themselves" (Ali 1983). Yet again, this passage from ar-Ra'd 13:11 was evoked to stir the spirit of reforming both self and nation.

As the designated master of ceremonies (and trainer in his own right), Pak Mukhlis tried his best to ramp up the audience before the arrival of the special guests. He began with the Gema Nusa call and response that had worked so well at the anti-pornography rally just two years earlier. He shouted into the microphone, "Gema Nusaaaaaa!" The handful of attendees who actually remembered then responded: "Peka, Peduli, Berbuat, Berjuang!" The cavernous training building seemed to swallow up those few voices and amplify the awkward lack of spirit. Pak Mukhlis then asked the audience if they remembered the other Gema Nusa acronym, SMS. Besides a few murmurs, it was clear that very few remembered the acronym, *Sukarelawan Membantu dengan Santun* (volunteers helping courteously). The band was getting back together—but only a few seemed to remember the music.

Pak Mukhlis invited Marwah Daud Ibrahim to join him onstage. He proceeded to explain how "Ibu Marwah" went to America to earn her doctorate degree, returning to Indonesia with a new paradigm for science, religion, and technology. During her time in America, he continued, Ibu Marwah was amazed at how parents and children planned ahead for their future. Hoping to instill this ethic in Indonesians whom she believed had become lazy, Ibrahim designed her own Islamic training seminar, "Managing Your Life and Planning Your Future" (MHMMD).[19] When it was Ibrahim's turn to speak, she embodied the demeanor and cadence of an aspiring political candidate. She shared several PowerPoint slides from her training program: "With MHMMD, I have tried to develop a program with which we can *bangkit bersama* [rise together] and achieve glory/prosperity. . . . It is a program to build the character of the nation [*karakter bangsa*] to be strong and benevolent." Invoking the first of Aa Gym's 3 Ms, she continued, "What Aa Gym says is true. We must begin with ourselves. We must return to our *qolbu*. . . . Before we read the *koran* [newspaper], we must read the Qur'an." As eloquent and clever as her comments were, they did little to assuage the fears of regional leaders that Gema Nusa had become just another ceremonial organization with no tangible impact. One participant later invoked the Indonesian acronym about bureaucratic inefficiency and political stagnation, NATO: No Action, Talk Only. During the question-answer period regional leaders wondered aloud about the same question Gema Nusa volunteers raised at the TOT in April 2006—could Gema Nusa maintain national prominence without a public figure like Aa Gym? It did not appear so, at least not yet.

After the morning's Gema Nusa festivities, I dashed off to have lunch with Yana and Sena, the two trainers who brought firewalking and talent mapping to Daarut Tauhiid. They were among the best trainers at Daarut Tauhiid, and both had recently resigned. Yana and Sena understood the market value of psychological and human resources discourses. Shortly after leaving Daarut Tauhiid, Sena even joined forces with Tung Desem Waringin for a training seminar, "The Secrets of a Successful Career." Once Yana and Sena left Daarut Tauhiid, they founded their own training company, MUVI. They have clients across Indonesia and are now among the most charismatic and financially successful trainers in Indonesia. When I arrived, they were both stretched out at a long table, a pile of finished plates before them. They surprised me with the presence of Abah Rama Royani, the engineer–turned–human resources consultant who invented "Talent Mapping" in Indonesia. I spoke with Rama on several occasions, first when he came to Daarut Tauhiid and later at human resources fairs in Bandung and Jakarta. Opening up his laptop, Rama showed me the new additions to his "Talent Mapping" data. Yana and Sena's new company, they proudly told me, was the only training company licensed to use his "Talent Mapping" software. Rama had the concept but lacked the trainer charisma. Rama brokered the psychological knowledge and methods, and Yana and Sena packaged and marketed the training to their clients, mostly national companies in Jakarta and local regency governments throughout Indonesia.

Yana and Sena told me that the training market was now saturated with too many trainers and seminars. They remarked that even ESQ Training was no longer as wildly popular as it had been between 2002 and 2007. In spite of Ary Ginanjar's efforts to encourage a family-like feeling among ESQ alumni, people began to feel as if they had, well, been there and done that. Trends are telling, but they can also be fleeting. Despite his best efforts, Ginanjar was unable to develop a second stage of ESQ Training that could fill the auditoriums. After hundreds of seminars in Indonesia, Singapore, Malaysia and beyond—in which over a million people joined the training— even ESQ had become somewhat passé. Many of those who once proudly donned their black ESQ alumni jackets in supermalls across Indonesia were now updating their wardrobe. As important as they might be in particular moments, training seminars and their celebrity gurus also experience what marketers refer to as a "product life cycle." Authority and economic viability, at least in the market niche of Islamic training, are intricately connected to the ability to reinvent oneself and one's magic. After lunch, Sena offered to go out of his way to take me back to Daarut Tauhiid in his brand-new, metallic blue BMW. Now, several years later, he co-owns a successful training company and broadcasts motivational quotes on Facebook and Twitter.

·   ·   ·

Ramadan had already begun when I passed back through Jakarta a few weeks later. I flipped on the television seven minutes prior to the *Maghrib* call to prayers that would end the day's fast, the time slot for what had become a staple of Ramadan television—*kultum*, an acronym meaning "seven-minute sermon." Every television station had its respective TV preacher. Indosiar featured the "funky preacher" popular with adolescents, Jefri al-Buchori. TPI touted Arifin Ilham, famous for his "national zikir." TransTV featured the rising star Ahmad al-Habsyi. But still no Aa Gym. Yet none of the others were able to command the market share that Aa Gym once enjoyed. Popular Islam was changing in Indonesia, and the allure of the television preacher appeared to be fading. Aa Gym's rise to fame was during a moment of both political uncertainty and religious aspiration in Indonesia. This political moment, coupled with the global traffic of psychological discourses, provided the context and means for the formation of affective and economic ties between new classes of preacher-producers and consuming devotees.

Aa Gym still held his monthly Sunday sermon at Istiqlal mosque. I was scheduled to meet with him before his sermon. On this day there were no television cameras; however, there were a couple thousand people in attendance, including women. Aa Gym arrived through the back entrance. He had abandoned the grand entrance of his celebrity days, when he would whip open the sliding door of his luxury van and wave to adoring fans awaiting his arrival. No one even noticed him arrive in the front seat of a modest blue sedan. When I met with him, Aa Gym was quietly preparing his sermon backstage. His copy of Quraish Shihab's book, *Parting the Curtain to God*, was open to the chapter on *riya* (pretending to be virtuous; showing off). It appeared that Aa Gym was still grappling with his own demons and doubts, wondering whether he had put himself before Allah.

During his sermon Aa Gym recounted, yet again, the story of the *muezzin* with an extraordinarily beautiful call to prayer. If performed with sincerity, surely Allah would count the call to prayer in the good deed column. But this one *muezzin*, Aa Gym told the audience, had become enchanted by the beauty of his own voice and his sincerity was suspect. Aa Gym told the audience that, to truly live sincerely (*ikhlas*), the *muezzin* needed to live by the "5 Nevers": (1) never seek attention; (2) never seek to be seen; (3) never seek praise; (4) never seek to be revered; (5) never seek reciprocity [for one's good deeds]. For Aa Gym, preaching continued to be a public reckoning of private introspection. He was much the same, but Indonesia had changed. New trainers and televangelists were on the horizon. As I walked out of the mosque after the sermon, a young man was handing out promotional fliers for a training seminar: "SEFT—Spiritual Emotional Freedom Technique! Over 200,000 already trained. Sign up Now! Early Bird Special!"

# Figuring Islam
## Popular Culture and the Cutting Edge of Public Piety

The post-authoritarian moment of hope and aspiration that provided the conditions of possibility for Aa Gym's rise to fame has given way to a renewed cynicism about Islamist politics and a skepticism about public proclamations of personal piety. The rise and fall of Aa Gym must be understood in the wider context of similar scandals that have played out on the public stage of popular culture over the last several years. In this brief conclusion, I examine the underlying moral logics of public scandal in Indonesia, explain how the rise and fall of public figures shed light on the cultural politics of public piety, and suggest that the search for new, cutting-edge ways of being modern Muslims will continue to influence the forms and figures of public piety in the future.

Those who placed their faith in Aa Gym were disappointed by his second marriage, but he was by no means the only icon of public piety who succumbed to his vices. In 2014 Anas Urbaningrum, Aa Gym's friend and adviser who was the former president of the prestigious Association of Muslim University Students (HMI) and who also served on Gema Nusa's executive council, was sentenced to eight years in prison for corruption involving bribery and kickback schemes. It was also suggested that he leveraged his prior position with the General Elections Commission (in which he traveled throughout Indonesia to implement direct local elections) to pay dubious forms of "transportation money" in exchange for support by regional Democrat Party leaders for his candidacy as chair of the Democrat Party. If the allegations were true, then some of the transgressions would have taken place precisely during the time that Urbaningrum presided over the "Civic

Voluntarism" session at Gema Nusa's "Training of Trainers" in 2006. He would have been lecturing trainees about the spirit of civic virtue while also distributing state funds, earmarked for democratic reform, in the pursuit of personal political gain. In defiance of the various charges against him, Urbaningrum proclaimed his innocence and publicly pledged to hang himself from the national monument if he were actually guilty of the alleged crimes. A wave of social media response encouraged him to do just that.

In recent years Indonesians have taken a certain delight in the public revelations of immorality and inauthenticity among self-proclaimed exemplars of piety, especially among members of the PKS. In the aftermath of disclosures of widespread corruption and massive state violence during Suharto's authoritarian rule, PKS leadership branded the political party as a clean party, free from the moral ills of public corruption and personal vice. In a quest for political power, PKS traded on its image of public piety. And, like Aa Gym, its brand suffered when the real fell short of the ideal.

President Obama's first official visit to Indonesia in 2010, broadcast live on national television, set the stage for another fall from grace. Political choreographers in both countries were eager to capitalize on the homecoming of Indonesia's adopted son. And Obama was eager to praise Indonesia as evidence that Islam and democracy can coexist. But during the official receiving line of senior government officials at the state palace, an unexpected media bombshell exploded over what might otherwise have been a routine handshake between Michelle Obama and a cabinet member, Tifatul Sembiring. As former chair of PKS and then minister of communication and information, Sembiring frequently cited Islamic ethics as his reason for routinely refusing to shake hands when meeting with Indonesian women (he also supported the anti-pornography bill, advocated state restrictions on Internet content, and proclaimed that a 2009 earthquake in his home province of West Sumatra was due to rampant immorality). But when President Obama's arrival to Indonesia was broadcast live on national television, a noticeably giddy Sembiring greeted Michelle Obama with a broad smile and double-clasped handshake.

Prominent female journalist Uni Lubis chided Sembiring via Twitter for his apparent double standard: "How is it that Tifatul [Sembiring] can shake Michelle Obama's hand, but he doesn't want to shake the hands of [Indonesian] women?" (*Kok Tifatul bersalaman dengan Bu Michelle, tapi dengan kita-kita perempuan tidak mau bersalaman*). Among the many young politicians who have cultivated quite a following on Twitter (Sembiring currently has over 840,000 followers), he tweeted his defense and blamed the "inadvertent" contact on Michelle Obama: "I was holding back my two hands, but then Michelle placed her hands way in front and [my hand] was inadvertently touched. [Then] @unilubis got offended" (*Sdh ditahan 2 tangan, eh bu michele nya nyodorin tangannya maju banget . . . kena deh. @unilubis jadi tersungging . . .* ☺). Lubis retweeted that the video footage suggested otherwise. The footage soon appeared on YouTube, was reposted on various social media, and any Indonesian with Internet access could judge for herself. Within hours, activists, politicians, and even porn stars stirred up a public campaign to challenge Sembiring's claims to sincerity, authenticity, and public piety. The controversy went viral and shortly thereafter even appeared on *The Colbert Report*.

Sembiring had to explain himself yet again in 2014 when, despite his training in computer engineering and his savvy online presence, he somehow managed to "accidentally" follow a pornographic Twitter account.

FIGURE C.I. Cartoon poking fun at Tifatul Sembiring. Courtesy of Fonda Lapod.

The public critique was more about Sembiring's insincerity than any moral stand against pornography.

Other high-ranking PKS officials also found themselves embroiled in ethical scandal. In April 2011, over two years after the anti-pornography bill was signed into law, critics of the political and religious elite took great joy in reports that PKS politician Arifinto—a vocal advocate for the anti-pornography bill—was allegedly photographed watching pornography on his laptop during a session of the DPR. One such critic reinscribed the acronym PKS (The Justice and Prosperity Party) with the unflattering name "The Sex Work Party" (*Partai Karya-Karya Seks*). Although Arifinto claimed that he immediately closed the file sent by someone supposedly unknown, the *Media Indonesia* reporter who took the photographs claimed that Arifinto actually took time to dust off the screen for a better view. At stake for PKS was a crisis of sincerity and authenticity.

More recently, in 2013, Indonesians expressed a mix of horror and pleasure when Luthfi Hasan Ishaaq, then president of PKS—the self-proclaimed "clean party that cares" (*bersih dan peduli*)—was indicted for corruption in a bribery case involving beef imports. Once again, PKS's detractors used digital and social media to challenge political authority and religious authenticity by reinscribing the acronym of PKS with uncomplimentary meanings. One critic referred to PKS as the "Corruption and Prosperity Party" (*Partai Korupsi Sejahtera*). As Karen Strassler has observed, "Political communications thus travel from medium to medium in a complex traffic, taking on, at each remediation, distinctive forms of address, authority, and authorship" (2009a, 95). In the cases of both PKS and Aa Gym, proud proclamations of piety were transformed into public unveilings of purported insincerity and hypocrisy. And logos, slogans, and visual images often become the locus of such critiques and served as the site for the remediation of personal and political brands. In marketing parlance, PKS was losing control of its brand narrative.

Scholars of Indonesia have sought to understand how the idea of authenticity figures into the forms and preoccupations of politics in post-authoritarian Indonesia. An excellent and expanding body of scholarship (Barker et al. 2009; Jones 2010b; Lindsey 2001; Siegel 1998; Strassler 2009a) explores the crisis of authenticity through the neologism *aspal*, derived from combining *asli* (genuine/original) and *palsu* (fake). It could be translated as "original but false" or "the authentic fake." This specter of the inauthentic, the *aspal*, loomed especially large in state-sanctioned corruption and mass violence during the New Order. For example, one could obtain authentic fake passport documents, legal logging stamps, counterfeit money, or Gucci handbags. The concept of *aspal* thus sheds light on anxieties about the authenticity of commodities, currency, and government documents.

Likewise, I would also suggest that we can understand the cultural politics of religious scandal in terms of what we might call "*aspal* piety." However, the public outcry against Aa Gym (and others who traded on public piety) is less about the material falsity connoted by the Indonesian term *palsu* than about his purported insincerity (*keikhlasan*). What is at stake is not the inauthenticity of a material commodity but the insincerity of publicly performed piety. Indeed, public displays of piety invite suspicion about one's motives and challenges to one's sincerity (Jones 2010b, 104–112). The mediated and marketized forms of public protest—whether against PKS or Aa Gym—relish in the revealing, the unveiling, of sin and scandal among those who show off their piety (*riya*), the self-proclaimed righteous who are referred to in Indonesian with the pejorative term *sok suci*, or what could be loosely translated as "[those who think they are] so pious." Thus, the cutting edge of modernity slices both ways. What launches one into stardom can also bring about one's demise.

The phenomenon of Aa Gym offers an instructive case study insofar as his rise, fall, and rebranding illuminate a type of public figure—the televangelist–cum–self-help guru—that is greater than Abdullah Gymnastiar as an individual person (Barker et al. 2009). As Michael Lambek has observed, figures of modernity are important insofar as they "condense entire worlds within them" (2013, 271). The figure of Aa Gym consolidated the aura of media technologies and global self-help psychology with the aspirations of middle-class Muslims in search of piety and prosperity and the anxieties of Indonesian women who try to balance their careers with demands of emotional labor at home. Aa Gym offered hope in an uncertain time. With "one foot in the future" (Lambek 2013, 273), he was a harbinger for the promises of religious revival and Islamic psychology, of digital technologies and capital accumulation. This is not to say, however, that figures of modernity can survive the future they usher in. Aa Gym embodied the futuristic ideal of a soft Muslim masculinity, but to his former admirers his polygamy was evidence that his other foot was still rooted firmly in the patriarchy of the past.

Aa Gym possessed an ephemeral sort of religious authority, quite different from the more enduring kind enjoyed by conventional Muslim clerics.

He did not wield a diploma earned at a reputable Islamic school; instead, he built a name brand by promoting his self-help psychology, ethical know-how, and heart-to-heart pastoral relationship to an increasingly affluent market of Indonesian Muslims who aspired to the very success that Aa Gym claimed to embody. His popularity and legitimacy depended on consumption. Aa Gym's female followers' public protests constituted a new mar-ketized form of power in which they mobilized boycotts to challenge his sincerity, authenticity, and legitimacy. Without brand credibility, Aa Gym's personal style and self-help slogans became fodder for mockery and parody.

During the last few years Aa Gym has methodically reclaimed some of his popularity, revamped his public image, and even returned to television. Once again, thousands come to listen to his monthly sermon at Istiqlal mosque. And social media platforms, nonexistent during his early years on television, have proved a great fit with his pithy, Twitter-friendly self-help slogans. His Facebook postings routinely receive twenty-five thousand "likes." In a manner that only a few would have predicted, Aa Gym has managed to carve out a new niche for himself in the landscape of public culture and political Islam. Of course, at fifty-three years old, he is no lon-ger the embodiment of youthful piety and exuberant entrepreneurship. He has repositioned himself as a more senior public figure, yet he still retains the popular appeal of an elder brother, not the religious authority of an elder cleric. Even those Indonesians who once decried him are still inter-ested in the gossip about his family life. Aa Gym's female detractors became angry once again when Aa Gym divorced his first wife, Ninih, in 2011, but were pleased to hear the news, in March 2012, that they had reconciled and remarried. Aa Gym once again maintains his schedule of Monday afternoon through Thursday in Jakarta with Teh Rini, and Thursday night through Monday morning in Bandung with Teh Ninih.

It appeared that many Indonesian women were willing to forgive Aa Gym, or at least to allow him back into the emotional turmoil of their personal lives. As one university psychology professor recounted, his col-leagues took turns preparing material for a weekly religious study group. One of Aa Gym's former admirers composed a deep and insightful, but also humorous and practical, lesson for that week. Apparently it went well, and everyone loved that week's material. When someone asked her about how she prepared, she smiled sheepishly and admitted that she had been rereading some of Aa Gym's books. Other women I interviewed suggested that, even though they no longer idolized Aa Gym, they missed his simple and humorous teachings. Many of these women now like to watch popular preacher Ustad Yusuf Mansur, yet he lacks Aa Gym's charismatic presence and rhetorical grace.

Over the last several years TV stations have broadcast programs titled "Nostalgia for Aa Gym" and "The Metamorphosis of Aa Gym." During Ramadan 2013, Aa Gym and fellow televangelists Yusuf Mansur and Arifin Ilham starred in the Sunday-afternoon program *3 Preachers*. And beginning February 2014, ANTV (owned by Aa Gym's friend Anindya Bakrie) broadcast MQTV's program *Cahaya Hati* (Radiant heart) during the 4:00 a.m. slot. On August 9, 2014, TV One (also owned by Bakrie) featured a one-hour special, "One Hour to Get Closer with Aa Gym" as part of a series of interviews with celebrity guests and their family. Similar to his 2008 appearance on the talk show *Kick Andy*, Aa Gym used the occasion to reflect on his fall from grace. Yet it was now a redemption narrative in which he rediscovered the oneness of God (*tauhid*) and, consequently, is no longer preoccupied with showing off his piety (*riya*) to maintain his public image.

Aa Gym was not trying to simply re-create his former fame. He was no longer concerned with neutrality or the mediating role of therapist-in-chief. Breaking with tradition, in 2014 Aa Gym openly endorsed and campaigned on behalf of the presidential candidate Prabowo Subianto, who narrowly lost to the populist candidate Joko Widowo. The left in Indonesia despises Prabowo, Suharto's son-in-law, for alleged human rights violations when he served as commander of Indonesia's special forces. Nevertheless, nearly every Islamic organization and political party officially supported Prabowo (despite some dissension in their ranks). As evidence of Aa Gym's political jockeying and contemporary relevance, he was asked to deliver the sermon on the morning that Prabowo and his vice presidential candidate, Hatta Rajasa, officially submitted their candidacy to the national elections commission. Whereas many Islamist leaders and politicians praised Aa Gym for his allegiance to their preference for Prabowo, others such as liberal commentator Wimar Witoelar castigated Aa Gym and other Muslim leaders as a bunch of "bad guys" serving Prabowo's political interests. In either case, Aa Gym had successfully reinserted himself into the moral and political debates of the nation.

The importance of Aa Gym as a figure of modernity, however, goes well beyond whether or not he can regain some semblance of his prior glory. I am not sure that anyone—even pre-polygamy Aa Gym—could once again achieve that particular kind of celebrity glory. To be sure, new figures have garnered public adoration, but not that Islamic celebrity status during the uncertain, yet hopeful, dawn of post-authoritarian Indonesia. That moment has passed. In this shifting landscape of religion, politics, and popular culture, political alliances are forged and broken, public figures rise and fall, and personal brands come and go. Many Indonesians continue to search for the "cutting edge," the *mutakhir* of Muslim modernity, and they try to emulate the public figures who purport to embody its aura (in whatever iteration that might take). The idea of the cutting edge remains, but its public icons change.

New ways of being Muslim, of practicing Islam, and of consuming Islam will continue to come in and out of fashion. The popularity of *Psikologi Islami*, self-help gurus, and Islamic training is not a given. These, too, will shift with the desires and anxieties of religious consumers in search of success in this life and the hereafter. Further still, the definition of *sukses* and the means by which Indonesian Muslims pursue it—through books, training sessions, or mobile devices—will undoubtedly change. Thus, broad conclusions about the "state of Islam" or the "nature" of religious authority in Indonesia are as fleeting as the empirical conditions on which such conclusions are drawn. The mosaic of Islam in Indonesia is never a finished piece, displayed in all of its grandiosity. New artisans are constantly adding (and selling) new materials, new colors, and new techniques. The people, products, and ideas that resonate with Muslims will be simultaneously rooted in Islamic traditions and reflect the aura of the cutting edge. And those who embody that cutting edge of modernity will continue to play an important role, if only for a while, in the political theater of popular Islam.

# Notes

*Notes to Acknowledgments*

  1. Anna Gade's illuminating book on emotion and Qur'anic recitation (2004) had not yet been published.

  2. There are actually two separate departments for Islamic training under MQ Corporation, one under the rubric of MQ Training, the other part of LP2ES (Institute for Education and Training in Sharia Economy). I will gloss these as MQ Training but will note when I am referring to specific modules of training, such as Entrepreneur Training or Civic Training.

  3. These other training programs included Marwah Daud Ibrahim's "Managing Your Life and Planning Your Future" (Mengelola Hidup dan Merencanakan Masa Depan, or MHMMD); Ary Ginanjar Agustian's ESQ (Emotional Spiritual Quotient) Training; and Jamil Azzaini's "Kubik Leadership." Although these were among the most popular training programs, there were also dozens of lesser-known training programs and business seminars. Indonesians have imported the English word *trainer*.


*Notes to Introduction*

  1. This is the literal translation of Daarut Tauhiid's designated term *wisata rohani*. Corporate trainees were managed by two different corporate entities within Daarut Tauhiid.

  2. I translate this from the Indonesian language used during MQ Training. However, all referenced passages of the Qur'an are from Ali (1983).

  3. See Kugle (2007) and Gianotti (2001) for a detailed account of the moral psychology of the heart in Sufism.

4. Hirschkind (2006) describes the necessary cultivation of affective and moral dispositions of the heart.

5. Geroulanos 2014; Kloos 2014; Lakoff 2005; Luhrmann 2001; Martin 2007; Rose 1996.

6. Hefner 2005; Hirschkind 2006; Jones 2010a; Mahmood 2005; Masquelier 2009; Peletz 2002, 2013; Schielke 2009; Schulz 2006; Soares and Osella 2009.

7. Hansen 1999; Hefner 2000; Navaro-Yashin 2002; Özyürek 2006; Pandey 2006; Peletz 2013.

8. Cushman 1995; Danziger 1990; Stearns 1994.

9. W. Anderson 2008; Good et al. 2008; Mahone and Vaughan 2007; Pols 2007.

10. Nandy was indebted, of course, to postcolonial theorists such as Frantz Fanon, Albert Memmi, and others. I also draw from more recent work by medical anthropologists working on psychology and postcolonial subjectivities, e.g., Good et al. (2008).

11. Aspinall 2013; Brenner 1998; Fealy 2008; George 1998; Hefner 2005; Heryanto 2014; Howell 2008; Jones 2010a, 2010c; Menchik 2014; Rinaldo 2013; Rudnyckyj 2010; Sasono 2010; Smith-Hefner 2007; Weintraub 2011; Widodo 2008.

12. See Bradley 2014; Laffan 2003; Ho 2006; Tagliacozzo 2009.

13. Mark Woodward (1989) offers a compelling corrective to Geertz; see also Lukens-Bull (2005).

14. Adding another lane of transnational traffic, the president-director of Mizan Press, Haidar Bagir, is an Indonesian of Arab descent who was a student of renowned scholar of Sufism Annemarie Schimmel.

15. Danforth (1989) offers an excellent ethnographic account of how the concept of neuro-linguistic programming influenced the New Age and corporate firewalking tradition in America.

16. See Moll (2012) and Wise (2003) for perspectives on Egyptian television preacher Amr Khaled; Schulz (2006) and Soares (2005) on Malian preacher Cherif Haidara; Yavuz and Esposito (2003) on Turkey's Fetullah Gülen.

17. In one respect, alternative voices of authority are nothing new. Popular preachers and religious scholars vied for religious authority and political patronage centuries before the onset of Muslim television preachers (Berkey 2001).

18. For accounts of new forms of religious authority beyond Indonesia, see Eickelman and Anderson (1999); Hirschkind (2006); Krämer and Schmidtke (2006); Mandaville (2001); Messick (1996); Moll (2010); Schulz (2012); Soares (2005).

19. See Eickelman and Anderson 1999; George 1998; Hefner 2009; Hirschkind 2006; Messick 1996; Schulz 2006.

20. Consider these titles at the popular bookstore, Gramedia: *Reach Riches, Attain Piety*; and *Brave to Be Pious, Brave to Be Rich: 15 Ways to Pack Your Money*

*Bags Based on the Qur'an and Sunnah.* I should note that these particular titles were even in the "Islam" section, not the applied psychology section.

21. For market Islam, see Haenni (2005) and Rudnyckyj (2009a). For approaches to the anthropological study of branding and economic globalization, see Einstein (2008); Foster (2007); Luvaas (2013); Mazzarella (2005); Newell (2013).

22. Anna Gade makes a compelling argument for this broader notion of "technologies of community" that goes beyond Foucault's interest in self-discipline (2004, 74).

23. See also Ferguson 2006; Freeman 2007; Gershon 2011; Little 2014; Peck, Theodore, and Brenner 2010.

24. Hefner (2012) makes a similar point and also outlines the plural meanings of neoliberalism even in the Western context.

25. I also build on the work of other scholars interested in the nexus of Islam and economy, including Hefner (1998, 2012); Kuran (2004); Nasr (2009). Muehlebach (2012) provides an excellent parallel example of the relationship between neoliberalism and Catholicism in Italy.

26. Gerakan Membangun Nurani Bangsa. The shortened Indonesian acronym, Gema Nusa, has another level of meaning that could be roughly translated as "an echo that reverberates across the nation."

27. See George 2010; Hefner 2007; Heryanto 2014; Hoesterey and Clark 2012; Howell 2008; Jones 2007; Lukens-Bull 2013; Sasono 2010; Smith-Hefner 2007.

28. The irony is not lost that such a question would come from Benedict Anderson, who has been critiqued for largely ignoring the role of Islam. I am indebted to Jeremy Menchik and Donald K. Emmerson for pointing me to the question that Anderson raised, yet never quite answered.

29. The acknowledgment of the public and political dimensions of emotion seems to me a more important endeavor than trying to affix specific qualities to one word or another as expressed in the English language, which may not have much bearing in how emotion terms, concepts, and embodied experiences are understood, experienced, and deployed in local languages.

30. Daromir Rudnyckyj (2009c) also offers an insightful discussion of "spiritual trainers" as figures of Indonesian modernity who emphasize the compatibility between work and worship.

## Notes to Chapter 1

1. This quote is taken from the introduction to Kartajaya et al., *Aa Gym: A Spiritual Marketer*, where Kartajaya outlines his "ten credos of compassionate marketing" (2005, vii). Indonesia's self-proclaimed "marketing guru," Kartajaya frequently shared the stage with Aa Gym at business seminars.

2. MQ Baroqah was a direct-marketing firm selling dozens of MQ products through a pyramid network of salespeople. Many of the products were household and hygiene products for women.

3. Aa Gym has authored and coauthored several books on marketing and business, including *Qalbu Marketing: 7 Kunci Menuju Kemenangan* (Qalbu marketing: 7 Keys toward victory) with Ippho Santosa and *The Power of Network Marketing: Hikmah Silaturahmi dalam Business* (The power of network marketing: The wisdom of maintaining good relations in business).

4. The five elements of *Pancasila* ideology include belief in One God; just and civilized humanity; the unity of Indonesia; representative and deliberative governance; and social justice for all citizens.

5. Feillard and Madinier (2011) provide a similar assessment of Aa Gym's involvement in anti-vice campaigns.

6. Aa Gym's close friend Deden Miqdad gives 1986 as the year (Gymnastiar 2003, 31), whereas Solahudin (1996, 17) reports 1987.

7. One person I interviewed was particularly bothered by the fact that Aa Gym was so wealthy. When I replied by saying that the Prophet Muhammad was also a savvy entrepreneur, this interlocutor reminded me that the Prophet sold tangible goods, whereas Aa Gym sold religion itself.

8. Hanafi and Henny are both pseudonyms.

9. In this respect, the religious authority embedded in the preacher-disciple relationship provides a stark contrast to Benedict Anderson's argument that Javanese concepts of power are arelational.

10. I confine my discussion of gender and Islam to explicitly hetero-normative discourses that were most common to this particular project. Elsewhere, I have examined Muslim masculinity in light of same-sex relations in cinematic versions of Islamic boarding schools (Hoesterey 2012). For readers interested in Islam and gender in Indonesia beyond these hetero-normative categories, there is a rich and burgeoning body of anthropological literature on Islam, gender, and queer theory (Blackwood 2010; Boellstorff 2005; Bennett and Davies 2014; Coppens and Levi 2013; see also Kugle 2010 for an excellent analysis beyond Indonesia).

11. "Polygyny" refers to a man who has multiple wives and is the more precise term; however, "polygamy" will be used throughout this book. Whereas the English term "polygamy" does not specifically denote whether it is a man or woman who has multiple spouses, Indonesians use the word *poligami*. In Islam, polygamy is strictly a male privilege.

12. We might consider this new celebrity type as the social and moral relief to James Siegel's (1998) much darker description of a "new criminal type" in Indonesia.

13. Tuti Oktoviany and Titi Kusrini, "Kisah Asmara KH Abdullah Gymnastiar

dan Ummu Ghaida Muthmainnah" [The love story of KH Abdullah Gymnastiar and Ummu Ghaida Muthmainnah], *Seputar Indonesia*, October 19–21, 2005.

14. See van der Pool (2005) for an interesting semiotic analysis of the popular MQTV program based on Aa Gym's family, *The Smiling Family*. Aa Gym's family also graces the cover of his book *Sakinah: Manajemen Qolbu untuk Keluarga* (Manajemen Qolbu for a harmonious family) (Gymnastiar 2004).

15. The belief that women are somehow naturally more emotional than men, and less capable of controlling their emotions, is a frequent theme of Gymnastiar's sermons. Anthropologists, especially those working in Islamic contexts, have interpreted such statements within relations of gender, power, and language (Brenner 1995; Lutz 1988; Lutz and Abu-Lughod 1990; Peletz 1996).

## *Notes to Chapter 2*

1. Badri 1996, 11.

2. Nancy Smith-Hefner (2007) offers an excellent linguistic analysis of al-Buchori's appeal to Muslim youth.

3. In Islam, physically performing the pilgrimage does not necessarily mean that Allah accepts that act of worship. In Indonesia, one common greeting for pilgrims who have just returned is to wish that Allah would accept their pilgrimage so they would become a *haji mabrur*.

4. The Indonesian translation kept the original English title.

5. Daromir Rudnyckyj (2009c) provides a similar analysis of the trainer, or *pelatih spiritual*, as a figure of Indonesian modernity.

6. Again I should qualify this as perceived scientific expertise. I once spoke with a molecular chemist who specialized in water. When I told him that Dr. Emoto's research on hexagonal crystal formations had become popular in Indonesia, he chuckled and informed me that all water crystals are hexagonal.

7. In recent years, Gray reinvented this popular (yet overly simplistic) explanation of gendered differences in emotion through a PBS series *Venus on Fire, Mars on Ice*, in which he romanticizes the fatalistic stoicism of the "ancient" Nepalese in the Himalayas.

8. Tung carefully used the word *dahsyat*, which had actually become his own favorite word—one might say his own discursive brand—to describe his financial and marketing seminars. Even in endorsement one finds self-promotion.

9. This section title alludes to Tanya Luhrman's (1989) insightful ethnography about the processes by which witchcraft comes to make sense to its practitioners.

10. Depending on the context, *ilmiah* can refer more specifically to scientific knowledge, but both are used interchangeably in everyday language. I generally use *ilmu* and will indicate when the speaker chooses the word *ilmiah*.

11. When I searched SEFT on YouTube, the first entry that popped up was a video testimonial by Tung Desem Waringin. With his own marketing voice, Tung ends his testimonial about SEFT and Ahmad with "Learn from the best, or die like the rest. I'm Tung Desem Waringin, wishing you *salam dahsyat* [amazing greetings, Tung's own trademark tagline]." Aa Gym also provides a testimonial in another posting.

12. Despite such claims, Faiz paid approximately $3,500 for his own training and certification. Faiz typically charges 1.4 million rupiah (approximately $150 at that time) for a two-day training session. He claimed to have trained two thousand people during the prior fifteen months.

13. Faiz next showed fMRI scans of people's brains that were intended to prove the EFT's ability to heal negative feelings after four, eight, and twelve sessions. Faiz told the audience that EFT "has the capacity to change the chemical structure of the brain."

14. Faiz did not perform the demonstration to stop smoking on that day, but it was part of his marketing materials. Daarut Tauhiid trainers soon picked up on this theme and also offered to rid people of their smoking habits in just five minutes. As Faiz later claimed in this presentation, he draws on hypnosis therapy (versions of which had become very popular in Indonesia and were promoted for personal health and wealth).

15. Tito is a pseudonym.

16. Faiz uses the Indonesian words *ridho* (sometimes spelled *ridha*) and *pasrah*, both of which imply giving one's problems up to God.

17. I refer here to supplicatory prayer, or *du'ā*, not ritual prayer, or *ṣalāh*.

18. Richard Bandler and John Grinder are credited with formulating NLP, although legal disputes and acrimonious relations have left some specifics in question. Even though academic psychology critiqued the lack of data to support claims for the therapeutic benefits of NLP, Bandler and Grinder transformed it into a huge sensation in the newly emerging New Age and self-help industries, especially in the Bay Area in Northern California. Newly emerging self-help gurus such as Anthony Robbins integrated NLP into their own training modules.

19. This process is loosely analogous to Danilyn Rutherford's notion of the "fetishization of the foreign" on the eastern Indonesian island of Biak (2003, 4).

20. Michael Peletz (2013, 617–619) provides an insightful analysis about how Japanese organizational management principles were integrated into Sharia courts in contemporary Malaysia.

21. Here I borrow from Lara Deeb's (2006) understanding of the processes of authentication.

*Notes to Chapter 3*

1. Osella and Osella 2009, S204.

2. The Indonesian title *Robohnya entrepreneur santri kita* invokes the famous Indonesian short story collection by A. A. Navis, *Robohnya surau kami* (The fall of our mosque).

3. Membangkitkan Khitah Wirausaha.

4. Translation by Ali (1983).

5. In the final line of the article, Bagir declares, "I am indebted to Salman [mosque in Bandung]." As previously discussed, Bagir was greatly influenced by the educational atmosphere at Salman mosque during the early years of Imaduddin's "mental training" programs.

6. Antonio cites the website Inspirational Words of Wisdom, www.wow4u.com/change-world/ (accessed November 20, 2014).

7. "Entrepreneurship Rasulullah," cybermq.com on, posted September 28, 2007 (accessed October 3, 2007; no longer available).

8. In this context, I translate the Indonesian word *mengendalikan* as "manage." This causative verb form of the word *kendali*, literally meaning "reins," is also used in the context of restraining, or reining in, one's emotions. Controlling one's emotions (i.e., managing one's *qolbu*) is thus presented as an integral aspect of financial success and *manajemen*.

9. For example, money earned through forbidden means would not bring (and itself constitute) blessing. In this written text Aa Gym consciously chose the Arabic transliteration for "blessing," not the Indonesian word *berkah*. Blessing is the real ethical aim. One can fulfill obligatory almsgiving only when that money was earned by halal means.

10. In Arabic, *ikhtiar* means "choice." However, in the Indonesian context, it refers more to a sense of self-initiative and personal effort.

11. These principles of entrepreneurship and capital accumulation are also featured in Aa Gym's 2006 book, *I Don't Want to Be Rich, I Have to Be Rich*.

12. Mizan Press has translated Seligman's work on positive psychology into Indonesian. The iconic yellow smiley face adorns the front cover of one of these books.

13. de Bono Consulting, "Drive Innovation," http://www.debonoconsulting.com; and Tony Buzan, www.tonybuzan.com (accessed November 20, 2014).

14. Here I have purposely translated the verse from the Indonesian-language slide into English. Translations from the Arabic tend to stress a person's manner and intentions, not necessarily his or her aptitudes per se. I would argue that this is not simply an error in translation by Pak Royani but rather a desire to reconcile positive psychology with Islamic teachings. The desire for commensurability can thus result in imperfect translation.

15. Kiyosaki is a popular American financial self-help guru whose book was on the *New York Times* best-seller list for 350 weeks. Following the success of *Rich Dad, Poor Dad* the national bookstore chain Gramedia heavily promoted a subsequent, coauthored book by Kiyosaki and Donald Trump.

16. The following verses were also popular among trainers: Q 2:267 (*Al-Baqara*); Q 57:7 (*Al-Ḥadīd*); Q 65:7 (*Al-Ṭalāq*); Q 92:5–7 (Al-Layl); Q 34:39 (*Saba'*). At the risk of not fully exploring the importance and authority of these verses, I restrict my analysis to those Qur'anic verses that kept appearing in various seminar settings and ethnographic contexts.

## Notes to Chapter 4

1. Gymnastiar 2004a, 9–11.

2. Inneke Koesherawati had once been protested for exposing too much flesh in her former career as an *artis panas*, or hot/sexy celebrity, who starred in films like *Metropolitan Woman*. According to Inneke, she saw the error of her ways, repented, and embraced Islam. Now she plays the moral protagonist on Islamic television and has become a model for the Islamic fashion company Shafira.

3. "Aa Gym Kritik film Buruan Cium Gue (BCG)," www.klikdt.com (accessed September 16, 2004; no longer available).

4. Gema Nusa is the abbreviated acronym for Gerakan Membangun Nurani Bangsa. This shortened version provides a second layer of meaning, as if a call ringing throughout the archipelago.

5. According to data provided by the Gema Nusa executive board.

6. Rudnyckyj (2010) argues that training in Indonesia is promoted as an Islamic corrective to what is perceived as the failed development initiatives of the New Order that privileged technology at the expense of religion and human resources development. Hefner (2012, 104–105) challenges this model of discrete periodization from secular technology-driven development to Islamic approaches to development.

7. Anna Gade (2004, 74) makes a similar point that moral comportment (*adab*) is also a technology of community.

8. I invoke Paul Willis's seminal book *Learning to Labor: How Working Class Kids Get Working Class Jobs* (1977). Whereas Willis was interested in the formation of socioeconomic class, in this chapter I explore the formation of a moral class of citizens who perform ethical labor for the nation.

"Training of Trainers" gatherings have become part of a widely used human resources development lexicon in Indonesia.

9. The local training sessions were named *Pembina Nurani*, or "The Cultivation of Conscience."

10. Interestingly, during the seminar Zohar critiqued Bahaudin's cognitive, biomedical understanding of the brain, offering instead her theory of the mind as understood from the viewpoint of quantum physics. And it was Ary Ginanjar, not Bahaudin, whom Zohar invited for an international symposium at Oxford University. Several months later, Ginanjar and Zohar hosted an "East Meets West" seminar in Jakarta. Approximately one thousand seats were available, most priced well over one hundred dollars per ticket.

11. Harvard psychologist Howard Gardner's pioneering research on "multiple intelligences" was translated into Indonesian by Mizan Press during the 1990s. In this regard, Haidar Bagir of Mizan Press plays an underappreciated role as cultural broker with respect to the transnational flows of psychological knowledge and expertise.

12. Many psychologists correctly note that Goleman merely brought several trends in the psychological study of emotion to a broad public audience (with the help of Oprah Winfrey, of course). As the present research makes abundantly clear, however, the importance of discourse lies less in the specificities of its genealogy than in the ways in which religious and political actors draw on its legitimacy in efforts to mobilize national reform.

13. The actual total of ESQ alumni was much greater. Rudnyckyj (2010, 93) provides more exact annual statistics about its exponential rise to popularity in the early to mid-2000s.

14. In this case of spoken speech I translate directly from Pak Naufaul's Indonesian language, which is comparable to that of Ali (1983).

15. For a sense of the range of contexts in which this passage is being summoned, see also Kenneth M. George's (2005) analysis of the meanings of this passage in the Islamic calligraphic art of Indonesian painter A. D. Pirous.

16. Rizky was an aspiring trainer. During our car ride from Bandung to Jakarta the day before, Rizky told me that his first book, *Pay Your Soul First*, was inspired by, and provided an Islamic corrective to, the Western self-help book *Pay Your Self First*.

17. Widjajakusuma plays on words here. *Biasa* (pronounced be-asa) means "average" or "normal," and he is playing on the combination of Indonesian and English meanings.

18. Pak Naufal cited American psychologist Bruce Tuckman as the theorist of these stages of group development.

19. This date is important in the sense that it was chosen as the date, in 2004, that marked the national response following the tsunami that devastated Aceh. Some Indonesians suggested that that date become a national holiday to honor civic voluntarism.

20. *Al-Fatihah* (The opening; Arabic, *Al-Fātiḥa*) is the first chapter of the Qur'an.

## Notes to Chapter 5

1. This quote is cited in Widhi Nugroho, "Culture of Shame," *Republika*, May 17, 2006, daily "Wisdom" (*hikmah*) section.

2. Asad 2003, 205.

3. Hirschkind (2006, 153–156) does examine Sayyid Qutb's analysis of visualization in the Qur'an; however, it is limited to Qutb's study of how Qur'anic narrative conjures visualization, what Hirschkind describes in terms of the cinematic image. While insightful and compelling, Hirschkind's analysis does not address the act of vision itself as an ethical act.

4. Elsewhere in the Qur'an (17:36) humans are told they will be questioned about their hearing, sight, and the content of their hearts.

5. "A'a Gym KH Abdullah Gymnastiar—Bab Menjaga Pandangan," January 22, 2008, http://www.youtube.com/watch?v=NLbAExnBbMo (accessed October 31, 2013).

6. This story is recounted in Al-Ghazālī 2005, 2:492.

7. As yet another example of the merging of politics and pop culture, the singer who sings the sound track in the film, Rhoma Irama, campaigned unsuccessfully for the 2014 presidential elections.

8. "Setan dan menjaga pandangan.mp4," May 28, 2011, http://www.youtube.com/watch?NR=1&v=52OaXvtuNoU&feature=endscreen (accessed November 24, 2014).

9. We might consider Neno Warisman as a *muslimah* version of the Kartini figure in the public sphere (Heider 1991a). In addition to being an actress and author, Warisman was also one of the celebrity judges on the popular "little tele-*dai*" contest, modeled after *American Idol*, in which young children compete to become the best young television preacher.

10. Muhammad Nur Hayid, "Ratna Sarumpaet *Nyolot* dengan Anggota Pansus RUU Pornografi," *Detik News*, August 2, 2006, http://news.detik.com/read/2006/02/08/113030/534847/10/ratna-sarumpaet-nyolot-dengan-anggota-pansus-ruu-pornografi (accessed November 24, 2014).

11. Talal Asad and colleagues (2009) offer an insightful analysis of the underlying assumptions of religion, affect, and secularism that sparked diverse reactions across the world. I restrict my analysis here to the way in which Aa Gym's public positioning to this controversy is consistent with his positioning as Indonesia's therapist-in-chief.

12. Muhammad Nur Hayid, "Hati Aa Gym Remuk dan Tersayat-sayat Lihat Kartun Nabi Muhammad," *Detik News*, August 2, 2006, http://news.detik.com/read/2006/02/08/142537/535022/10/hati-aa-gym-remuk-dan-tersayat-lihat-kartun-nabi-muhammad?nd993303605 (accessed November 24, 2014).

13. The program, previously on SCTV, was now broadcast by TPI and used a new title, *The Beauty of Mercy and Compassion* (*Indahnya Kasih Sayang*).

14. Aa Gym often uses the verb *mengendalikan*, which refers to pulling back on a horse's reins.

15. The word *join* here is an imperfect translation of the word *turun*, literally, "to come down from something." Although SBY's phrase was somewhat vague, it also could have implied *turun ke jalan*, or "taking to the streets," which might be read as tacit approval for hard-liner groups such as the Islamic Defenders Front to conduct their sweeping raids. Such an implication is much more problematic when considering the bill that eventually passed includes an article in the "enforcement" section that permits nonstate actors to enforce state law.

16. Hidayat Nur Wahid was mentioned in all of the promotional materials but was not able to attend because he was campaigning for the PKS candidate for governor of Papua.

17. *Santri Siap Guna* is an ongoing weekend training program that, at least in its first fourteen cohorts, mostly comprises young college students.

18. The 3 Ms were Aa Gym's trademark formula for piety and prosperity: *Mulai* (begin) with yourself; *Mulai*, with small things; *Mulai*, right now.

19. On this point I am indebted to a conversation with David Nugent, who has advanced a similar argument with respect to the surveillance of the Peruvian state by an underground political party in the latter half of the twentieth century (Nugent 2011).

## *Notes to Chapter 6*

1. For more details on the history of this debate in late colonial and independent Indonesia, see Brenner (2011); Nurmila (2009); van Doorn Harder (2006); van Wichelen (2009).

2. The "Friday Dialogue" insert of the Islamic newspaper *Republika* on the next Friday (December 8, 2006) featured an article by Islamic scholar Quraish Shihab, who also argued the case that in Islam polygyny is allowed as an "emergency exit" (*pintu darurat*).

3. *Cek & Ricek*, July 16–22, 2008, 28. Name of interviewer not provided.

4. Interestingly, Aa Gym's production house deleted these comments when they produced and distributed the audio CD of Aa Gym's explanation of polygamy recorded during this gathering. They also edited out a later comment by a senior female executive who indirectly criticized Aa Gym for spending too much time with politicians and celebrities who were purportedly less pious than religious scholars.

5. I selected the following excerpts from approximately one hour of audio recording.

6. Siti is a pseudonym.

7. Miftah Farid was the head of the West Java branch of the MUI. He was a close friend of Aa Gym and a frequent guest on MQTV religious talk shows. Weeks later, after Aa Gym returned from the pilgrimage at a time when employee morale was still low, Aa Gym invited Miftah Farid to provide textual justification for polygamy and to inspire employees. Farid was more successful at the former. He began by suggesting that those against polygyny were being duped by liberal and "Orientalist" understandings of Islam. As Farid claimed (and accused), "To judge a verse of the Qur'an as wrong [*salah*] is not permitted!"

8. Arif is a pseudonym.

9. *Selingkuh* can also be translated as dishonest, corrupt, and unfair. In this context it refers to marital infidelity. I am grateful to Jolanda M. Pandin for her expertise concerning this specific translation.

10. Within weeks, Achmad Setiyaji (2006), Aa Gym's loyal friend and media adviser (if not always sufficiently disclosed), had already written a book in defense of polygamy, *Aa Gym: Why Polygamy? Testimony of a Journalist.*

11. The term *rela* implies an affective tone and, in everyday speech, is more commonly referred to as *rela hati* (resigned/consenting heart).

12. This was the harshest of the many jokes and plays on words that circulated widely at the time. The woman changed MQ to MS, or Manajemen Syahwat (Lust/Orgasm Management).

13. "Kejamnya Aa, ambil isteri muda / Kejamnya Aa, ambil isteri muda." This video has been removed from YouTube. Accessed August 17, 2009.

14. Noor Yanto, 2007, "Repositioning Aa Gym," *Marketing*, May, 48–49.

15. Bambang Sulistyo, "Tujuh Hari Berbagi Cinta," *Gatra*, April 2007, 114.

16. A new television preacher, Ahmad Alhabsyi, became popular during Ramadan in 2007. None of the new preachers, however, have managed to attain the celebrity status of Aa Gym.

17. An important difference is that Ary Ginanjar was careful not to build the brand around himself. He marketed himself as the creator, not the exemplar, of ESQ.

18. Kartajaya is the author of a book on Aa Gym (Kartajaya et al. 2005) and the coauthor of another (Gymnastiar and Kartajaya 2004). Pak Taufik at MarkPlus graciously provided a copy of this program.

19. *Megelola Hidup dan Merencanakan Masa Depan.* When I joined this training seminar in 2007, trainees were asked to fill out and discuss our "life calendar." At that session, Ibu Marwah shared her own personal goal—to run for national office in 2014.

# References

Abrams, Philip. 1988. "Notes on the Difficulty of Studying the State." *Journal of Historical Sociology* 1 (1): 58–89.

Akbar, Sa'dun. 2000. "Prinsip-prinsip dan Vektor-vektor Percepatan Process Internalisasi Kewirausahaan: Studi pada Pendidikan Visi Pondok Pesantren Daarut Tauhiid Bandung" [Principles and velocity vectors in the process of internalization of entrepreneurial values: A study of the educational vision of Pesantren Daarut Tauhiid, Bandung]. PhD diss., University Pendidikan Indonesia.

Ali, A. Yusuf. 1983. *The Holy Qur'an: Text, Translation, and Commentary*. Brentwood, MD: Amana Corp.

Althusser, Louis. 1972. *Lenin and Philosophy, and Other Essays*. New York: Monthly Review Press.

Amin, A. Riawan. 2004. *The Celestial Management: Zikr, Pikr, Mikr*. Jakarta: Senayan Abadi.

Anderson, Benedict. 1977. "Religion and Politics in Indonesia since Independence." In *Religion and Social Ethos in Indonesia*, edited by Benedict R. O'G. Anderson, Mitsuo Nakamura, and Mohammad Slamet, 21–32. Clayton, Victoria, Australia: Centre for Southeast Asian Studies.

———. 1990. *Language and Power: Exploring Political Cultures in Indonesia*. Ithaca, NY: Cornell University Press.

Anderson, Warwick. 2008. *The Collectors of Lost Souls: Turning Kuru Scientists into Whitemen*. Baltimore: Johns Hopkins University Press.

Antonio, Syafi'i. 2007. *Muhammad SAW: The Super Leader, Super Manager*. Jakarta: Prophetic Leadership and Management Centre.

Appiah, Kwame Anthony. 1997. "Cosmopolitan Patriots." *Critical Inquiry* 23 (3): 617–639.

————. 2006. *Cosmopolitanism: Ethics in a World of Strangers*. New York: W. W. Norton.

Aretxaga, Begoña. 2000. "A Fictional Reality: Paramilitary Death Squads and the Construction of State Terror in Spain." In *Death Squad: The Anthropology of State Terror*, edited by Jeffrey A. Sluka, 46–69. Philadelphia: University of Philadelphia Press.

————. 2003. "Maddening States." *Annual Review of Anthropology* 32:393–410.

Asad, Talal. 1986. *The Idea of an Anthropology of Islam*. Occasional Paper Series. Washington, DC: Georgetown University Center for Contemporary Arab Studies.

————. 1993. *Genealogies of Religion: Discipline and Reasons of Power in Christianity and Islam*. Baltimore: Johns Hopkins University Press.

————. 2003. *Formations of the Secular: Christianity, Islam, Modernity*. Stanford, CA: Stanford University Press.

Asad, Talal, Wendy Brown, Judith Butler, and Saba Mahmood. 2009. *Is Critique Secular? Blasphemy, Injury, and Free Speech*. Townsend Papers in the Humanities. Berkeley: Townsend Center for the Humanities. Accessed November 1, 2101. http://politics-of-religious-freedom.berkeley.edu/files/2011/05/Is-Critique -Secular-Blasphemy-Injury-and-Free-Speech.pdf.

Aspinall, Edward. 2013. "A Nation in Fragments." *Critical Asian Studies* 45 (1): 27–54.

Ayoob, Mohammed. 2008. *The Many Faces of Political Islam: Religion and Politics in the Muslim World*. Ann Arbor: University of Michigan Press.

Azzaini, Jamil, Farid Poniman, and Indrawan Nugroho. 2006. *Kubik Leadership*. Bandung: Mizan Publika.

Badri, Malik B. 1996. *Dilema Psikolog Muslim* [The dilemma of a Muslim psychologist]. Jakarta: Penerbit Al-Kautsar.

Bahaudin, Taufik. 1999. *Brainware Management: Generasi kelima Manajemen Manusia* [Brainware management: The fifth generation of People Management]. Jakarta: Gramedia.

Barker, Joshua. 2005. "Engineers and Political Dreams: Indonesia in the Satellite Age." *Current Anthropology* 19 (1): 703–727.

Barker, Joshua, Erik Harms, and Johan Lindquist. 2013. "Introduction to Special Issue: Figuring the Transforming City." *City & Society* 25 (2): 159–172.

Barker, Joshua, and Johan Lindquist, with Tom Boellstorff, Daromir Rudnyckyj, Rachel Silvey, Karen Strassler, Chris Brown, Aryo Danusiri, Dadi Darmadi, Sheri Gibbings, Jesse Hession Grayman, James Hoesterey, Carla Jones, and Doreen Lee. 2009. "Figures of Indonesian Modernity." *Indonesia* 87 (April): 35–72.

Baswardono, Dono. 2007. *Poligami Itu Selingkuh* [Polygamy is an extra-marital affair]. Yogyakarta: Galang Press.

Batmanghelidj, Fereydoon. 1995. *Your Body's Many Cries for Water: You Are Not Sick, You Are Thirsty! Don't Treat Thirst with Medications*. Falls Church, VA: Global Health Solutions.

Bayat, Asef. 1996. "The Coming of a Post-Islamist Society." *Critique: Critical Middle East Studies* 9 (Fall): 43–52.

———. 2005. "What Is Post-Islamism?" *ISIM Review* 16:5.

———. 2007. *Making Islam Democratic: Social Movements and the Post-Islamist Turn*. Stanford, CA: Stanford University Press.

———, ed. 2013. *Post-Islamism: The Changing Faces of Political Islam*. New York: Oxford University Press.

Bennett, Linda Rae, and Sharyn Graham Davies, eds. 2014. *Sex and Sexualities in Contemporary Indonesia: Sexual Politics, Health, Diversity, and Representations*. New York: Routledge.

Berkey, Jonathan P. 2001. *Popular Preaching and Religious Authority in the Medieval Islamic Near East*. Seattle: University of Washington Press.

———. 2003. *The Formation of Islam: Religion and Society in the Near East, 600–1800*. New York: Cambridge University Press.

Bhabha, Homi K. 1994. *The Location of Culture*. London: Routledge.

———. 1996. "Unsatisfied: Notes on Vernacular Cosmopolitanism." In *Text and Nation*, edited by Laura Garcia-Morena and Peter C. Pfeifer, 191–207. London: Camden House.

Blackwood, Evelyn. 2010. *Falling into the Lesbi World: Desire and Difference in Indonesia*. Honolulu: University of Hawaii Press.

Boellstorff, Tom. 2005. "Between Religion and Desire: Being Muslim and *Gay* in Indonesia." *American Anthropologist* 107 (4): 575–585.

Bradley, Francis C. 2014. "Islamic Reform, the Family, and Knowledge Networks Linking Mecca to Southeast Asia in the Nineteenth Century." *Journal of Asian Studies* 73 (1): 89–112.

Brenner, Suzanne. 1995. "Why Women Rule the Roost: Rethinking Javanese Ideologies of Gender and Self-Control." In *Bewitching Women, Pious Men: Gender and Body Politics in Southeast Asia*, edited by Aihwa Ong and Michael G. Peletz, 19–50. Oakland: University of California Press.

———. 1998. *The Domestication of Desire: Women, Wealth, and Modernity in Java*. Princeton, NJ: Princeton University Press.

———. 2011. "Private Moralities in the Public Sphere: Democratization, Islam, and Gender in Indonesia." *American Anthropologist* 113 (3): 478–490.

Buehler, Michael. 2008. "The Rise of Shari'a By-laws in Indonesian Districts: An Indication of Changing Patterns of Power Accumulation and Political Corruption." *South East Asia Research* 16 (2): 255–285.

Burhani, Najib. 2002. *Tarekat Tanpa Tarekat: Jalan Baru Menjadi Sufi* [Sufism without Sufi orders: The new way of becoming Sufi]. Jakarta: Serambi.

Bush, Robin. 2008. "Regional Sharia Regulations in Indonesia: Anomaly or Symptom?" In *Expressing Islam: Religious Life and Politics in Indonesia*, edited by Greg Fealy and Sally White, 174–191. Singapore: Institute for Southeast Asian Studies.

Cahn, Peter S. 2006. "Building Down and Dreaming Up: Finding Faith in a Multilevel Marketer." *American Ethnologist* 33 (1): 126–142.

Calhoun, Craig J., ed. 1992. *Habermas and the Public Sphere*. Cambridge, MA: MIT Press.

Carnegie, Dale. (1936) 1970. *Guide to Enjoying Your Life and Work*. Reprint, New York: Simon and Schuster.

Casanova, José. 1994. *Public Religions in the Modern World*. Chicago: University of Chicago Press.

Clark, Marshall. 2010. *Maskulinitas: Culture, Gender, and Politics in Indonesia*. Caulfield, Australia: Monash University Press.

Comaroff, Jean, and John L. Comaroff. 1999. "Occult Economies and the Violence of Abstraction: Notes from the South African Postcolony." *American Ethnologist* 26 (2): 279–303.

———. 2001. "Millennial Capitalism: First Thoughts on a Second Coming." In *Millennial Capitalism and the Culture of Neoliberalism*, edited by Jean Comaroff and John L. Comaroff, 1–56. Durham, NC: Duke University Press.

Cooke, Miriam, and Bruce Lawrence, eds. 2005. *Muslim Networks: From Hajj to Hip Hop*. Chapel Hill: University of North Carolina Press.

Coppens, Laura, and Angelika Levi, producers. 2013. *Children of Srikandi*. New York: Outcast Films.

Cornell, Vincent J. 1998. *Realm of the Saint: Power and Authority in Moroccan Sufism*. Austin: University of Texas Press.

Covey, Steven. 1989. *The Seven Habits of Highly Effective People*. New York: Simon and Schuster.

Cushman, Philip. 1995. *Constructing the Self, Constructing America: A Cultural History of Psychotherapy*. Boston: Addison-Wesley.

Danforth, Loring M. 1989. *Firewalking and Religious Healing: The Anastenaria of Greece and the American Firewalking Movement*. Princeton, NJ: Princeton University Press.

Danziger, Kurt. 1990. *Constructing the Subjects: Historical Origins of Psychological Research*. New York: Cambridge University Press.

Darmadi, Dadi. 2001. "Urban Sufism: The New Flourishing Vivacity of Contemporary Indonesian Islam." *Studia Islamika* 8 (1): 205–207.

Deeb, Lara. 2006. *An Enchanted Modern: Gender and Public Piety in Shi'i Lebanon*. Princeton, NJ: Princeton University Press.

Diamond, John. 1998. *Life Energy: Using the Meridians to Unlock the Hidden Power of Your Emotions*. New York: Paragon House.

Dinsi, Valentino. 2005. *Jangan Mau Seumur Hidup Jadi Orang Gajian* [Don't be an employee for the rest of your life]. Jakarta: Let's Go Indonesia.

Dossey, Larry. 1993. *Healing Words: The Power of Prayer and the Practice of Medicine*. San Francisco: Harper Publishing.

Duncan, Christopher R. 2013. *Violence and Vengeance: Religious Conflict and Its Aftermath in Eastern Indonesia*. Ithaca, NY: Cornell University Press.

Eickelman, Dale F., and Jon W. Anderson, eds. (1999) 2003. *New Media in the Muslim World: The Emerging Public Sphere*. Reprint, Bloomington: Indiana University Press.

Eickelman, Dale, and James Piscatori. 1996. *Muslim Politics*. Princeton, NJ: Princeton University Press.

Einstein, Mara. 2008. *Brands of Faith: Marketing Religion in a Commercial Age*. New York: Routledge.

Emoto, Masaru. 2001. *The Hidden Messages in Water*. Hillsboro, OR: Beyond Books Publishing.

———. 2006. *The True Power of Water*. Bandung: MQS Publishing.

Esposito, John, and Ibrahim Kalin. 2009. *The 500 Most Influential Muslims in the World*. Royal Islamic Strategic Studies Centre. Accessed November 16, 2014. http://thebook.org/files/500.pdf.

Ewing, Katherine Pratt. 2010. "The Misrecognition of a Modern Islamist Organization: Germany Faces 'Fundamentalism.'" In *Rethinking Islamic Studies: From Orientalism to Cosmopolitanism*, edited by Carl Ernst and Richard Martin, 52–71. Columbia: University of South Carolina Press.

Fadjar, Abdullah. 2006. *Khasanah Islam Indonesia: Monografi Penerbit Buku-Buku Islam* [Treasure box of Indonesian Islam: A book about Islamic publishing]. Jakarta: The Habibie Center.

Fanon, Frantz. 1963. *The Wretched of the Earth*. New York: Grove Press.

———. 1967. *Black Skin White Masks*. New York: Grove Press.

Fealy, Greg. 2008. "Consuming Islam: Commodified Religion and Aspirational Pietism in Contemporary Indonesia." In *Expressing Islam: Religious Life and Politics in Indonesia*, edited by Sally White and Greg Fealy, 15–39. Singapore: Institute of Southeast Asian Studies.

Federspiel, Howard M. 1995. *A Dictionary of Indonesian Islam*. Athens: Ohio University, Center for International Studies.

Feillard, Andrée, and Rémy Madinier. 2011. *The End of Innocence? Indonesian Islam and the Temptations of Radicalism*. Honolulu: University of Hawaii Press.

Ferguson, James. 2006. *Global Shadows: Africa in the Neoliberal World*. Durham, NC: Duke University Press.

Formichi, Chiara. 2012. *Islam and the Making of the Nation: Kartosuwiryo and Political Islam in 20th Century Indonesia*. Leiden, Netherlands: KITLV Press.

Foster, Robert J. 2007. "The Work of the New Economy: Consumers, Brands, and Value Creation." *Cultural Anthropology* 22 (4): 707–731.

Foucault, Michel. 1988. "Technologies of the Self." In *Technologies of the Self: A Seminar with Michel Foucault*, edited and translated by Luther Martin, Huck Gutman, and Patrick Hutton, 16–49. Amherst: University of Massachusetts Press.

Freeman, Carla. 2007. "The 'Reputation' of Neoliberalism." *American Ethnologist* 34:252–267.

Gade, Anna M. 2004. *Perfection Makes Practice: Learning, Emotion, and the Recited Qur'an in Indonesia*. Honolulu: University of Hawaii Press.

Gade, Anna M., and Michael R. Feener. 2004. "Muslim Thought and Practice in Contemporary Indonesia." In *Islam in World Cultures: Comparative Perspectives*, edited by Michael R. Feener, 183– 215. Santa Barbara, CA: ABC-CLIO.

Gal, Susan. 2002. "A Semiotics of the Public/Private Distinction." *differences: A Journal of Feminist Cultural Studies* 13 (1): 77–95.

Geertz, Clifford. 1959. "The Javanese Village." In *Local, Ethnic and National Loyalties in Village Indonesia*, edited by William Skinner, 34–41. New Haven, CT: Southeast Asia Program, Yale University.

———. 1960a. "The Javanese Kijaji: The Changing Role of a Cultural Broker." *Contemporary Studies in Society and History* 2 (2): 228–249.

———. 1960b. *Religion of Java*. Chicago: University of Chicago Press.

———. 1963. *Peddlers and Princes: Social Change and Economic Modernization in Two Indonesian Towns*. Chicago: University of Chicago Press.

———. 1973. *The Interpretation of Cultures*. New York: Basic Books.

George, Kenneth M. 1998. "Designs on Indonesia's Muslim Communities." *Journal of Asian Studies* 57 (3): 693–713.

———. 2005. "Picturing Aceh: Violence, Religion, and a Painter's Tale." In *Spirited Politics: Religion and Public Life in Contemporary Southeast Asia*, edited by Andrew Willford and Kenneth George, 185–208. Ithaca, NY: Southeast Asia Publication Series, Cornell University.

———. 2009. "Ethics, Iconoclasm, and Islamic Art in Indonesia." *Cultural Anthropology* 24 (4): 589–621.

———. 2010. *Picturing Islam: Art and Ethics in a Muslim Lifeworld*. Malden, MA: Wiley-Blackwell.

Geroulanos, Stefanos. 2014. "The Plastic Self and the Prescription of Psychology: Ethnopsychology, Crowd Psychology, and Psychotechnics, 1890–1920." *Republics of Letters: A Journal for the Study of Knowledge, Politics, and the Arts* 3 (2): 1–31.

Gershon, Ilana. 2011. "Neoliberal Agency." *Current Anthropology* 52 (4): 537–555.

Al-Ghazālī, Abū Ḥāmid. 1982. *The Revival of the Religious Sciences* [*Iḥyā' 'ulūm al-*

*dīn*]. 4 vols. Translated by Al-haj Maulana Fazul-ul-Karim. New Delhi: Kitab Bhavan.

———. 2005. *The Alchemy of Happiness*. 2 vols. Translated by Jay R. Crook. Chicago: KAZI Publications.

Gianotti, Timothy. 2001. *Al-Ghazali's Unspeakable Doctrine of the Soul: Unveiling the Esoteric Psychology and Eschatology of the Ihya'*. Leiden, Netherlands: Brill.

Giddens, Anthony. 1991. *Modernity and Self-Identity: Self and Society in the Late Modern Age*. Stanford, CA: Stanford University Press.

Göle, Nilüfer. 2002. "Islam in Public: New Visibilities and New Imaginaries." *Public Culture* (14) 1: 173–190.

Goleman, Daniel. 1995. *Emotional Intelligence*. New York: Bantam Books.

Good, Byron J. 2012. "Theorizing the Subject of Medical and Psychiatric Anthropology." *Journal of the Royal Anthropological Institute* 18 (3): 515–535.

Good, Mary-Jo DelVecchio, and Byron J. Good. 1988. "Ritual, the State, and the Transformation of Emotional Discourse in Iranian Society." *Culture, Medicine, and Psychiatry* 12 (1): 43–63.

Good, Mary-Jo DelVecchio, Sandra Teresa Hyde, Sarah Pinto, and Byron J. Good, eds. 2008. *Postcolonial Disorders*. Berkeley: University of California Press.

Gray, John. 1992. *Men Are from Mars, Women Are from Venus: A Practical Guide for Improving Communication and Getting What You Want in Your Relationships*. New York: HarperCollins.

Gymnastiar, Abdullah. 2003. *Aa Gym, Apa Adanya: Sebuah Qolbugrafi* [Aa Gym, just as he is: A biography of the heart]. Bandung: Khas MQ.

———. 2004a. *Refleksi untuk Membangun Nurani Bangsa* [Reflections on building the conscience of the nation]. Bandung: MQS.

———. 2004b. *Sakinah: Manajemen Qolbu untuk Keluarga* [Manajemen Qolbu for a harmonious family]. Bandung: Khas MQ.

———. 2006. *Saya tidak ingin kaya. Saya harus kaya* [I don't want to be rich. I have to be rich]. Bandung: MQS.

———. 2007. "Entrepreneurship Rasulullah." Abatasa. Accessed October 3, 2007. cybermq.com (no longer available).

Gymnastiar, K. H. Abdullah, and Hermawan Kartajaya. 2004. *Berbisnis dengan Hati* [Doing business with the heart]. Jakarta: MarkPlus.

Haenni, Patrick. 2005. *L'Islam de marché: L'autre révolution conservatrice* [Market Islam: The other conservative revolution]. Paris: Le Seuil / La République des Idées.

Hansen, Thomas Blom. 1999. *The Saffron Wave: Democracy and Hindu Nationalism in Modern India*. Princeton, NJ: Princeton University Press.

Harding, Susan. 1991. "Representing Fundamentalism: The Problem of the Repugnant Cultural Other." *Social Research* 58 (2): 373–393.

———. 2000. *The Book of Jerry Falwell: Fundamentalist Language and Politics.* Princeton, NJ: Princeton University Press.

Hare, Robert D. 1999. *Without Conscience: The Disturbing World of the Psychopaths among Us.* New York: Guilford Press.

Harvey, David. 2005. *A Brief History of Neoliberalism.* Oxford: Oxford University Press.

Hefner, Robert W. 1996. "Islamizing Capitalism: On the Founding of Indonesia's First Islamic Bank." In *Toward a New Paradigm: Recent Developments in Indonesian Islamic Thought,* edited by Mark Woodward, 291–322. Tempe: Arizona State University Program for Southeast Asian Studies.

———, ed. 1998. *Market Cultures: Society and Morality in the New Asian Capitalisms.* Boulder, CO: Westview Press.

———. 2000. *Civil Islam: Muslims and Democratization in Indonesia.* Princeton, NJ: Princeton University Press.

———, ed. 2005. *Rethinking Muslim Politics: Pluralism, Contestation, Democratization.* Princeton, NJ: Princeton University Press.

———, ed. 2007. *Schooling Islam: The Culture and Politics of Muslim Education.* Princeton, NJ: Princeton University Press.

———, ed. 2009. *Making Modern Muslims: The Politics of Islamic Education in Southeast Asia.* Honolulu: University of Hawaii Press.

———. 2012. "Islam, Economic Globalization, and the Blended Ethics of Self." *Bustan: The Middle East Book Review* 3:91–108.

Heider, Karl G. 1988. "The Rashomon Effect: When Ethnographers Disagree." *American Anthropologist* 90 (1): 73–81.

———. 1991a. *Indonesian Cinema: National Culture on Screen.* Honolulu: University of Hawaii Press.

———. 1991b. *Landscapes of Emotion: Mapping Three Cultures of Emotion in Indonesia.* Cambridge: Cambridge University Press.

Helminski, Kabir. 2000. *The Knowing Heart: A Sufi Path to Transformation.* Boston: Shambhala.

Hendricks, Gay, and Kate Ludeman. 1997. *The Corporate Mystic: A Guidebook for Visionaries with Their Feet on the Ground.* New York: Bantam Books.

Hernowo, and M. Deden Ridwan, eds. 2001. *Aa Gym dan Phenomena Daarut Tauhiid* [Aa Gym and the phenomenon of Daarut Tauhiid]. Bandung: Mizan.

Heryanto, Ariel. 2008. "Pop Culture and Competing Identities." In *Popular Culture in Indonesia: Fluid Identities in Post-authoritarian Politics,* edited by Ariel Heryanto, 1–36. New York: Routledge.

———. 2014. *Identity and Pleasure: The Politics of Indonesian Screen Culture.* Singapore: National University of Singapore Press.

Hirschkind, Charles. 2001a. "Civic Virtue and Religious Reason: An Islamic Counter-Public." *Cultural Anthropology* 16 (1): 3–34.

————. 2001b. "The Ethics of Listening: Cassette-Sermon Audition in Contemporary Egypt." *American Ethnologist* 28 (3): 623–649.

————. 2006. *The Ethical Soundscape: Cassette Sermons and Islamic Counterpublics.* New York: Columbia University Press.

Ho, Engseng. 2006. *The Graves of Tarim: Genealogy and Mobility across the Indian Ocean.* Berkeley: University of California Press.

Hodgson, Marshall. 1974. *The Venture of Islam: Conscience and History in a World Civilization.* Vol. 2, *The Expansion of Islam in the Middle Periods.* Chicago: University of Chicago Press.

Hoesterey, James B. 2008. "Marketing Morality: The Rise, Fall, and Re-branding of Aa Gym." In *Expressing Islam: Religious Life and Politics in Indonesia,* edited by Sally White and Greg Fealy, 95–112. Singapore: Institute of Southeast Asian Studies.

————. 2009. "The Muslim Television Preacher." In "Figures of Indonesian Modernity," by Joshua Barker and Johan Lindquist, with Tom Boellstorff et al., *Indonesia* 87 (April): 41–43.

————. 2012. "Prophetic Cosmopolitanism: Islam, Pop Psychology, and Civic Virtue in Contemporary Indonesia." *City & Society* 24 (1): 38–61.

Hoesterey, James, and Marshall Clark. 2012. "*Film Islami*: Gender, Piety, and Pop Culture in Post-authoritarian Indonesia." *Asian Studies Review* 36 (2): 201–226.

Hollan, Douglas. 1988. "Staying 'Cool' in Toraja: Informal Strategies for the Management of Anger and Hostility in a Nonviolent Society." *Ethos* 16 (1): 52–72.

Howell, Julia Day. 2001. "Sufism and the Indonesian Islamic Revival." *Journal of Asian Studies* 60 (3): 701–729.

————. 2007. "Modernity and Islamic Spirituality in Indonesia's New Sufi Networks." In *Sufism and the "Modern" in Islam,* edited by Martin van Bruinessen and Julia Day Howell, 217–240. London: I. B. Tauris.

————. 2008. "Modulations of Active Piety: Professors and Televangelists as Promoters of Indonesian 'Sufisme.'" In *Expressing Islam: Religious Life and Politics in Indonesia,* edited by Sally White and Greg Fealy, 40–62. Singapore: Institute of Southeast Asian Studies.

Ibn 'Aṭā' Allāh al-Iskandarī. 1984. *Kitab Al-Ḥikam* [Sufi aphorisms]. Translated by Victor Danner. Leiden, Netherlands: E. J. Brill.

Illouz, Eva. 2008. *Saving the Modern Soul: Therapy, Emotions, and the Culture of Self-Help.* Berkeley: University of California Press.

Jones, Carla. 2004. "Whose Stress: Emotion Work in Middle-Class Javanese Homes." *Ethnos* 69 (4): 509–528.

————. 2007. "Fashion and Faith in Urban Indonesia." *Fashion Theory* 11 (2/3): 211–232.

————. 2010a. "Better Women: The Cultural Politics of Gendered Expertise in Indonesia." *American Anthropologist* 112 (2): 270–282.

————. 2010b. "Images of Desire: Creating Virtue and Value in an Indonesian Islamic Fashion Magazine." *Journal of Middle East Women's Studies* 6 (3): 91–117.

————. 2010c. "Materializing Piety: Gendered Anxieties about Faithful Consumption in Contemporary Urban Indonesia." *American Ethnologist* 37 (4): 617–637.

Kartajaya, Hermawan, and Muhammad Syakir Sula. 2006. *Syariah Marketing.* Bandung: Mizan Pustaka.

Kartajaya, Hermawan, Yuswohady, Sunarto, Anke Dwi Saputro, and Mas Waris. 2005. *Aa Gym: A Spiritual Marketer.* Jakarta: MarkPlus.

Kassam, Zayn, ed. 2010. *Women and Islam.* Santa Barbara, CA: Praeger.

Keane, Webb. 2007. *Christian Moderns: Freedom and Fetish in the Mission Encounter.* Berkeley: University of California Press.

Keeler, Ward. 1990. "Speaking of Gender in Java." In *Power and Difference: Gender in Island Southeast Asia,* edited by Jane Atkinson and Shelly Errington, 127–152. Stanford, CA: Stanford University Press.

Kepel, Gilles. 2002. *Jihad: The Trail of Political Islam.* Cambridge, MA: Harvard University Press.

————. 2004. *The War for Muslim Minds.* Cambridge, MA: Harvard University Press.

Kipnis, Andrew. 2007. "Neoliberalism Reified: Suzhi Discourses and Tropes of Neoliberalism in the People's Republic of China." *Journal of the Royal Anthropological Institute* 13 (2): 383–400.

Kiyosaki, Robert. 2000. *Rich Dad, Poor Dad: What the Rich Teach Their Kids about Money That the Poor and Middle Class Do Not.* New York: Warner Books.

Klinken, Gerry van, and Joshua Barker, eds. 2009. *State of Authority: The State in Society in Indonesia.* Ithaca, NY: Southeast Asia Programs.

Kloos, David. 2014. "Becoming Better Muslims: Religious Authority and Ethical Improvement in Aceh, Indonesia." PhD diss., Free University, Amsterdam.

Krämer, Gudrun, and Sabine Schmidtke, eds. 2006. *Speaking for Islam: Religious Authorities in Muslim Societies.* Boston: Brill.

Kugle, Scott. 2007. *Sufis and Saints' Bodies: Mysticism, Corporeality, and Sacred Power in Islam.* Chapel Hill: University of North Carolina Press.

————. 2010. *Homosexuality in Islam: Critical Reflection on Gay, Lesbian, and Transgender Muslims.* Oxford: Oneworld Publications.

Kuran. 2004. *Islam and Mammon: The Economic Predicaments of Islamism.* Princeton, NJ: Princeton University Press.

Laffan, Michael Francis. 2003. *Islamic Nationhood and Colonial Indonesia: The Umma below the Winds.* New York: Routledge.

————. 2011. *The Makings of Indonesian Islam: Orientalism and the Narration of a Sufi Past.* Princeton, NJ: Princeton University Press.

Lakoff, Andrew. 2005. *Pharmaceutical Reason: Knowledge and Value in Global Psychiatry*. New York: Cambridge University Press.

Lambek, Michael. 1993. *Knowledge and Practice in Mayotte: Local Discourses of Islam, Sorcery and Spirit Possession*. Toronto: University of Toronto Press.

———. 2013. "Afterword: How the Figure Figures." *City & Society* 25 (2): 271–277.

Li, Tanya. 2007. *The Will to Improve: Governmentality, Development, and the Practice of Politics*. Durham, NC: Duke University Press.

Lindquist, Johan. 2009. *The Anxieties of Mobility: Migration and Tourism in the Indonesian Borderlands*. Honolulu: University of Hawaii Press.

Lindsey, Timothy. 2001. "Abdurrahman, the Supreme Court, and Corruption: Viruses, Transplants, and the Body Politic in Indonesia." In *Indonesia: The Uncertain Transition*, edited by Arief Budiman and Damien Kingsbury, 43–67. Hindmarsh, S. Australia: Crawford House.

Little, Peter D. 2014. *Economic and Political Reform in Africa: Anthropological Perspectives*. Bloomington: Indiana University Press.

Lofton, Kathryn. 2011. *Oprah: The Gospel of an Icon*. Berkeley: University of California Press.

Luhrmann, Tanja Marie. 1989. *Persuasions of the Witch's Craft: Ritual Magic in Modern Culture*. Cambridge, MA: Harvard University Press.

———. 2001. *Of Two Minds: An Anthropologist Looks at American Psychiatry*. New York: Knopf.

———. 2012. *When God Talks Back: Understanding the American Evangelical Relationship with God*. New York: Vintage Books.

Lukens-Bull, Ronald. 2005. *A Peaceful Jihad: Negotiating Identity and Modernity in Muslim Java*. New York: Palgrave.

———. 2013. *Islamic Higher Education in Indonesia: Continuity and Conflict*. New York: Palgrave Macmillan.

Lutz, Catherine A. 1988. *Unnatural Emotions: Everyday Sentiments on a Micronesian Atoll and Their Challenge to Western Theory*. Chicago: University of Chicago Press.

Lutz, Catherine A., and Lila Abu-Lughod, eds. 1990. *Language and the Politics of Emotion*. New York: Cambridge University Press.

Luvaas, Brent. 2013. "Material Interventions: Indonesian DIY Fashion and the Regime of the Global Brand." *Cultural Anthropology* 28 (1): 127–143.

Mahmood, Saba. 2005. *Politics of Piety: The Islamic Revival and the Feminist Subject*. Princeton, NJ: Princeton University Press.

Mahone, Sloan, and Megan Vaughan, eds. 2007. *Psychiatry and Empire*. Cambridge: Cambridge University Press.

Mandaville, Peter. 2001. *Transnational Muslim Politics: Re-imagining the Umma*. New York: Routledge.

———. 2007. *Global Political Islam*. New York: Routledge.

Marcus, George. 1998. *Ethnography through Thick and Thin*. Princeton, NJ: Princeton University Press.

Martin, Emily. 2007. *Bipolar Expeditions: Mania and Depression in American Culture*. Princeton, NJ: Princeton University Press.

Masquelier, Adeline Marie. 2009. *Women and Islamic Revival in a West African Town*. Bloomington: Indiana University Press.

Massumi, Brian. 2002. *Parables for the Virtual: Movement, Affect, Sensation*. Durham, NC: Duke University Press.

Mazzarella, William. 2003. "'Very Bombay': Contending with the Global in an Indian Advertising Agency." *Cultural Anthropology* 18 (1): 33–71.

Menchik, Jeremy. 2014. "Productive Intolerance: Godly Nationalism in Indonesia." *Comparative Studies in Society and History* 56 (3): 591–621.

Messick, Brinkley. 1996. "Media Muftis: Radio Fatwas in Yemen." In *Islamic Legal Interpretation: Muftis and Their Fatwas*, edited by Muhammad Khalid Masud, Brinkley Messick, and David Powers, 311–320. Cambridge, MA: Harvard University Press.

Meyer, Birgit, and Jojada Verrips. 2008. "Aesthetics." In *Key Words in Religion, Media, and Culture*, edited by David Morgan, 20–30. New York: Routledge.

Mitchell, Timothy. 1998. *Colonising Egypt*. New York: Cambridge University Press.

———. 2002. *Rule of Experts: Egypt, Technopolitics, Modernity*. Berkeley: University of California Press.

Moll, Yasmin. 2010. "Islamic Televangelism: Religion, Media, and Visuality in Contemporary Egypt." *Arab Media and Society* 10 (Spring). Accessed December 1, 2013. http://www.arabmediasociety.com/?article=732.

———. 2012. "Storytelling, Sincerity, and Islamic Televangelism in Egypt." In *Global and Local Televangelism*, edited by Pradip Ninan and Philip Lee, 21–44. New York: Saint Martin's Press.

Moosa, Ebrahim. 2005. *Ghāzāli and the Poetics of Imagination*. Chapel Hill: University of North Carolina Press.

Mrazek, Rudolf. 2002. *Engineers of Happy Land: Technology and Nationalism in a Colony*. Princeton, NJ: Princeton University Press.

Muehlebach, Andrea. 2012. *The Moral Neoliberal: Welfare and Citizenship in Italy*. Chicago: University of Chicago Press.

Mujani, Syaiful, and R. William Liddle. 2010. "Personalities, Parties, and Voters." *Journal of Democracy* 21 (2): 35–49.

Mujib, Abdul. 2005. "Pengembangan Psikologi Islam Melalui Studi Islam" [The growth of Islamic psychology through the study of Islam]. *Jurnal Psikologi Islami* 1 (1): 17–32.

Al-Mukaffi, Abdurrahman. 2003. *Rapot Merah Aa Gym: MQ di Penjara Tasawuf* [The red report on Aa Gym: MQ in the prison of Sufism]. Jakarta: Darul Falah.

Mustika, Shodiq. 2007. *Seandainya Saya Istri Aa Gym* [Supposing I were Aa Gym's wife]. Jakarta: Hikmah.

Myers, Isabel Briggs. 1962. *Manual: The Myers-Briggs Type Indicator*. Palo Alto, CA: Consulting Psychologists Press.

An-Naim, 'Abd Allah Ahmad. 2008. *Islam and the Secular State: Negotiating the Future of Shari'a*. Cambridge, MA: Harvard University Press.

Nakamura, Mitsuo. 1984. "The Cultural and Religious Identity of Javanese Muslims." *Prisma* 31:67–75.

Nakassis, Constantine V. 2013. "Brands and Their Surfeits." *Cultural Anthropology* 28 (1): 110–126.

Nandy, Ashis. 1983. *The Intimate Enemy: The Loss and Recovery of Self under Colonialism*. Delhi: Oxford University Press.

Nasr, Vali. 2009. *Forces of Fortune: The Rise of the New Muslim Middle Class and What It Will Mean for Our World*. New York: Free Press.

Navaro-Yashin, Yael. 2002. *Faces of the State: Secularism and Public Life in Turkey*. Princeton, NJ: Princeton University Press.

———. 2009. "Affective Spaces, Melancholic Objects: Ruination and the Production of Anthropological Knowledge." *Journal of the Royal Anthropological Institute* 15:1–18.

———. 2012. *Make-Believe Space: Affective Geography in a Postwar Polity*. Durham, NC: Duke University Press.

Newell, Sasha. 2013. "Brands as Masks: Public Secrecy and the Counterfeit in Côte d'Ivoire." *Journal of the Royal Anthropological Institute* 19 (1): 138–154.

Nugent, David. 2011. "On the Study of Social Optics: Foucault, Counter-surveillance, and the Political Underground in Northern Peru." *Review* 34 (3): 311–331.

Nurmila, Nina. 2009. *Women, Islam, and Everyday Life: Renegotiating Polygamy in Indonesia*. New York: Routledge.

Ohnuki-Tierney, Emiko. 2002. *Kamikaze, Cherry Blossoms, and Nationalisms: The Militarization of Aesthetics in Japanese History*. Chicago: University of Chicago Press.

Öncü, Ayşe. 2006. "Becoming 'Secular Muslims': Yaşar Nuri Öztürk as a Super-Subject on Turkish Television." In *Religion, Media, and the Public Sphere*, edited by Birgit Meyer and Annelies Moors, 227–250. Bloomington: Indiana University Press.

Ong, Aihwa. 1999. *Flexible Citizenship: The Cultural Logics of Transnationality*. Durham, NC: Duke University Press.

———. 2006. *Neoliberalism as Exception: Mutations in Citizenship and Sovereignty*. Durham, NC: Duke University Press.

Ong, Aihwa, and Stephen Collier, eds. 2005. *Global Assemblages: Technology, Politics, and Ethics as Anthropological Problems*. Malden, MA: Blackwell Publishing.

Osella, Filippo, and Caroline Osella. 2009. "Muslim Entrepreneurs in Public Life between India and the Gulf: Making Good and Doing Good." *Journal of the Royal Anthropological Institute* 15:202–221.

Özyürek, Esra. 2004. "Miniaturizing Atatürk: Privatization of State Imagery and Ideology in Turkey." *American Ethnologist* 31 (3): 374–391.

———. 2006. *Nostalgia for the Modern: State Secularism and Everyday Politics in Turkey*. Durham, NC: Duke University Press.

Pandey, Gyanendra. 2006. *Routine Violence: Nations, Fragments, Histories*. Stanford, CA: Stanford University Press.

Parker, Ian. 2006. "Critical Psychology and Critical Practice in Great Britain." *Annual Review of Critical Psychology* 5:89–100.

Peacock, James L. 1978a. *Muslim Puritans: Reformist Psychology in Southeast Asian Islam*. Berkeley: University of California Press.

———. 1978b. *Purifying the Faith: The Muhammadijah Movement in Indonesian Islam*. Menlo Park, CA: Benjamin Cummings.

Peck, Jamie, Nick Theodore, and Neil Brenner. 2010. "Postneoliberalism and Its Malcontents." *Antipode* 41 (S1): 94–116.

Peletz, Michael G. 1995. "Neither Reasonable nor Responsible: Contrasting Representations of Masculinity in a Malay Society." In *Bewitching Women, Pious Men: Gender and Body Politics in Southeast Asia*, edited by Aihwa Ong and Michael G. Peletz, 76–123. Berkeley: University of California Press.

———. 1996. *Reason and Passion: Representations of Gender in a Malay Society*. Berkeley: University of California Press.

———. 2002. *Islamic Modern: Religious Courts and Cultural Politics in Malaysia*. Princeton, NJ: Princeton University Press.

———. 2013. "Malaysia's Syariah Judiciary as Global Assemblage: Islamization, Corporatization, and Other Transformations in Context." *Comparative Studies in Society and History* 55 (3): 603–633.

Pols, Hans. 2007. "The Nature of the Native Mind: Contested Views of Dutch Colonial Psychiatrists in the Former Dutch East Indies." In *Psychiatry and Empire*, edited by Sloan Mahone and Megan Vaughan, 172–196. Cambridge: Cambridge University Press.

Prakash, Gyan. 1999. *Another Reason: Science and the Imagination of Modern India*. Princeton, NJ: Princeton University Press.

Al-Qarni, Aidh bin Abdullah. 2004. *Laa Tahzan* [Don't be sad]. Bandung: Irsyad Baitus Salam.

Ridwan, M. Deden. n.d. "Kyai Haji Abdullah Gymnastiar: Membangun Manusia Unggul Lewat Manajemen Qalbu" [K. H. Abdullah Gymnastiar: Developing superior people through heart management]. Unpublished manuscript. Jakarta, Indonesia.

Rinaldo, Rachel. 2013. *Mobilizing Piety: Islam and Feminism in Indonesia.* New York: Oxford University Press.

Robbins, Tony. 1992. *Awaken the Giant Within: How to Take Immediate Control of Your Mental, Emotional, Physical, and Financial Destiny!* New York: Free Press.

Rosaldo, Michelle Z. 1983. "The Shame of Headhunters and the Autonomy of Self." *Ethos* 11 (3): 135–151.

Rose, Nikolas S. 1989. *Governing the Soul: The Shaping of the Private Self.* New York: Free Association Books.

———. 1996. *Inventing Ourselves: Psychology, Power, and Personhood.* New York: Cambridge University Press.

———. 1999. *Powers of Freedom: Reframing Political Thought.* New York: Cambridge University Press.

Rose, Nikolas S., and Peter Miller. 2008. *Governing the Present: Administering Economic, Social, and Personal Life.* Cambridge, UK: Polity.

Roth, Ron. 2000. *Prayer and the Five Stages of Healing.* Carlsbad, CA: Hay House.

Roy, Olivier. 1994. *The Failure of Political Islam.* Cambridge, MA: Harvard University Press.

———. 2004. *Globalized Islam: The Search for a New Ummah.* New York: Columbia University Press.

Rudnyckyj, Daromir. 2009a. "Market Islam in Indonesia." *Journal of the Royal Anthropological Institute* 15 (1): 182–200.

———. 2009b. "Spiritual Economies: Islam and Neoliberalism in Contemporary Indonesia." *Cultural Anthropology* 24 (1): 104–141.

———. 2009c. "Spiritual Trainer." In "Figures of Indonesian Modernity," by Joshua Barker and Johan Lindquist, with Tom Boellstorff et al., *Indonesia* 87 (April): 43–45.

———. 2010. *Spiritual Economies: Globalization and the Afterlife of Development.* Ithaca, NY: Cornell University Press.

Rutherford, Danilyn. 2003. *Raiding the Land of the Foreigners: The Limits of the Nation on an Indonesian Frontier.* Princeton, NJ: Princeton University Press.

———. 2009. "Sympathy, State Building, and the Experience of Empire." *Cultural Anthropology* 24 (1): 1–32.

Salvatore, Armando, and Dale F. Eickelman, eds. 2004. *Public Islam and the Common Good.* Boston: Brill.

Saputro, Suhendro, and Joko Erwanto, eds. 2004. *Kisah Sukses: Pebisnis Muslim di Indonesia* [Success stories: Muslim businesspeople in Indonesia]. Jakarta: Pustaka Al-Kautsar.

Sasono, Eric. 2010. "Islamic-Themed Films in Contemporary Indonesia: Commodified Religion or Islamization?" *Asian Cinema* 21 (2): 48–68.

Schielke, Samuli. 2009. "Being Good in Ramadan: Ambivalence, Fragmentation, and the Moral Self in the Lives of Young Egyptians." *Journal of the Royal Anthropological Institute* 15 (S1): S24–S40.

Schmidt, Leigh Eric. 2000. *Hearing Things: Religion, Illusion, and the American Enlightenment.* Cambridge, MA: Harvard University Press.

Schulz, Dorothea E. 2006. "Promises of (Im)mediate Salvation: Islam, Broadcast Media, and the Remaking of Religious Experience in Mali." *American Ethnologist* 33 (2): 210–229.

———. 2012. *Muslims and New Media in West Africa: Pathways to God.* Bloomington: Indiana University Press.

Setiyaji, Achmad. 2006. *Aa Gym: Mengapa Berpoligami? Testimoni Seorang Jurnalis* [Aa Gym: Why polygamy? Testimony of a journalist]. Jakarta: Qolbun Media.

Shihab, M. Quraish. 1998. *Menyingkap Tabir Ilahi* [Parting the curtain to God]. Jakarta: Lentera Hati.

Siegel, James T. 1998. *A New Criminal Type in Jakarta: Counter-revolution Today.* Durham, NC: Duke University Press.

Smith-Hefner, Nancy J. 2007. "Youth Language, *Gaul* Sociability, and the New Indonesian Middle Class." *Journal of Linguistic Anthropology* 17 (2): 184–203.

———. 2009. "Language Shift, Gender, and Ideologies of Modernity in Central Java, Indonesia." *Journal of Linguistic Anthropology* 19 (1): 57–77.

Soares, Benjamin F. 2005. *Islam and the Prayer Economy: History and Authority in a Malian Town.* Ann Arbor: University of Michigan Press.

Soares, Benjamin F., and Filippo Osella. 2009. "Islam, Politics, Anthropology." *Journal of the Royal Anthropological Institute* 15 (S1): S1–S23.

Sokoloff, Kiril. 2005. *Personal Transformation: An Executive's Story of Struggle and Spiritual Awakening.* New York: Crossroad Publishing.

Solahudin, Dindin. 1996."The Workshop for Morality: The Islamic Creativity of Pesantren Daarut Tauhiid in Bandung, Java." Master's thesis, Australian National University, Canberra.

Stange, Paul. 1984. "The Logic of Rasa in Java." *Indonesia* 38: 113–134.

Starrett, Gregory. 1995. "The Political Economy of Religious Commodities in Cairo." *American Anthropologist* 97 (1): 51–68.

———. 1998. *Putting Islam to Work: Education, Politics, and Religious Transformation in Egypt.* Berkeley: University of California Press.

Stearns, Peter N. 1994. *American Cool: Constructing a Twentieth Century Emotional Style.* New York: New York University Press.

Stoler, Ann. 2009. *Along the Archival Grain: Epistemic Anxieties and Colonial Common Sense.* Princeton, NJ: Princeton University Press.

Strassler, Karen. 2009a. "The Face of Money: Currency, Crisis, and Remediation in Contemporary Indonesia." *Cultural Anthropology* 24 (1): 68–103.

———. 2009b. "Telecommunications and Multimedia Expert." In "Figures of

Indonesian Modernity," by Joshua Barker and Johan Lindquist, with Tom Boellstorff et al., *Indonesia* 87 (April): 38–41.

Sukidi, Mulyadi. 2006. "Max Weber's Remarks on Islam: The Protestant Ethic among Muslim Puritans." *Islam and Christian-Muslim Relations* 17 (2): 195–205.

Sundari, Betty Y. 2007. *Muslimah Goes to CEO: Ayo, Jadi Momtrepreneur!* [Muslim woman becomes a CEO: Come on, become a momtrepreneur!]. Bandung: Khansa.

Suryakusuma, Julia I. 1996. "The State and Sexuality in New Order Indonesia." In *Fantasizing the Feminine in Indonesia*, edited by Laurie J. Sears, 92–119. Durham, NC: Duke University Press.

Tagliacozzo, Eric, ed. 2009. *Southeast Asia and the Middle East: Islam, Movement and the Longue Durée*. Stanford, CA: Stanford University Press.

———. 2013. *The Longest Journey: Southeast Asians and the Pilgrimage to Mecca*. New York: Oxford University Press.

Tiller, William A. 1997. *Science and Human Transformation: Subtle Energies, Intentionality, and Consciousness*. Walnut Creek, CA: Pavior Publishing.

Tuckerman, Bruce. 1965. "Developmental Sequence in Small Groups." *Psychological Bulletin* 63 (6): 384–399.

van der Pool, M. W. H. 2005. "An Islamic Sitcom: *Keluarga Senyum*." Master's thesis, Vrije University, Amsterdam.

van Doorn-Harder, Pieterenella. 2006. *Women Shaping Islam: Indonesian Women Reading the Qur'an*. Urbana: University of Illinois Press.

van Klinken, Gerry, and Joshua Barker, eds. 2009. *State of Authority: The State in Society in Indonesia*. Ithaca, NY: Cornell Southeast Asia Program.

van Wichelen, Sonja. 2009. "Polygamy Talk and the Politics of Feminism: Contestations over Masculinity in a New Muslim Indonesia. *Journal of International Women's Studies* 11 (1): 173–188.

Volpi, Frederic, and Bryan S. Turner. 2007. "Introduction: Making Islamic Authority Matter." *Theory, Culture, and Society* 24 (1): 1–19.

Watson, C. W. 2005a. "Islamic Books and Their Publishers: Notes on the Contemporary Indonesian Scene." *Journal of Islamic Studies* 16 (2): 177–210.

———. 2005b. "A Popular Indonesian Preacher: The Significance of AA Gymnastiar." *Journal of the Royal Anthropological Institute* 11 (4): 773–792.

Weintraub, Andrew, ed. 2011. *Islam and Popular Culture in Indonesia and Malaysia*. New York: Routledge.

Werbner, Pnina. 2001. "The Limits of Cultural Hybridity: On Ritual Monsters, Poetic License, and Contested Postcolonial Purifications." *Journal of the Royal Anthropological Institute* 7: 133–152.

———. 2007. "Intimate Disciples in the Modern World: The Creation of Translocal Amity among South Asian Sufis in Britain." In *Sufism and the "Modern" in*

*Islam*, edited by Martin van Bruinesses and Julia Day Howell, 195–216. London: I. B. Tauris.

Whyte, William F. 1943. *Street Corner Society: The Social Structure of an Italian Slum*. Chicago: University of Chicago Press.

Widjajakusuma, Muhammad Karebet. 2007. *Be the Best, Not Be "Asa."* Jakarta: Gema Insani Press.

Widjajakusuma, Muhammad Karebet, and Muhammad Ismail Yusanto. 2002. *Menggagas Bisnis Islami* [Designing Islamic business]. Jakarta: Gema Insani Press.

Widodo, Amrih. 2008. "Writing for God: Piety and Consumption in Popular Islam." *Inside Indonesia* 93 (August–October). Accessed November 17, 2014. http://insideindonesia.org/weekly-articles/writing-for-god.

Willford, Andrew C., and Kenneth M. George, eds. 2005. *Spirited Politics: Religion and Public Life in Contemporary Southeast Asia*. Ithaca, NY: Cornell Southeast Asia Program.

Williams, Raymond. 1976. *Keywords: A Vocabulary of Culture and Society*. New York: Oxford University Press.

———. 1978. *Marxism and Literature*. Oxford: Oxford University Press.

Willis, Paul E. 1977. *Learning to Labor: How Working Class Kids Get Working Class Jobs*. Farnborough, UK: Saxon House.

Wilson, Ian Douglas. 2008. "As Long as It's *Halal*: Islamic *Preman* in Jakarta." In *Expressing Islam: Religious Life and Politics in Indonesia*, edited by Greg Fealy and Sally White, 192–210. Singapore: Institute of Southeast Asian Studies.

Wise, Lindsay. 2003. "Words from the Heart: New Forms of Islamic Preaching in Egypt." Master's thesis, St. Anthony's College, Oxford University.

Woodward, Mark. 1989. *Islam in Java: Normative Piety and Mysticism in the Sultanate of Yogyakarta*. Tucson: University of Arizona Press.

Yavuz, M. Hakan, and John L. Esposito, eds. 2003. *Turkish Islam and the Secular State: The Gülen Movement*. Syracuse, NY: Syracuse University Press.

Zaman, Muhammad Qasim. 2006. "Consensus and Religious Authority in Modern Islam: The Discourses of the '*Ulamā*.'" In *Speaking for Islam: Religious Authorities in Muslim Societies*, edited by Gudrun Krämer and Sabine Schmidtke, 153–180. Boston: Brill.

Zohar, Danah, and Ian Marshall. 2000. *SQ: Connecting with Our Spiritual Intelligence*. New York: Bloomsbury.

———. 2004. *Spiritual Capital: Wealth We Can Live By*. Oakland, CA: Berrett-Koehler Publishers.

# Index

Page references followed by "*f*" refer to figures and photographs.